Author: Jennifer Margell

Layout:
Baseline Co. Ltd
61A-63A Vo Van Tan Street
4th Floor
District 3, Ho Chi Minh City
Vietnam

ISBN: 978-1-78160-239-3

Printed in Croatia

Jennifer Margell

ENCAUSTIC ART

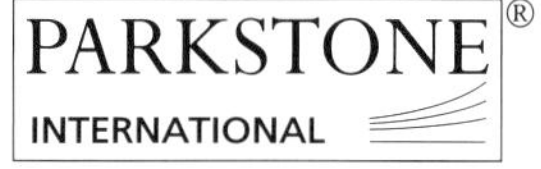

Featuring Artwork by:

Kristy Battani
Steven DaLuz
Brandy Eiger
Karen Freedman
Lorraine Glessner
Carrie Goller
Stephanie Hargrave
Miriam Karp
Cheryl D. McClure
Edie Morton
Debra Neiman
Jeremy Penn
Richard Purdy
Amy Royce
Adele Shaw
Tony Scherman

Lovingly dedicated to my mother and father whose support, encouragement, and constant love have supported me throughout my life.

Contents

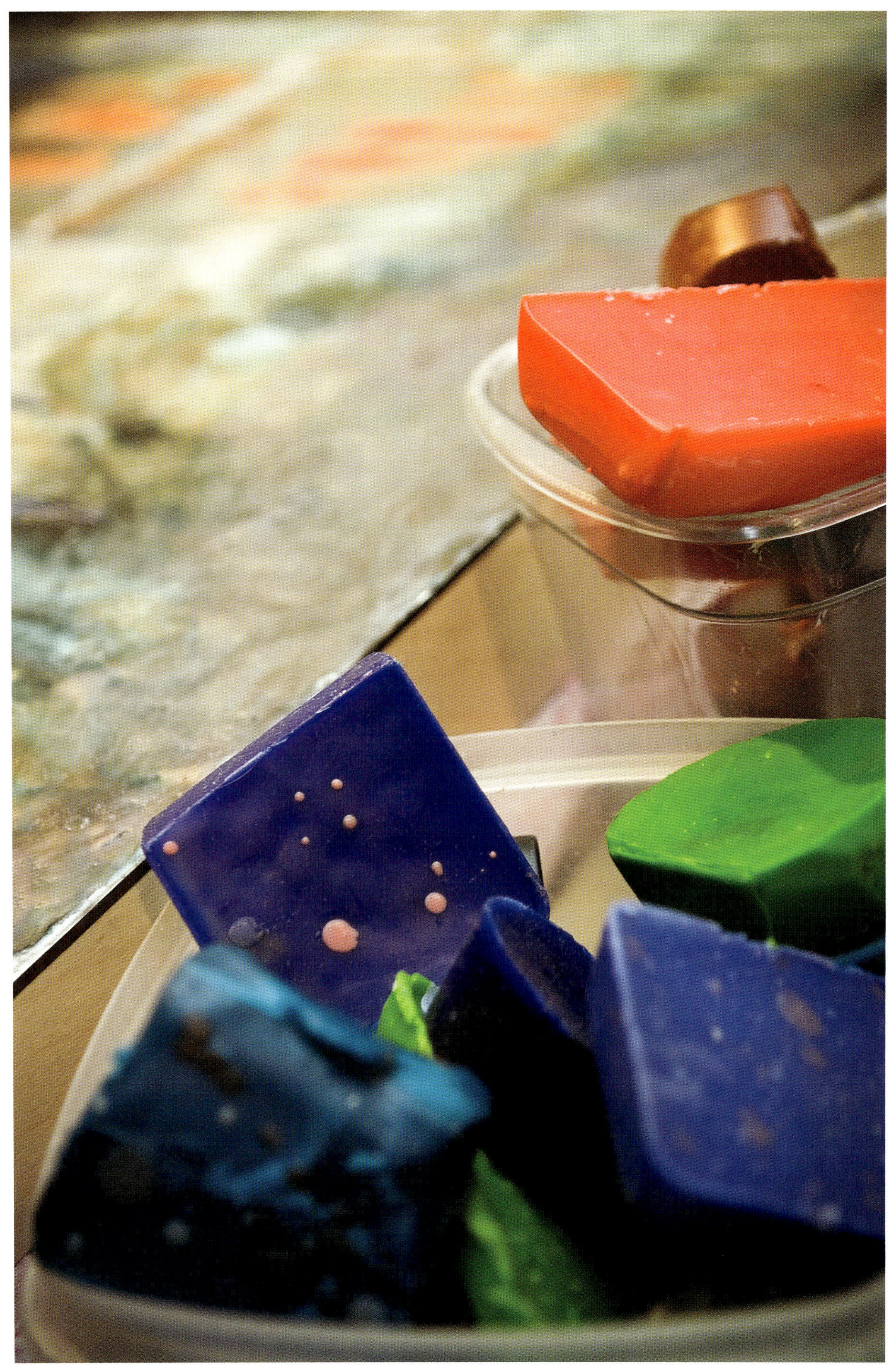

Introduction

The first time I saw an encaustic painting I was mesmerized by its beautiful surface, incredible texture, and translucency. I wanted to reach out and touch it. I was determined to try encaustic painting for myself, and as soon as I did, I was hooked. This is not only my story, but I have heard it echoed by so many encaustic artists who have also fallen in love with the possibilities of the medium.

Encaustics are like no other form of painting, in that there are endless techniques and fleeting seconds before your medium solidifies. It is a medium where you have to trust your instincts and paint in the moment. You have to take leaps of faith. In the beginning there are many frustrations, but over time you learn how to work with the beautiful accidents which incur.

The best way to learn the art of painting encaustics is not to create beautiful paintings. The best way to work with the medium is to create painting after painting, focusing on a different technique each time. Even a technique which you do not plan to use will later be another option added to your repertoire.

So many times I have gone to a gallery and marveled at the fantastic work of artists. I wondered how the artists created the piece I was admiring. I wanted to know what motivated the artists, what they were thinking of, what they were feeling, and what physical steps they used to create their artwork. So many times these questions were not answered, and they have become the inspiration behind this book. In this book, for the first time, is a collection of the voice from these encaustic artists. They are successful, talented individuals who have been gracious enough to share the work, their advice, and even their techniques.

Encaustics are a very fresh art form in the grand scheme of things. They were first used by the Greeks three thousand years ago, but have only recently been resurrected as a popular art form. They are rapidly gaining momentum. Although encaustics are now becoming well known in the art community, many people still do not know what they are and have questions about the medium. So many contemporary artists with vastly different styles have the same beautiful story of their relationship with the medium.

The encaustic painting community is a wonderful group because they are so willing to share their advice and experiences with each other. It is a fresh and exciting time for encaustics because the possibilities are endless. Artists around the world are trying new techniques and experimenting in ways which bring to mind the exciting times of the French Impressionists in the early 1900s.

This book brings together one of the largest collection of encaustic paintings printed in one place, featuring over one hundred and fifty paintings by talented contemporary artists. By looking through the pages, you can see that the range of painting styles you can create with encaustics are endless. The wonderful thing about this project is that it is not only a dazzling collection of work, but it also features the voices of these artists. The pages of this book reveal, in the artists' words, their passion, motivation, and advice.

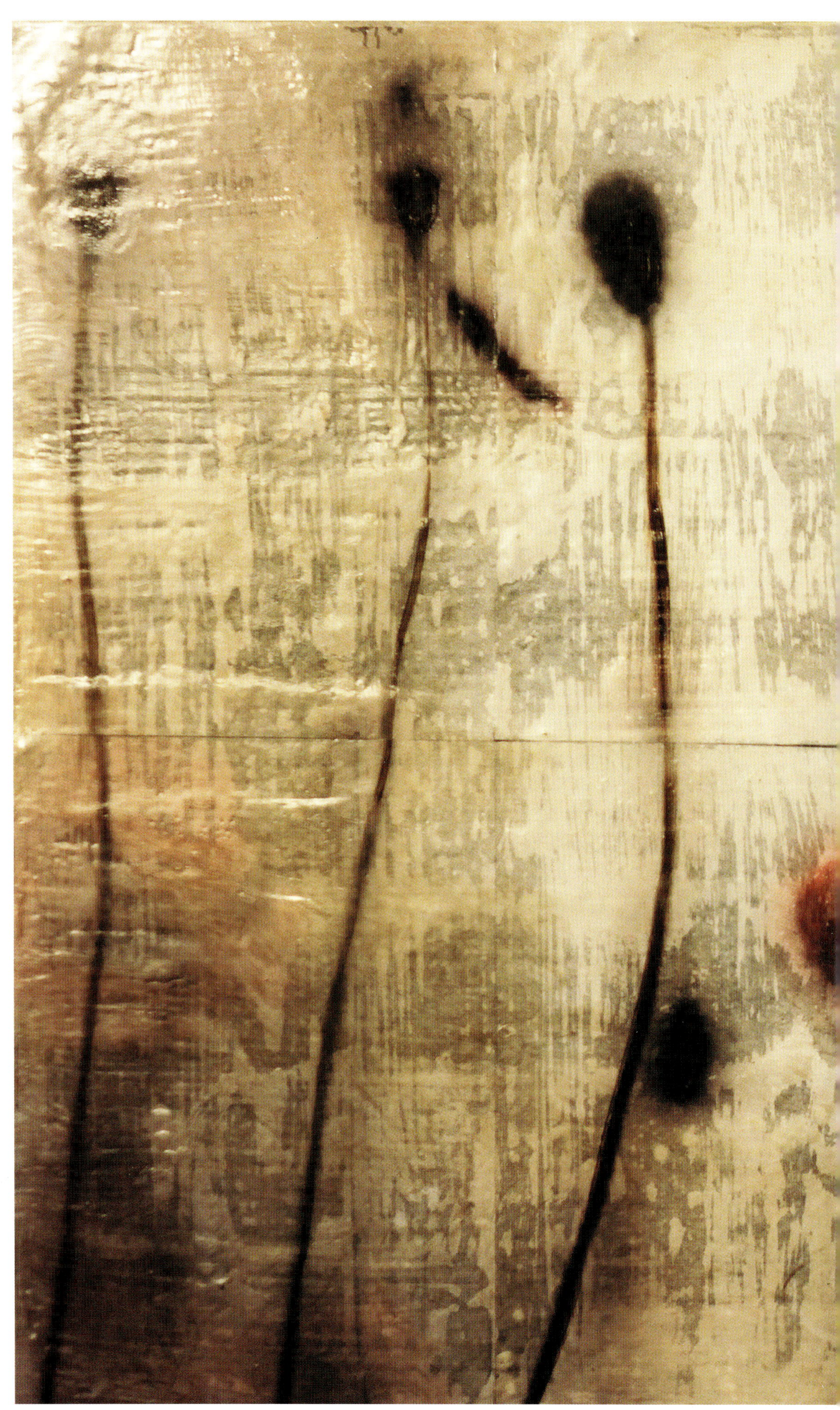

Jennifer Margell, *Poppy Fields*, 2011. Encaustic and photography on birch plywood, 91.4 x 61 cm.

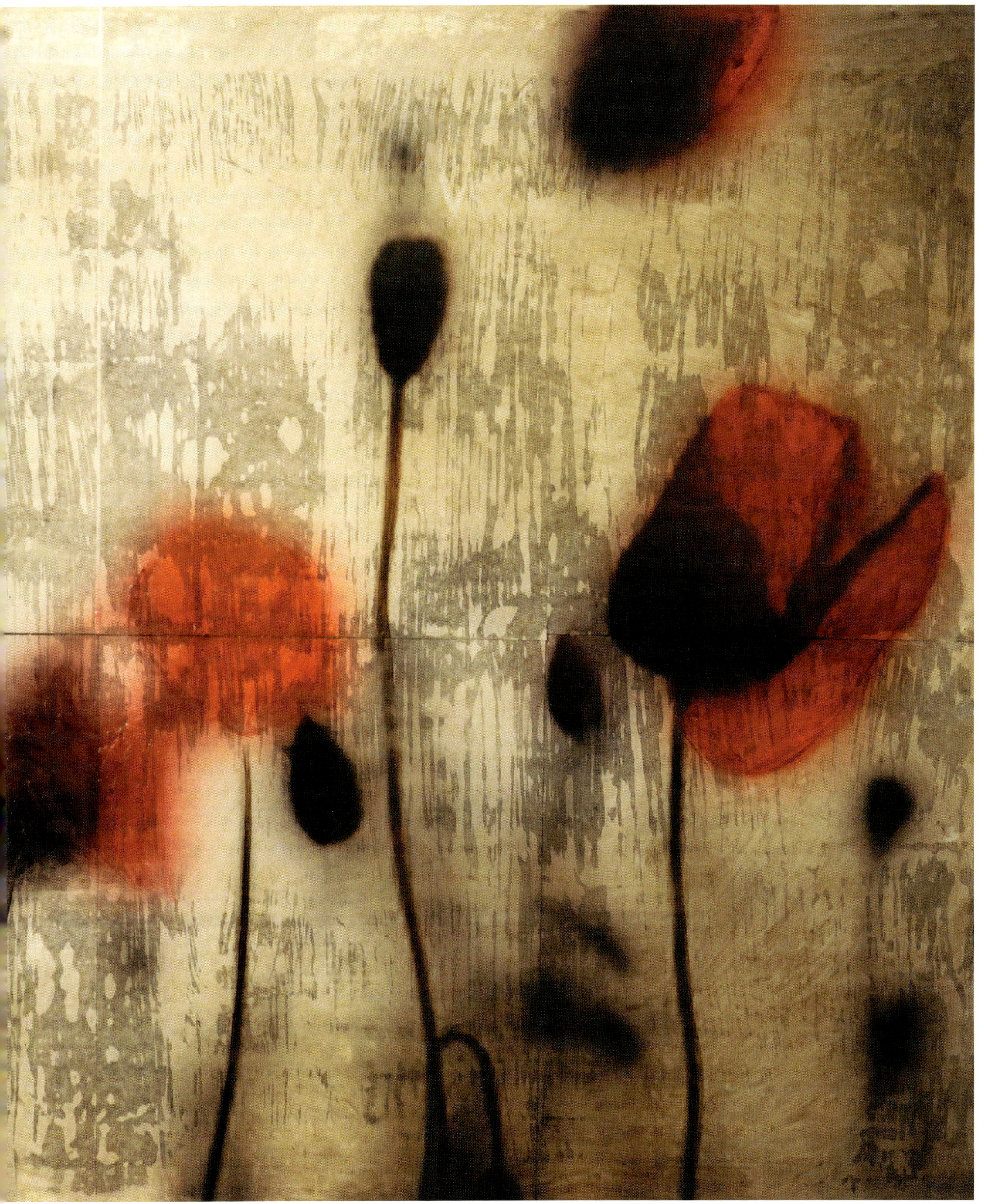

This workbook is intended for artists of all levels. An advanced artist can learn from the personal artist interviews, advice on ground-breaking techniques, and be inspired by the collection of work. This workbook also includes the information needed for anyone brand new to encaustics such as the basic tools and techniques to get started.

Encaustic is not an easy medium to learn, but for myself and so many other artists, it has been by far the most rewarding medium I have painted with. It is great to do a local workshop to learn firsthand how to paint with encaustics, but there are many ways to go about getting started with the medium on your own as well. This workbook also includes information about the materials required, creating encaustic medium, and ten lessons demonstrating the range of techniques available.

When I start a painting, I often wonder what I would like to say. I think about how I can show my individual style and what I want the viewers to feel. I always think of what one artist said in her interview. She was told that if you do not know your voice, you should paint and paint, then lay all of these paintings out. Look to see what thread ties them together. What shapes and colors weave throughout your pieces; this will demonstrate your individual style. This is a thing which you cannot hide if you wanted, so it is best to seek it out and embrace it. Creating this workbook has been a joy and a blessing. Like creating an encaustic painting, it has changed over time from what I originally imagined it to be. I hope the paintings in this book are an inspiration to the readers, the intimate stories and revelations by artists are appreciated, and this project helps to encourage more artists to learn about all the possibilities of encaustic.

The History

Encaustic painting is one of the oldest forms of painting, and stems from the word *Enkaustikos*, which means "to burn in". It originated in Ancient Greece three thousand years ago when ancient ship builders would use a combination of wax and resin to seal and waterproof their hulls. Pigments were then added to the medium and led to the decoration of warships.

Most likely the most famous encaustic paintings of all time are the Fayum mummy funeral portraits from the late 1st century BCE or the early 2nd century CE onwards. They were painted by a large community of Greeks who settled in Egypt and adapted to Egyptian customs after the conquest of Alexander the Great. As tradition, funeral portaits were placed over a person's mummy as a memorial. These portraits were painted either in the person's prime of life or after death. Many of these mummies have survived to present day, and the portraits maintain their bright and vivid colors because the pigments remain suspended in the wax medium; thereby retaining their vibrance. After the decline of the Roman Empire, encaustic painting fell by the wayside as the country faced instability and economic turmoil. At this time encaustic was largely replaced by tempura, which was easier to work with and more economical. Some painting continued as late as the 7th century, but encaustics soon became a lost art.

Encaustic was briefly revived in the late 18th century by the French archeologist Anne-Claude de Caylus. He studied the ancient murals of Pompeii and experimented with encaustic techniques. Later in the 19th century mural painters in northern climates experimented with encaustics to battle problems of dampness in mural paintings, but success was limited.

Adele Shaw, Studio detail.

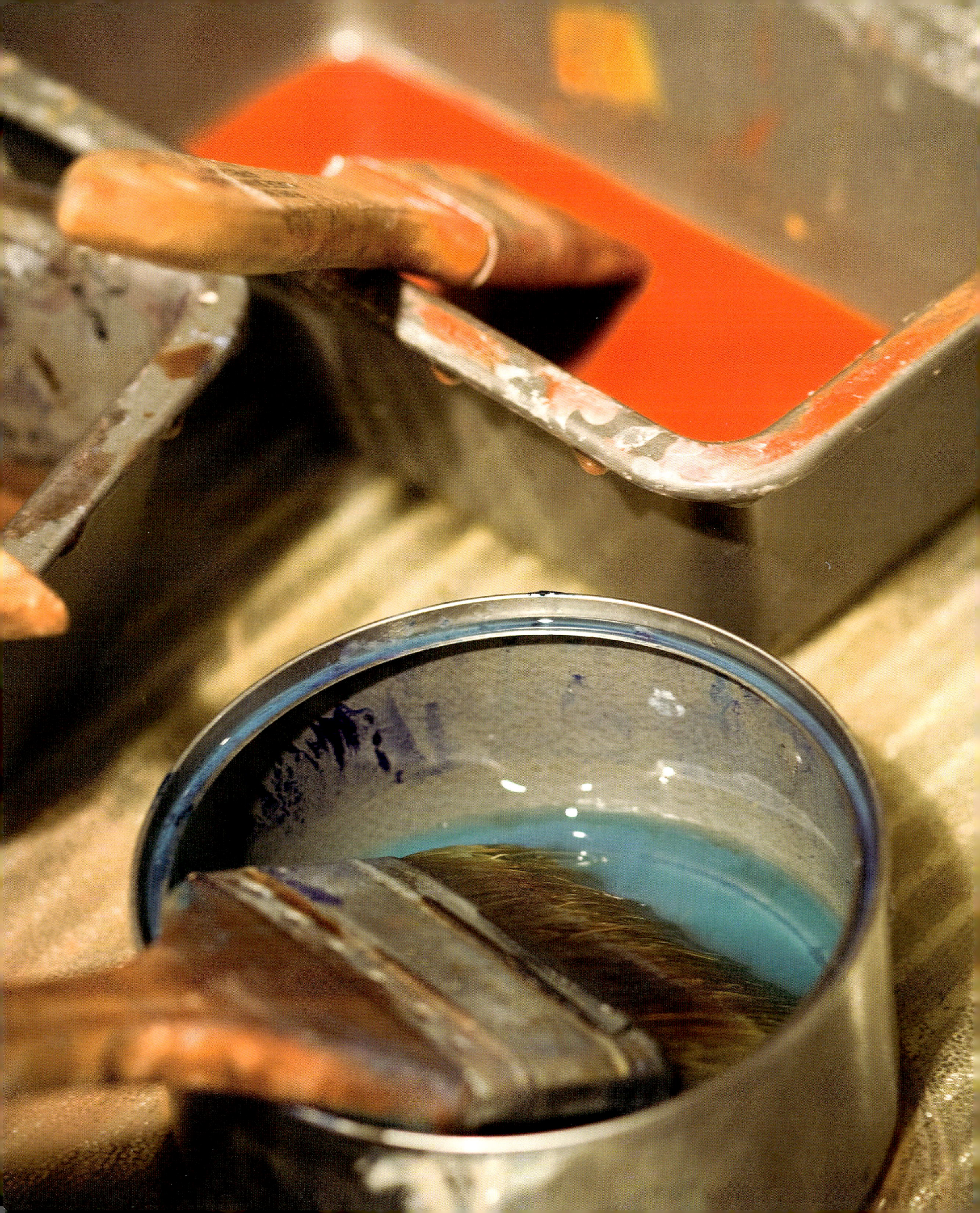

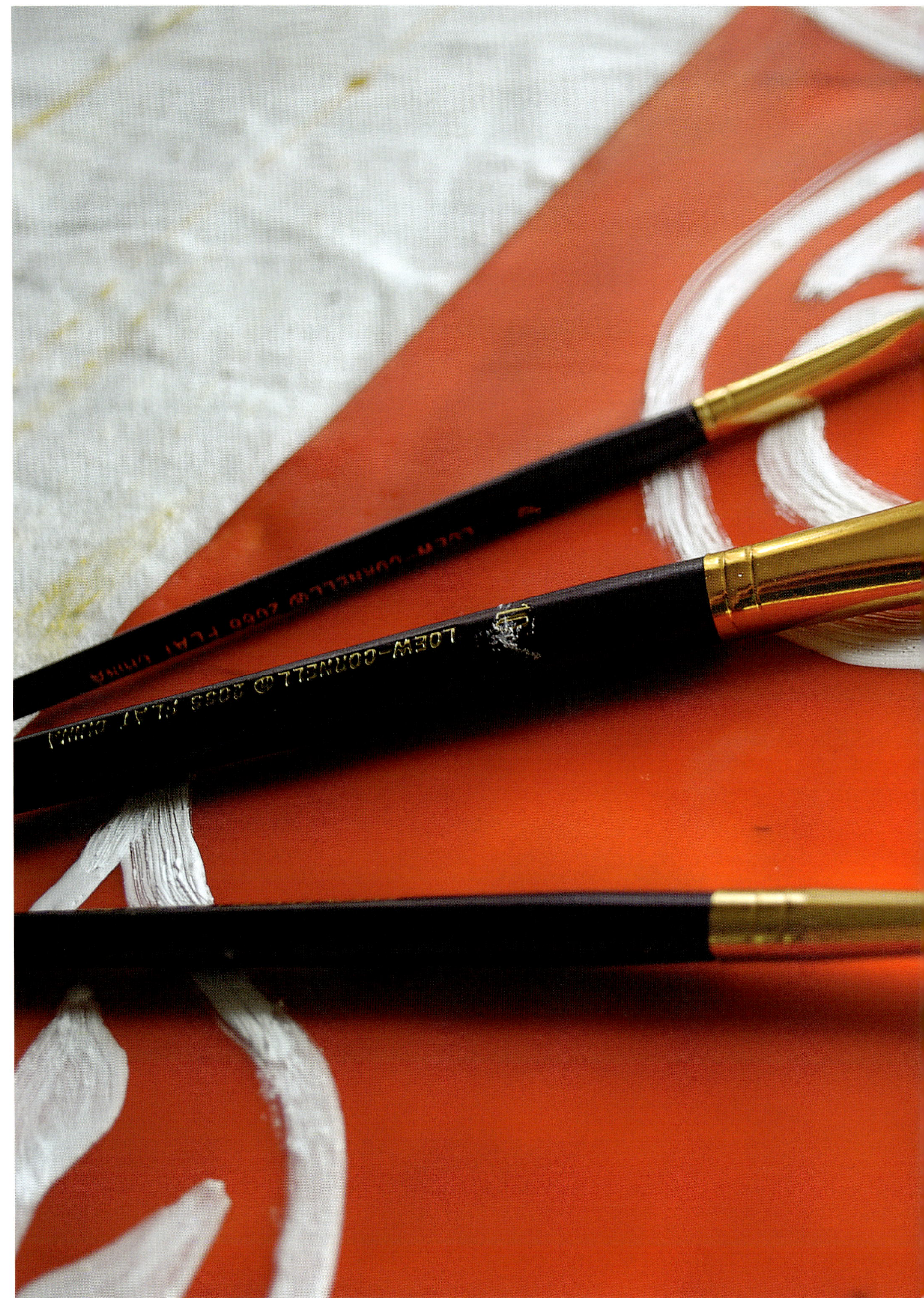
LOEW-CORNELL
LOEW-CORNELL

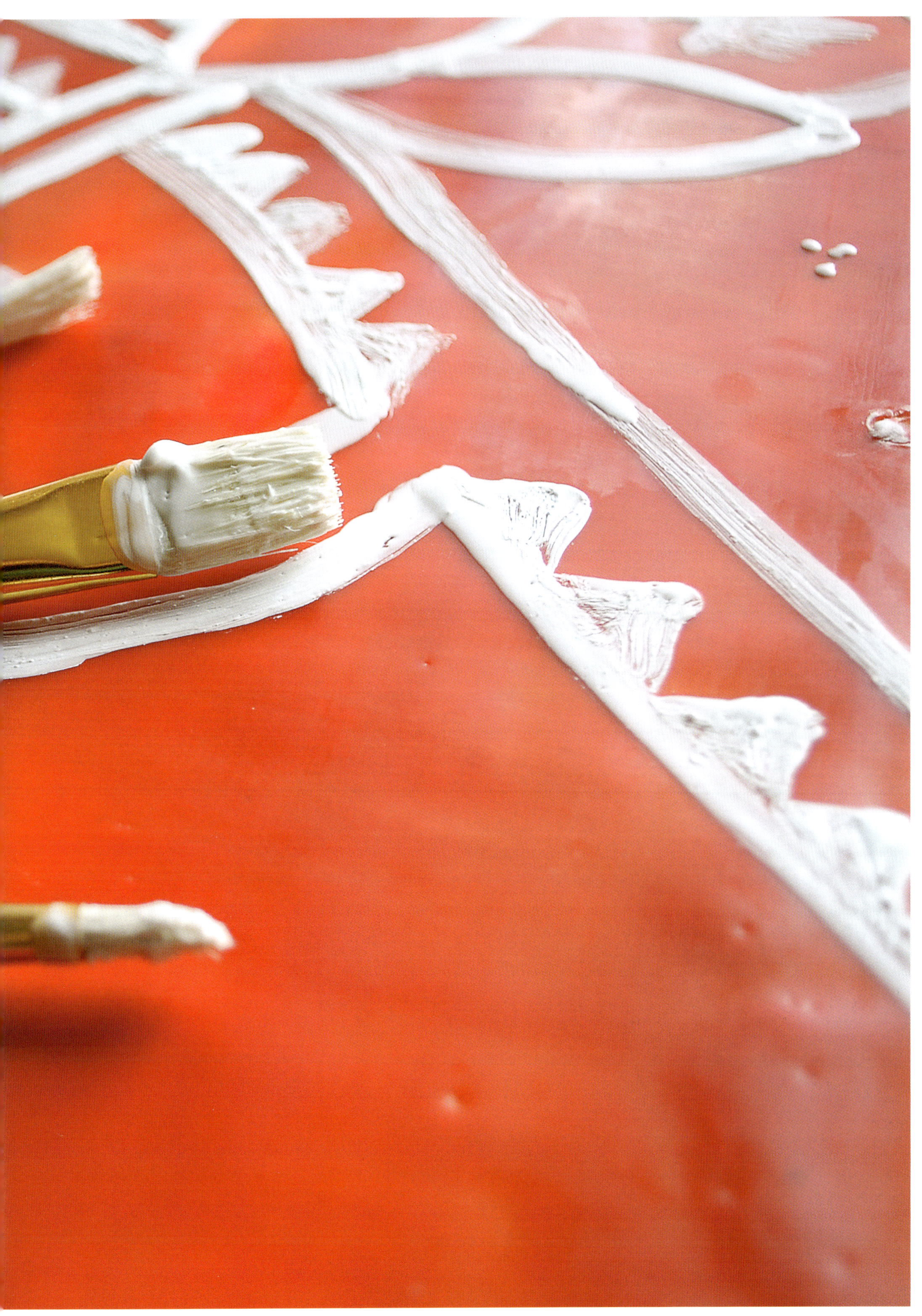

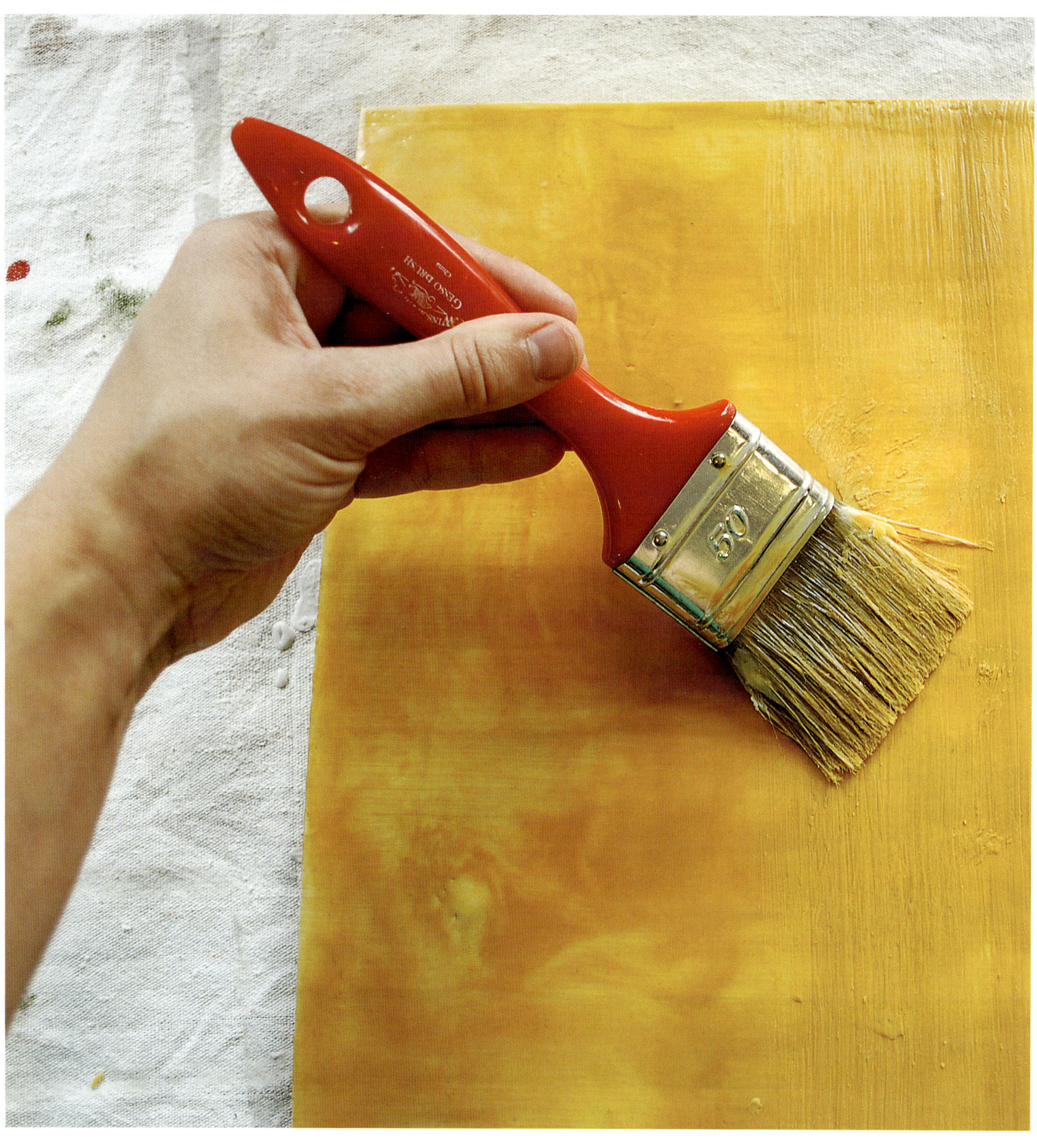
50

Leonardo da Vinci experimented with using encaustics in his work, but was not successful. Other European artists including Vincent van Gogh and Julius Schnorr von Carolsfeld used wax in their oil paintings to separate layers of paint with translucent layers.

One of the primary problems of working with encaustics was finding a way to melt the wax. In the 20th century, the invention of portable electronic heating implements revolutionized the art form and made encaustics much more attainable. This factor and the success of early encaustic painters gave rise to the resurrection of encaustic painting.

The founding father of Pop Art, Jasper Johns, is hugely responsible for popularizing the art form and increasing awareness about the medium. He used it in a number of his pieces, including his series of *American Flags*. Other artists who were responsible for reviving the art form include Alfonso Ossorio, Lynda Benglis, Robert Morris, Nancy Graves, and Tony Scherman. Encaustic is now a modern painting technique which continues to gain popularity.

Wax has many qualities that last the test of time, and encaustic may be the most durable form of painting. Beeswax is moisture resistant, it is a natural adhesive, it does not attract insects, and it resists mildew. Solvents and oils can darken or yellow over time, but beeswax does not change color at all. Because it is an ancient technique which has only recently been revived from obscurity, encaustic is a very exciting medium to experiment in. As it has continued to gain momentum in recent decades, contemporary artists push the limits by exploring the possibilities through materials and techniques. Encaustic is still a fairly new medium in the contemporary artist's repertoire; many of the pages of history remain to be written.

TOOLS FOR ENCAUSTICS

Many tools for encaustics come from unexpected sources; food tins can be used for mixing colors and an iron can be used to melt wax. Experiment with using different tools to create interesting looks. Here is a list of the basic tools required for painting with encaustics:

HEAT SOURCE:

-A griddle or hot plate is required to melt the wax.
-A hand held heat gun is needed to fuse layers together. A propane torch could also be used instead.

ENCAUSTIC MEDIUM:

-Encaustic medium is a mix of beeswax and Dammar Resin. You can purchase encaustic medium or, for a more cost effective option, you can mix your own.

ENCAUSTIC PAINT:

-Encaustic paint is a mix of encaustic medium (wax and Dammar Resin) with pigment. It is colored and can be purchased professionally mixed, or again you can mix your own. You can dilute encaustic paint with encaustic medium to make it last longer.

SUPPORT:

-A rigid surface is required to paint onto. Experiment with different surfaces such as birch wood, luan, bamboo, or Masonite. Canvas alone can stretch over time, so if you prefer to paint on canvas it is best to stretch it over a solid wood support.

APPLICATION:
- Natural bristle paint brushes such as hog bristle brushes from the hardware store. Do not use plastic brushes because they will melt with heat.
- Paper towels.

OPTIONAL TOOLS:
- A thermometer is a handy tool to help keep the wax in a temperature range from 180-200° Fahrenheit.
- Wood carving tools are fantastic for carving and incising lines into the wax.
- Mixed media materials such as interesting papers, organic materials, small objects, and fabrics.

CREATING ENCAUSTIC PAINT

Mixing your own encaustic medium is not difficult and is a great way to save money on supplies. Encaustic medium is a mixture of beeswax and Dammar Resin. Adding the Dammar Resin to the wax increases the melting temperature of the encaustic medium and makes it more rigid, thereby making it harder to damage.

Beeswax is available filtered or unfiltered. Unfiltered beeswax has a golden tint because of suspended particles of flower pollen and has a stronger smell. It is not very translucent so most artists use filtered beeswax, which has a translucent clear white color. It can be purified naturally using filters. It can also be purified through chemical or solar bleaching, however chemically bleached wax may yellow over time.

Beeswax comes in a number of forms. Most encaustic artists prefer pellets but blocks also work well. To break a large block of wax, you can freeze the block, put it in a paper bag, and then hit it with a hammer. Paraffin wax is petroleum based and a good choice for encaustic art. It is much harder than beeswax but if put under pressure it can crack. It is also cheaper than filtered beeswax, so some artists add a percentage of paraffin to their encaustic medium.

Dammar Resin, pronounced da-mahr, is actually hardened tree sap. It should not be confused with Dammar varnish. Dammar Resin is readily available at art supply stores or online. Most artists prefer to buy it as Dammar Crystals, which is hard Dammar Resin broken up into chunks.

SUPPLIES:
- Filtered Beeswax
- Dammar Resin
- Heat Source & Stir Stick
- Thermostat (recommended)
- Muffin Tins or Containers to pour wax
- Well-Ventilated Workspace

1. Use a scale to weigh 8 parts filtered beeswax to 1 part Dammar Resin. You can experiment with different ratios, but do not use too much resin or your medium will be brittle. If your chunks of Dammar Resin are very large, break them into smaller pieces with a hammer.

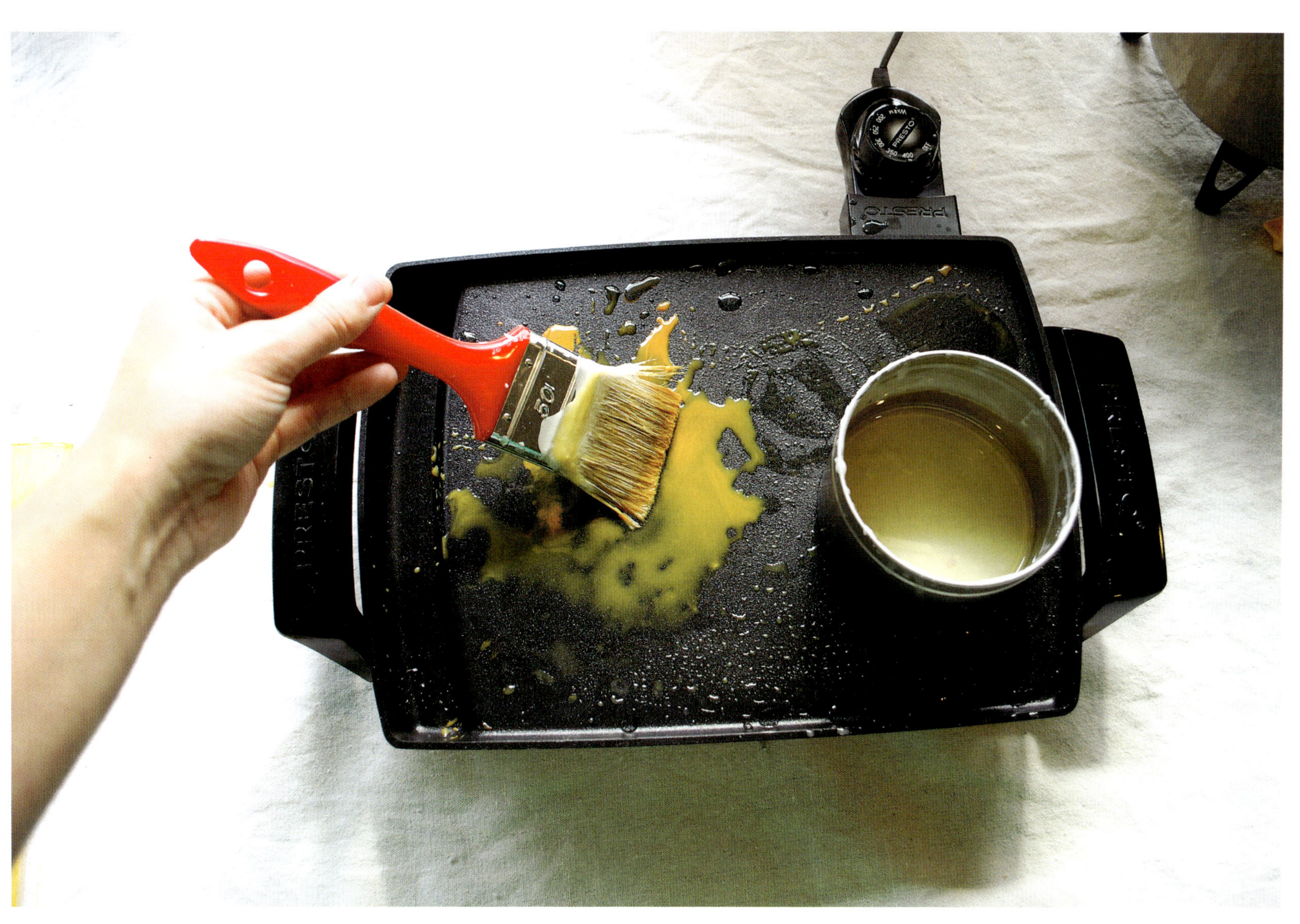
PRESTO

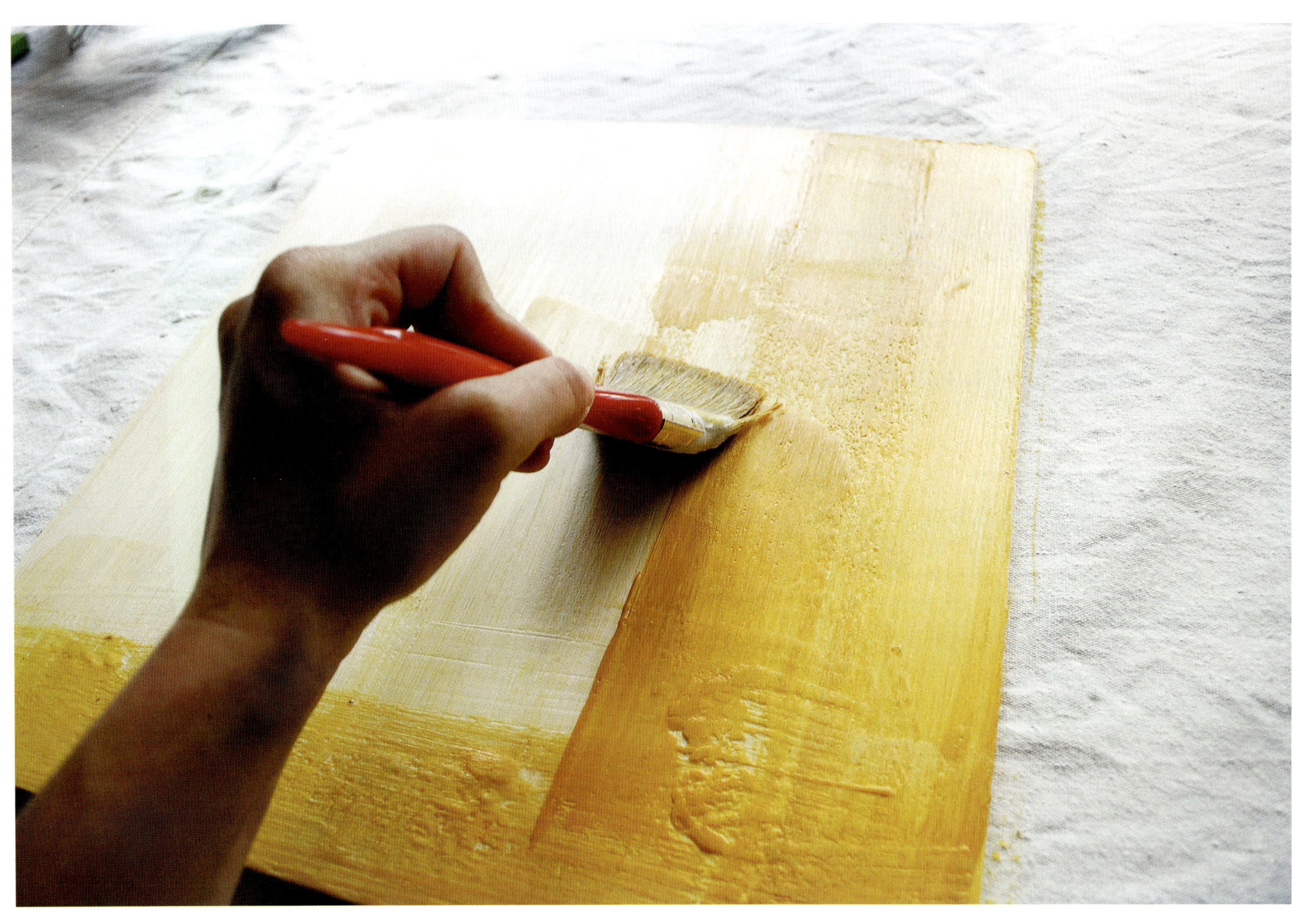

2. In a well-ventilated space, add a small amount of wax to your heat source. It will melt at about 140-150° Fahrenheit. You can use a crock pot, electric griddle, or a double boiler over water. Use the thermometer to keep an eye on the temperature and do not leave the wax unattended.

3. Bring the temperature up to 180 - 200°, which is the melting point for Dammar Resin. Slowly add all of the Dammar Resin and use a chopstick or the end of a long paintbrush to stir until it is completely incorporated. Do not bring the temperature above 250°. At any point if you see smoke when painting with encaustics, turn the heat down.

4. Once the Dammar Resin is completely smooth in consistency, add the rest of the beeswax. Reduce the temperature to 175° and stir until all the ingredients are completely mixed together.

5. Next pour the medium into small containers for cooling. If you use muffin tins, later put the tins in the freezer for 20 minutes and the wax cubes will pop right out. Do not allow the tins to come in contact with food after using them with encaustic medium. There are small impurities in Dammar Crystals which you will see at the bottom of your cubes of encaustic medium. If you want to avoid these, you can pour your medium through a metal strainer with a coffee filter or cheesecloth. Your medium is now ready for use.

COLORS & PIGMENTS

Encaustic paint is simply encaustic medium with pigment added for color. Pigment can be added using oil paint, powdered pigments, or Lyra Encaustic crayons. The amount of color that you add to the encaustic determines how transparent your medium will be. You can also choose to buy pre-made encaustic paint blocks with color already added. These blocks have quite a bit of color and are more often pricier, so you can dilute them with encaustic medium to make them last longer and add transparency to your medium.

The most common methods for adding color are to buy colored blocks of medium, or to add oil paints to your medium. The other option is to add powdered pigments, which can also be used to create oil paints. However, you should not use powdered pigments unless you use the correct safety precautions. You will require gloves, respiratory protection, and a controlled airflow. It is not safe to breathe powdered pigments, but once they are incorporated into the encaustic medium they are safe to use like normal encaustic paints.

Adding powdered pigments requires precautions such as using gloves, respiratory protection, and controlling airflow. We will focus on creating encaustic paint using oil paint tubes.

1. Add oil paint to melted encaustic paint either straight on your griddle or in individual containers. Oil paint will slightly soften your medium. If you would like, you can squeeze your oil paint onto paper towels or an oil absorbent material from an auto supply store.

2. Mix well to incorporate.

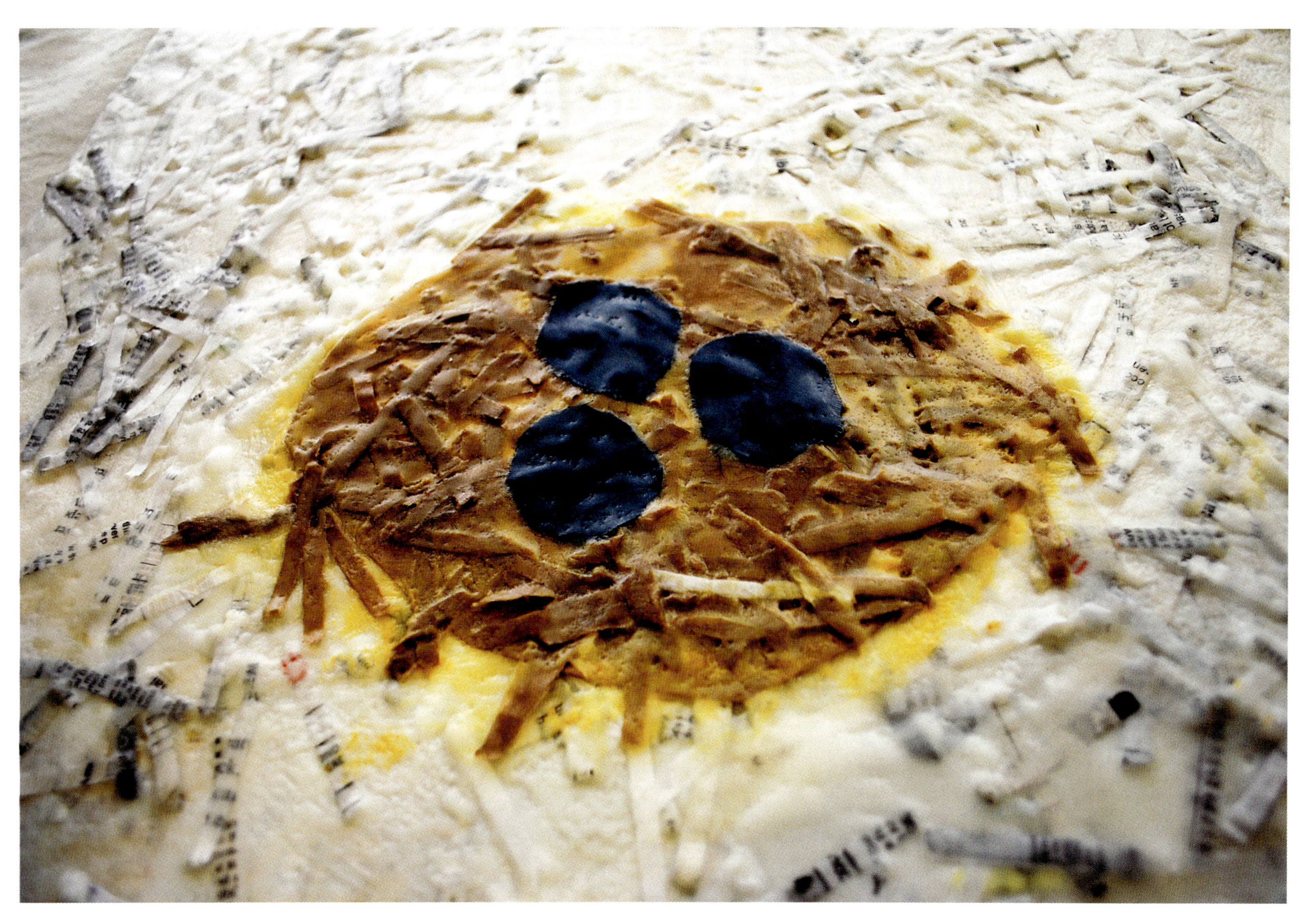

Jennifer Margell, *Nesting,* 2011.
Encaustic and mixed media on birch, 91.4 x 91.4 cm.

Lessons

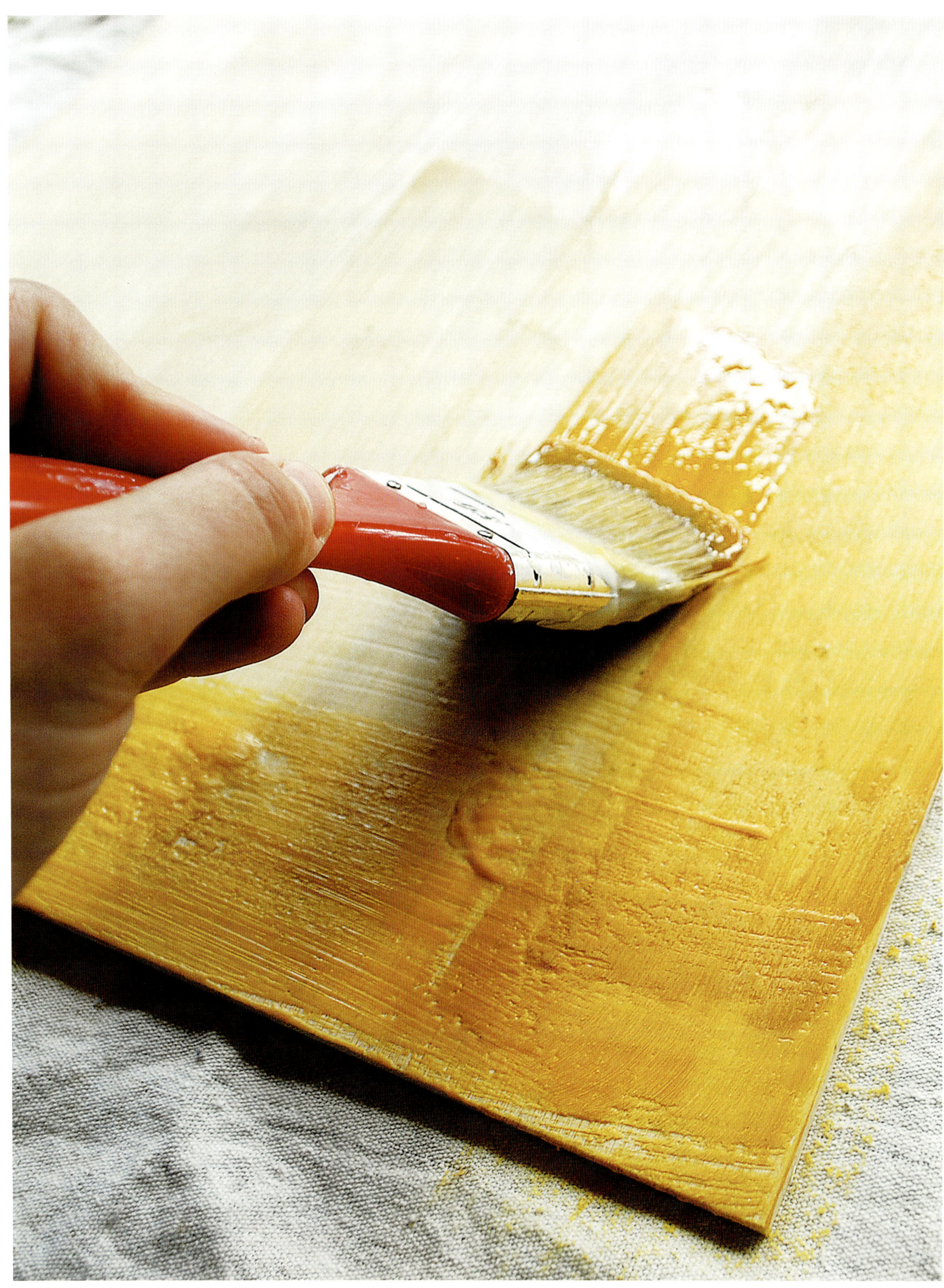

Lesson 1: Painting & Fusing

It is easy to get started painting with encaustics. Get together all of your tools including a heat source, encaustic medium, and paint, brushes, and a heat gun (see "Tools For Encaustics").

1. Use your hot plate or griddle to melt encaustic medium. You may want to use encaustic medium tinted with color to build up a translucent surface. You can mix encaustic medium and encaustic color together right on a heated griddle surface, or use individual tins to hold different colors. Experiment with both methods to see what works best for you.

2. Use a wide natural fiber brush to apply the wax to the substrate in long strokes. A 2" wide hog bristle brush from the hardware store works great. Do not use a brush with plastic or synthetic bristles or they will melt. A solid and porous substrate such as wood or Masonite works well for the painting surface. As you paint with the brush, the wax will solidify quickly. Continue to dip it into the wax often as you paint the initial layer of paint onto your ground.

3. Next you must fuse the layer of wax to the substrate. Most artists use a heat gun, but a propane torch will also work. Use a circular motion to lightly melt the wax and then continue to move to other parts of the painting. It is only necessary to melt the wax until it adheres to the surface below. If you heat an area too long, it will become an uneven mess. You will see the surface of the wax become smooth and glossy after it has been fused. It is common to have air bubbles in the wax, which look like little holes receding into the surface. To alleviate these simply continue to lightly circle the area with the heat source.

4. Paint on an additional layer of wax, fuse, and continue to build up your painting. It is always necessary to fuse the wax between every layer to ensure it adheres to the layer below and will not chip off. After painting two or more layers of wax, continue to paint with different colors, materials, and techniques to develop your piece.

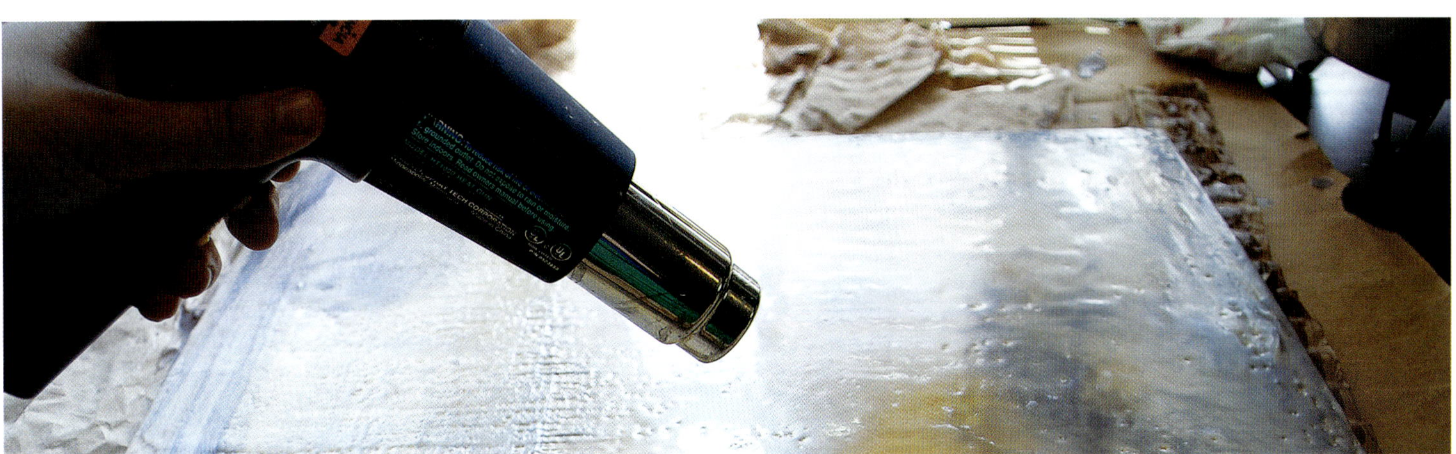

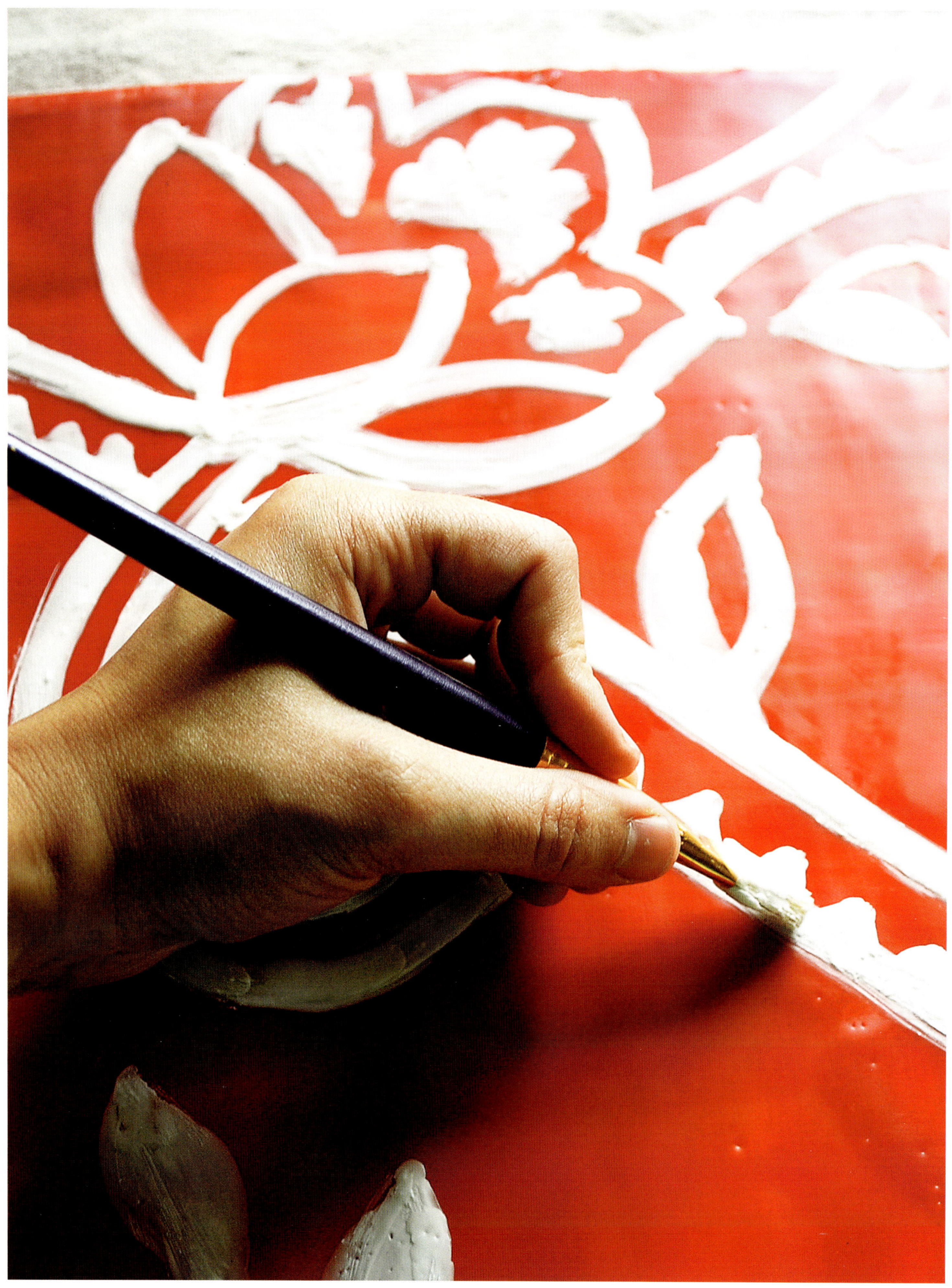

Lesson 2: Brush application

1. After starting your painting by applying and fusing at least two base layers, tint your background layers to create a colored surface to work on. You can do this by melting and painting with pre-colored encaustic paint, or by adding oil color from the tub and mixing it into your melted encaustic medium over a heat source.

2. Use a large brush with the melted colored wax to paint large areas of color or geometric shapes onto your canvas. Paint additional layers to create the amount of opacity or transparency that you would like, and remember to lightly fuse between each layer.

3. Now use a smaller brush and a new color to paint additional detail to your piece with melted encaustic paint. Notice that by changing brushes, the appearance of detail greatly changes in the painting. Move from large to small brushes as your composition approaches completion. Lightly fuse after each layer, and remember you only need to fuse for a moment until you see the that wax is melted and glistening. If you over-fuse, the painting may smear. One nice thing about encaustic is that you can always scrape off any mistakes and start again.

4. As you learn to paint with encaustics, do not worry about making a beautiful painting, but instead experiment with different brush sizes and methods to see what is possible within the medium. Now that you have created a basic encaustic painting, experiment with the lessons on the following pages to learn the range of techniques available.

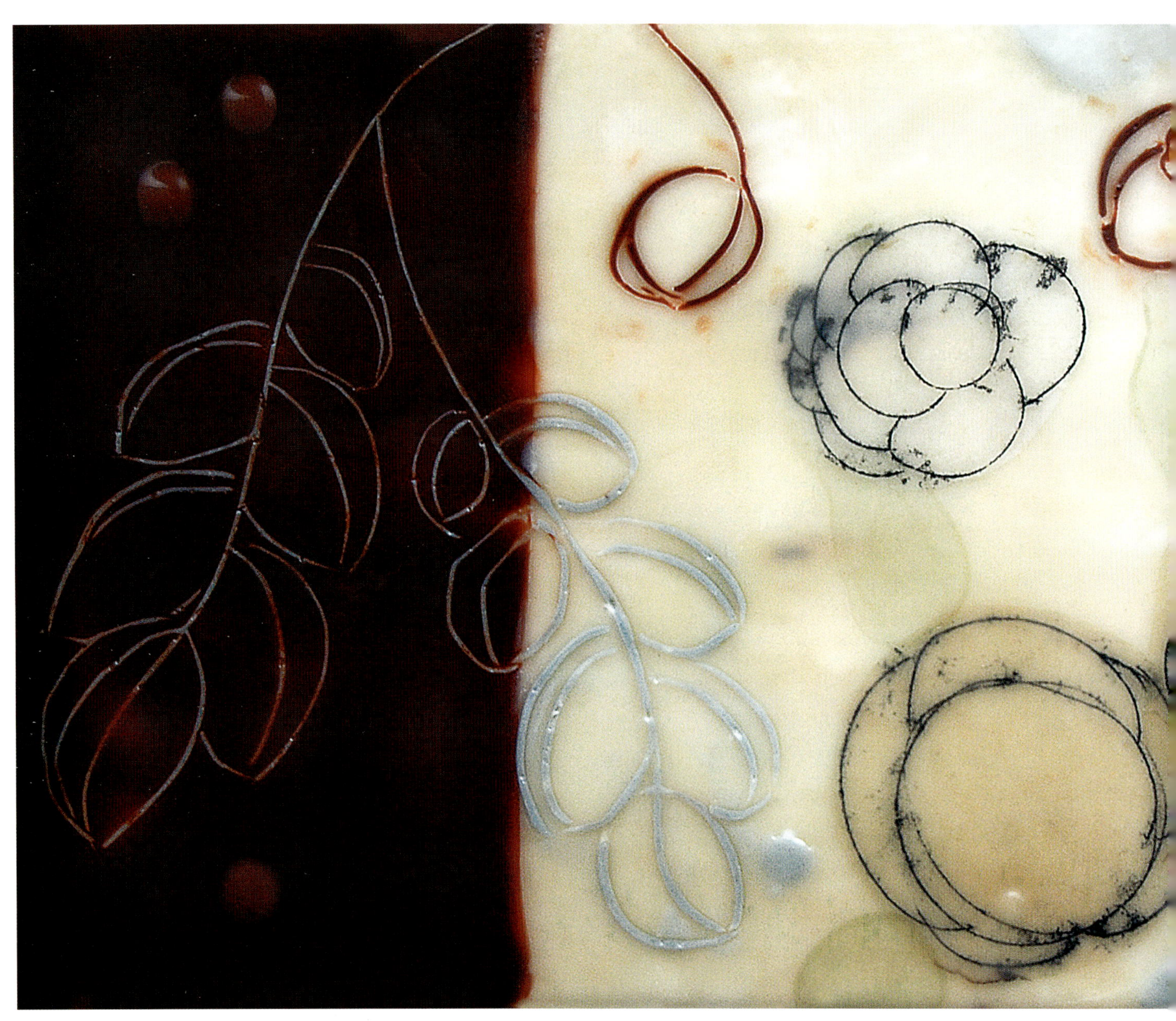

Stephanie Hargrave, *Lucidity 9*, 2009. Encaustic, 20.3 x 50.8 cm.

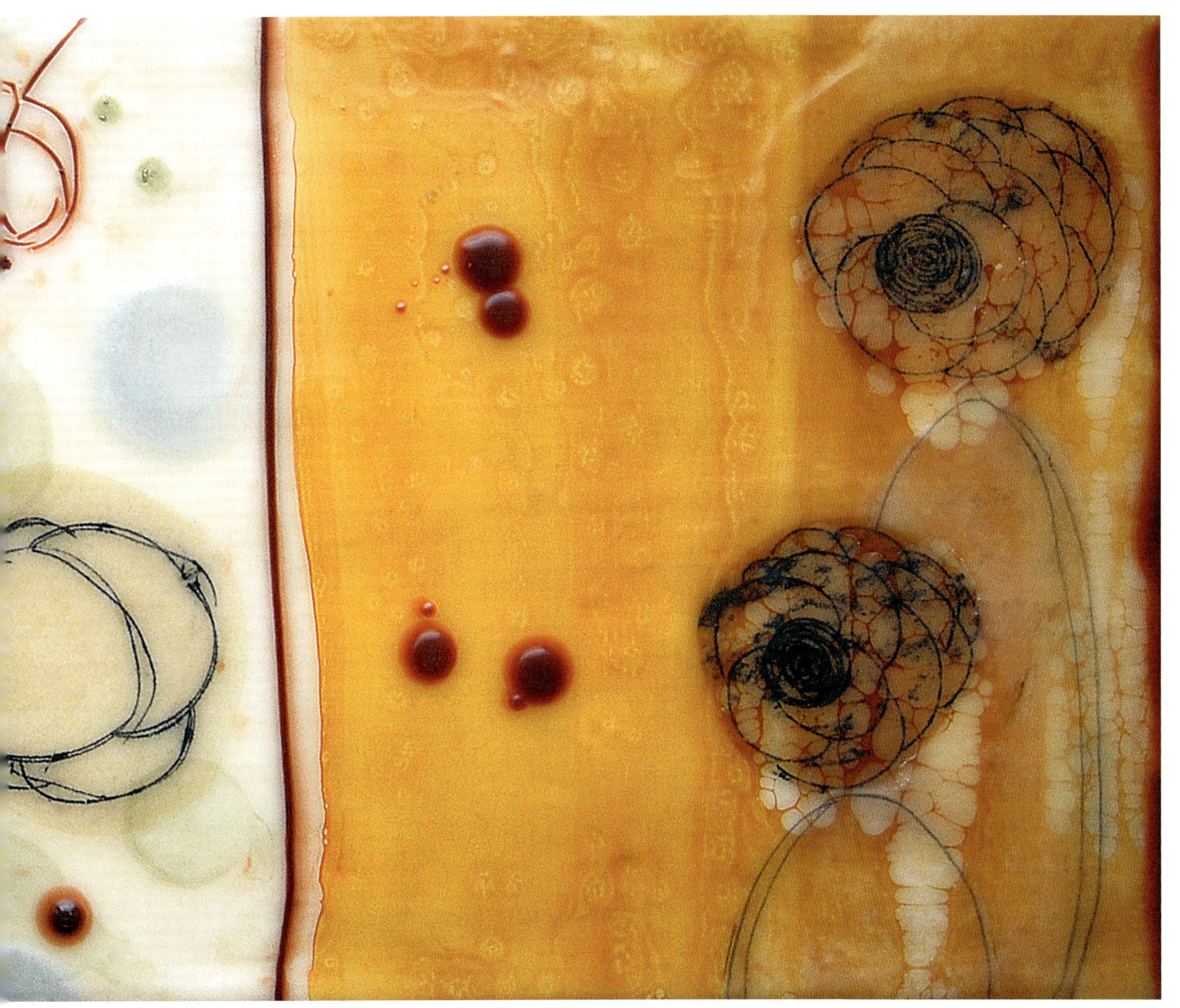

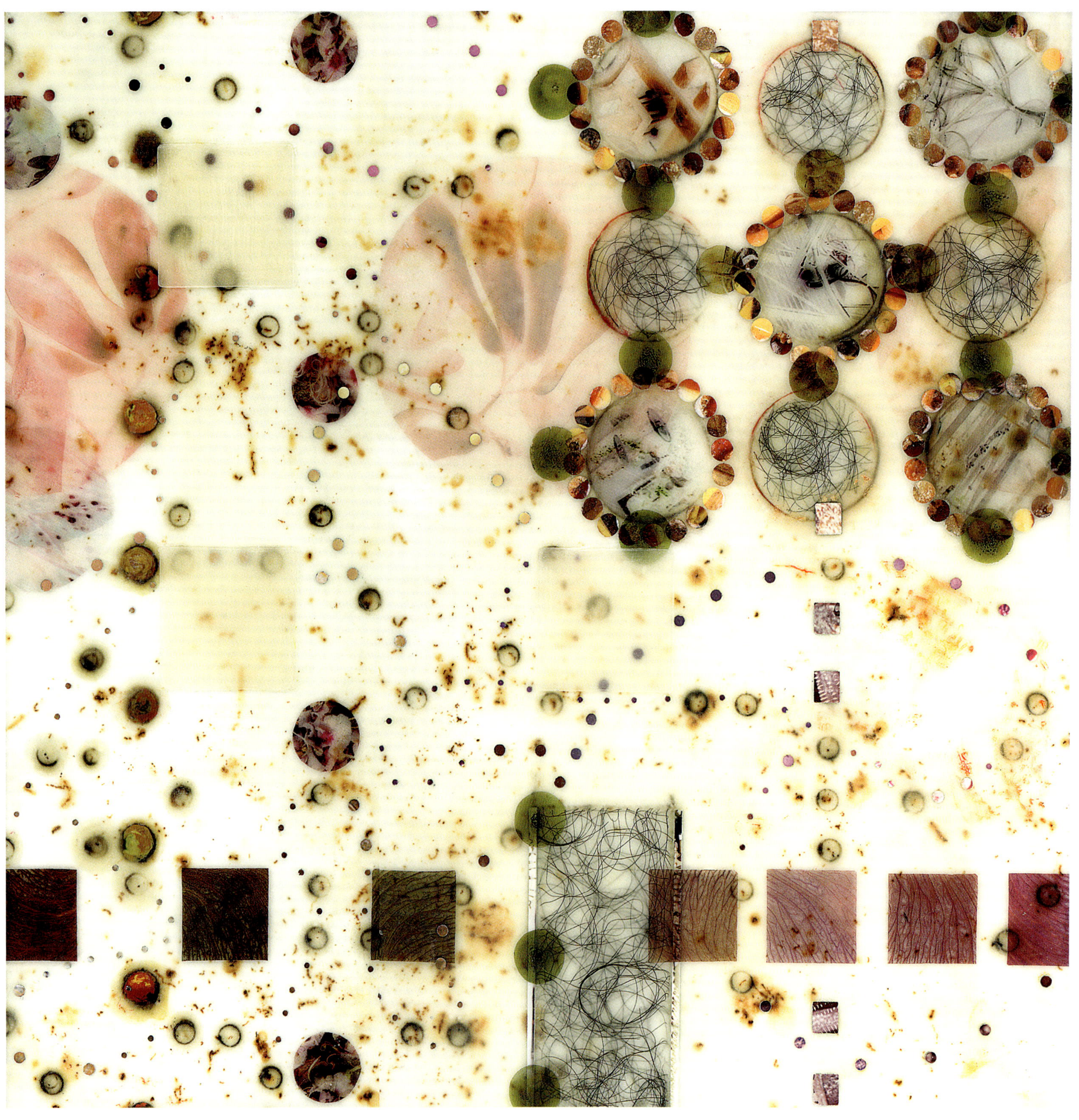

Lesson 3: Mixed media

1. There are many interesting options for adding different materials into encaustic paintings, first start by using paper in your paintings. Start by applying three layers of color-tinted wax to your piece. Fuse well between each layer to create a smooth working surface.

2. Next, sketch onto a piece of paper with a pencil, or use paper which already has a print on it. Lay the paper onto the painting and paint over it with a brush saturated in clear wax. Fuse to adhere the paper completely to the piece. Standard-weight paper will become translucent after fusing, and this it how you can tell is has completely adhered to the painting surface.

3. Experiment by also sketching onto tissue paper. Cut the tissue paper with scissors, lay it onto your painting surface, and brush over it with melted wax. After fusing this layer, the tissue paper becomes completely transparent. Mixing this technique with incised lines (as you will learn in Lesson 8) can create very interesting compositions.

4. Add additional layers of clear medium while fusing between each layer. You will still be able to see the images on paper receding into the wax. Add more collage elements to create an interesting depth with objects which are on the surface and receding into the wax.

5. Experiment with larger collage elements. If you use an object such as a large button, first apply wet wax to your composition with a brush. While the wax is still wet, press the large button into the painting. When the wax has dried, paint additional layers of medium over the top and lightly fuse. Large objects may not adhere so easily to the painting, so gently try to move them to check that they are attached securely.

The options for collage elements are only limited by your imagination. Be sure that any object you use in a painting is archival and will not deteriorate over time. Mixed media materials may include origami paper, small rocks, sticks, feathers, dried leaves, doilies, ribbons, wire, and string.

Lorraine Glessner, *Circulation*, 2006.
Encaustic, digital prints, photographs, hair, paper, oil paint on rusted, composted, and burned silk on panel, 30.5 x 30.5 x 2.5 cm.

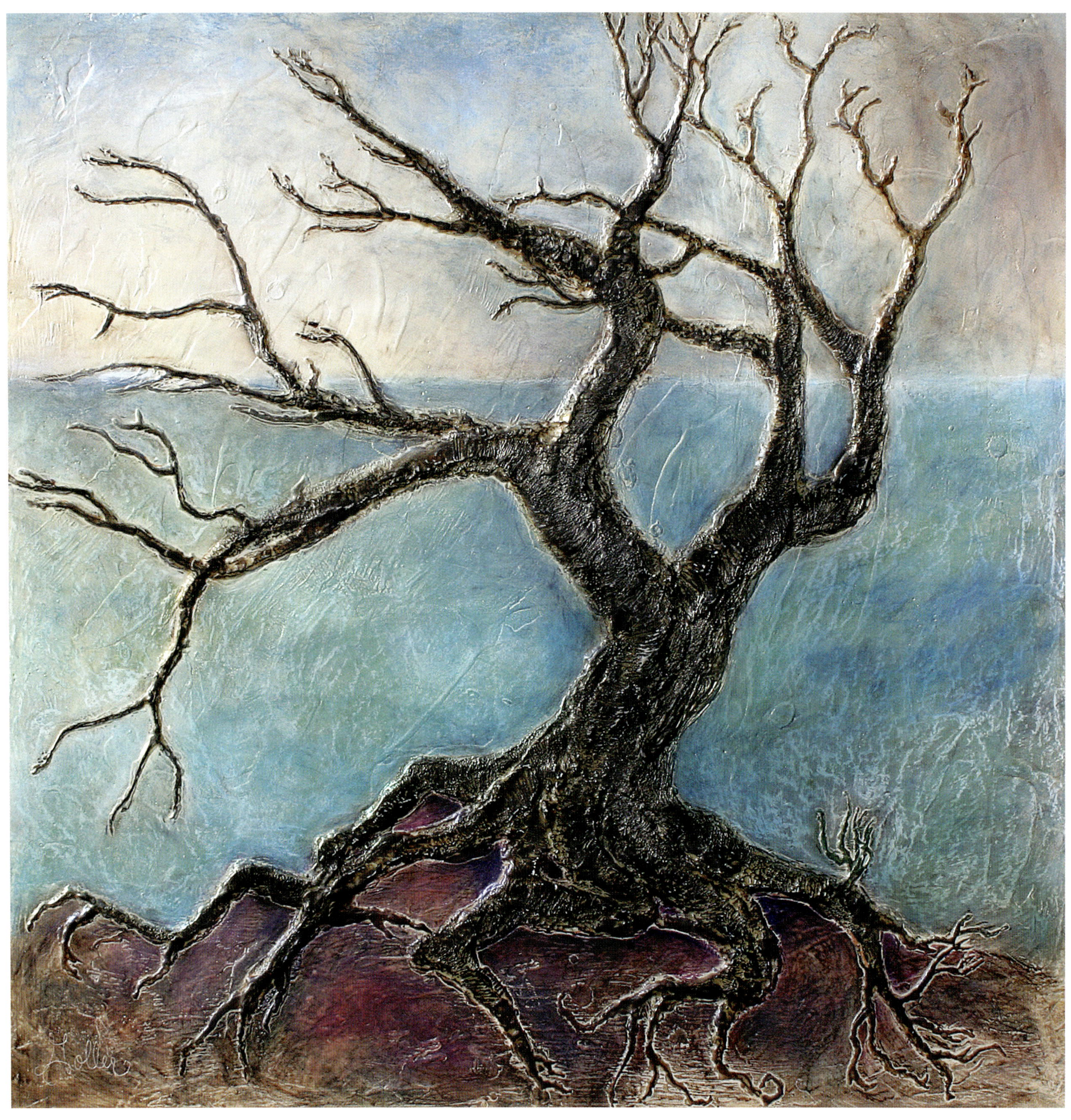

Lesson 4: Dimensional objects

1. It is possible to build dimensional objects in your compositions using encaustics. Start by applying three layers of color-tinted wax to your piece. Fuse well between each layer to create a smooth working surface. Build up subtle colors for the background of the piece. Add either oil paint or tinted encaustic medium to your melted encaustic paint, you do not need to add a lot of color. Building more layers with tinted color will produce transparency in your piece and help it to glow from within. Paint at least three layers.

2. Choose a concentrated color that you would like to use for a dimensional object. Use a wide hog bristle brush and lay down the initial layers. Lightly fuse the wax using a heat gun in a circular motion. Use a smaller hog bristle brush to create smaller lines and details in the same color. Continue to brush on additional layers and watch as the object grows dimensionally on your surface. Fuse lightly with a heat gun between each layer so that you can see the wax become glossy and melted, and then pull the heat gun away.

3. You can experiment with opacity by adding a low concentration of color to medium in the top layers. Also try slightly changing the color of the wax as your layers grow. As you finish your piece, move toward using smaller brushes. If a painting is executed using only one size brush it will show, however, if you use multiple size brushes you can create a more dynamic composition if this is the look you desire.

4. You can create texture by fusing very lightly, while still allowing the texture to remain from applying the wax with the hog bristle brush. Also try waiting until the wax is almost cool and dab it with the end of the brush for an interesting variation.

"For the larger tree areas, I built up layers while heat sealing every layer, using hog bristle brushes. For smaller branches, I used a wire brush of heated tool with a stylus on the end. For texture I simply brush the wax on and allow it to stay textured, or sculpt it with a brush or heated tool. I am careful with each heat sealing not to melt the texture. For iridescence, I usually use mica powders which I build up in many layers. It is messy and there is sometimes cleanup with a damp cloth before heat sealing."

- Carrie Goller

Carrie Goller, *Leaving II.*
Encaustic with iridescent minerals on two box panels, 61 x 61 x 55.8 cm. Pagosa Springs Art Gallery.

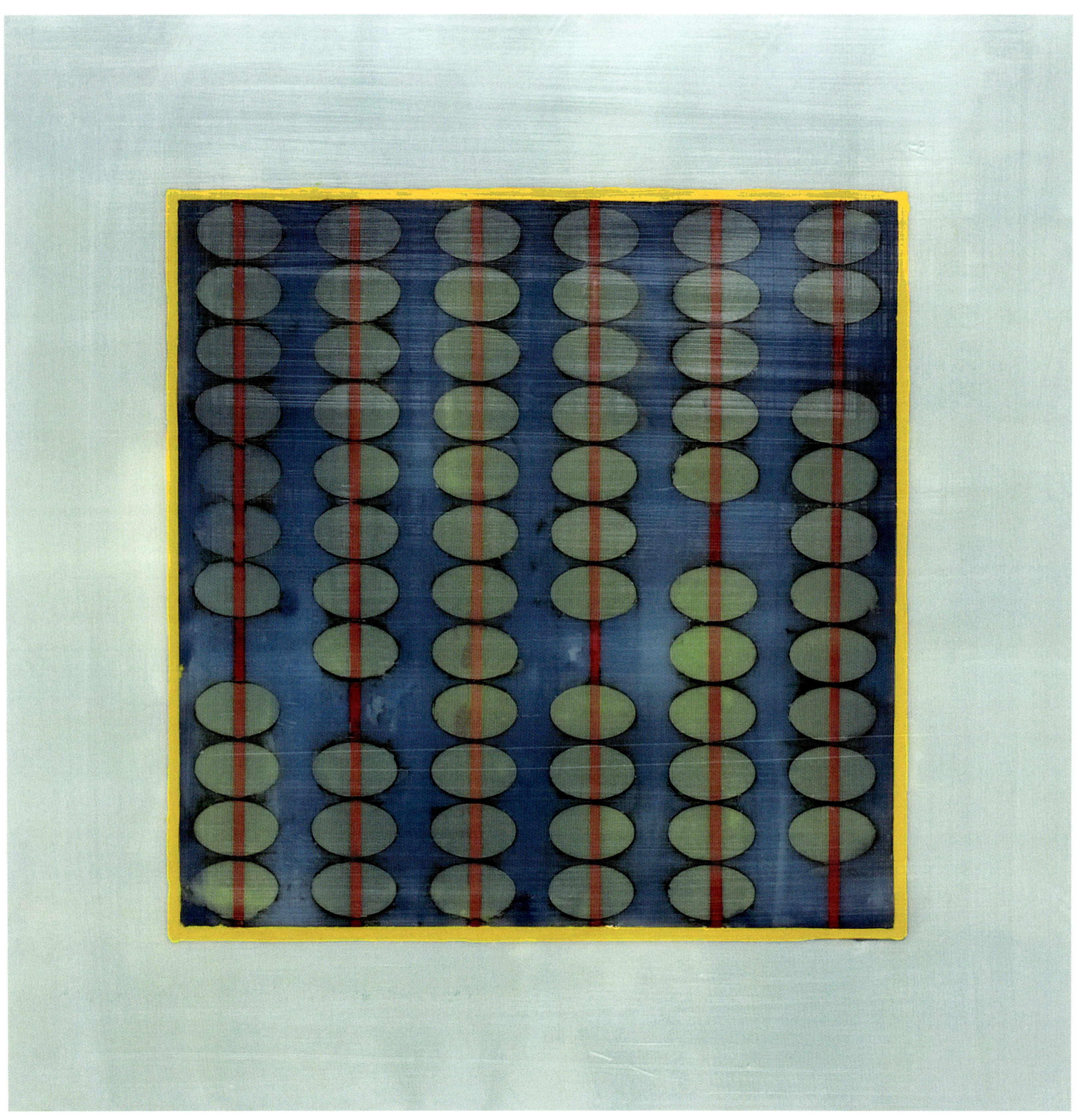

Lesson 5: Using masks

1. Paint and fuse at least two background layers with medium or medium tinted with encaustic paint. Be sure to remove all air bubbles and create a very smooth surface as you fuse; the smoother your surface the better contact the mask can have with the wax.

2. Create your mask by first choosing a material, such as standard paper, heavy-weight paper, clear plastic materials, vellum, or tape. Clear projector film sheets work well because they are designed to withstand heat. Many materials can work well for a mask, so get creative. In this example, we will use a clear plastic sheet. Use a razor blade to cut a shape out of the clear plastic sheet. Next place your mask on your painting and press down hard to ensure good contact. You can burnish with the back of a spoon or other improvised tool.

3. Next, use a brush to paint layers of encaustic medium in a different color over the mask and onto the painting surface. Paint over the exposed area in the mask and onto the mask so that you do not miss any places. Lightly fuse between each layer.

4. Next gently remove the mask and fuse again. You can now apply additional masks to the piece if you would like. Try creating the background in one color, and applying a dimensional mask with about three layers of medium in the same color. After removing the mask and fusing, you can rub an oil stick on the painting and wipe off the excess with paper towels. Leave a little bit of excess oil stick color around the perimeter of the dimensional masked area to emphasize the dimensionality.

"Once the background is laid down I have to scrape that back smooth and level. Then I will apply a stencil and I will lay down the ovals. That is usually a couple of layers. I scrape those back then go in with either a clear medium or tinted medium. I fill in those elements up until it covers the ovals that were made. When I do that, first I will go and kind of outline each of the ovals with a really fine brush so that I will hold my edges and I will minimize the tendency to create air bubbles. So, it is a lot of gentle fusing and laying down of very, very thin layers of wax."

- Karen Freedman

Karen Freedman, *Abacus: Summation*, 2009.
Encaustic on wood panel, 30.5 x 30.5 x 2.7 cm.

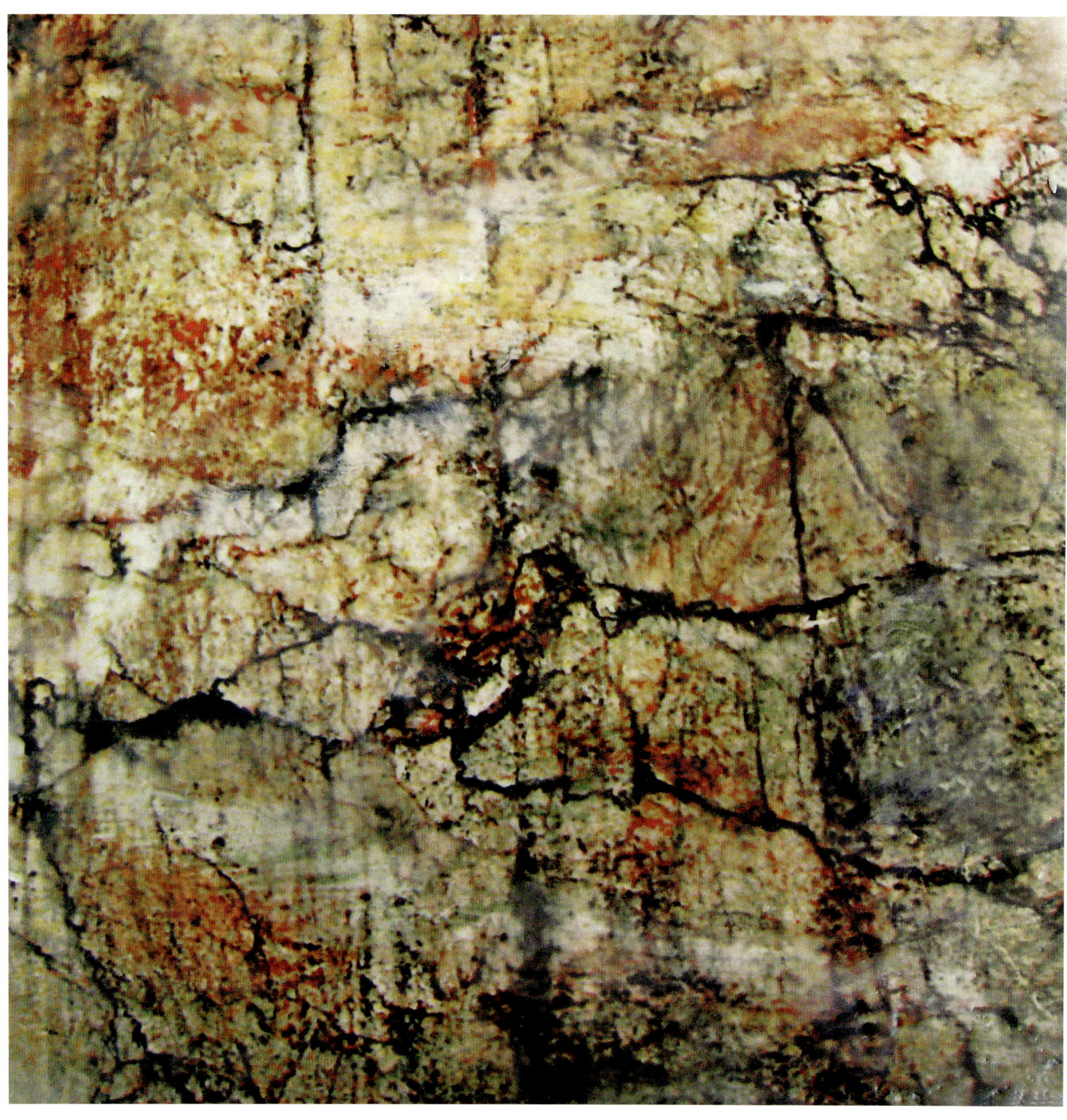

Lesson 6: Photography

1. Creating an encaustic painting over photography adds interesting detail and translucency. Use a ground which has some texture, such as wood. Choose an image which you would like to adhere to either the entire background or part of the background of the piece. It can be a photo printed onto paper with an inkjet printer, an archival-quality photograph, or even an image printed onto a cotton rag or fabric.

2. Use a neutral pH glue, such as Elmer's Glue, to paint a thin layer onto your ground. It works well to dilute the glue in a mix of 2 parts glue to 1 part water. Next lay your photograph onto the surface and remove air bubbles. A brayer works well to remove bubbles. Let the glue completely dry and check that the photograph is well adhered before proceeding.

3. Next paint a layer of clear medium over the photograph, and fuse. You can now add layers of tinted wax; paint directly onto the art piece with brushes, incise lines, or draw with an oil stick to create an interesting composition.

4. You can also try printing onto tissue paper or thin white Japanese paper. Apply the paper, paint on a top layer of medium, and fuse. After fusing the paper into the wax, it becomes translucent and all that remains is the image. Layering this effect over background photography works well to add an interesting depth to your piece.

"You can draw right on the wax with oil pastels and wax crayons, then coat it with a layer of medium on top of that. You just have to be really careful not to heat it too quickly or you will melt it and lose the detail."

- Brandy Eiger

Brandy Eiger, *Passages II*, 2008.
Encaustic on mixed medium, 25.4 x 25.4 cm.

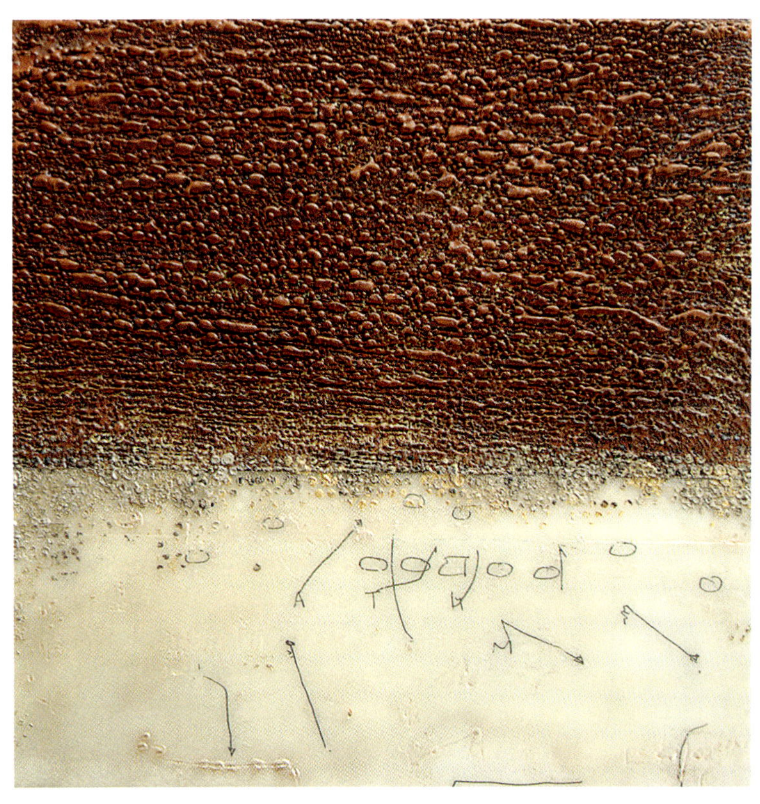

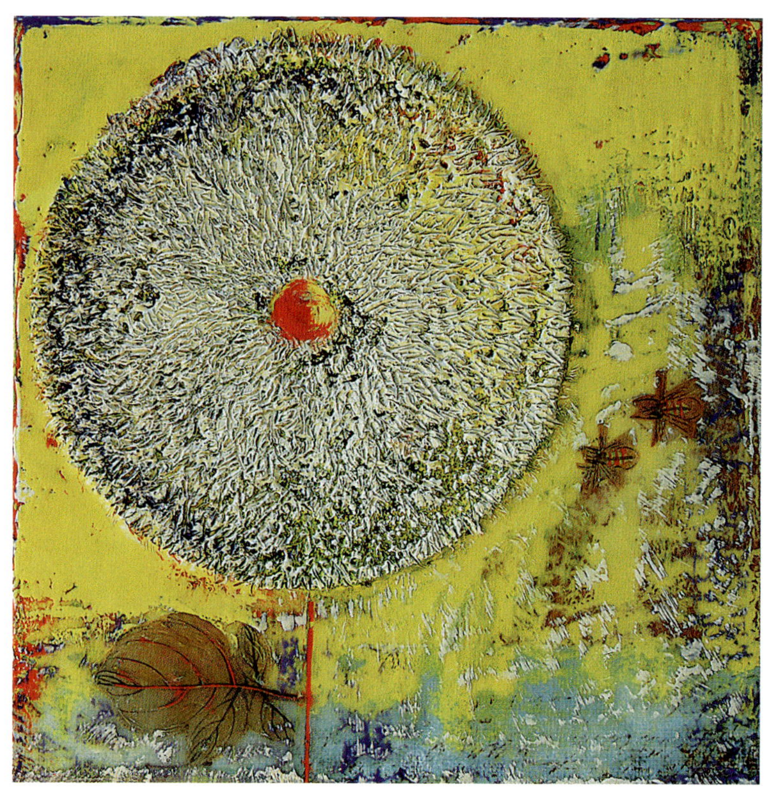

Kristy Battani, *Short Zoro*, 2008. Encaustic, 30.5 x 30.5 cm.

Kristy Battani, *Sunburst*, 2009. Encaustic, 25.4 x 25.4 cm.

Lesson 7: Textural background

1. Start by applying two background layers to your piece, fusing between each layer.

2. To begin creating texture in your piece, first decide what kind of composition you would like to create. Using brightly colored textures next to each other can create high contrast or, by fusing one part of the piece, you can create a texture which is part smooth as water, and part highly textured. To create texture, use a large hog bristle brush to lay down layer after layer of wax in your desired color. Dip your brush into the wax, then wait for a moment while it cools slightly before painting a layer of wax. When the wax is slightly cooler it creates more texture as you build up layers. Use your heat gun to fuse very lightly between layers.

3. Continue to build up layers until you have the amount of texture you desire. Experiment by using different brush strokes. You will achieve different textures by always brushing horizontally in the same direction, or by alternating the direction of the strokes.

"On the top I used a dry brush technique. Usually a wide brush works nicely. As you dip it into your paint, you hold just for a second so it is actually getting cool before you brush it on. You are just brushing and brushing over in the same spot."

- Kristy Battani

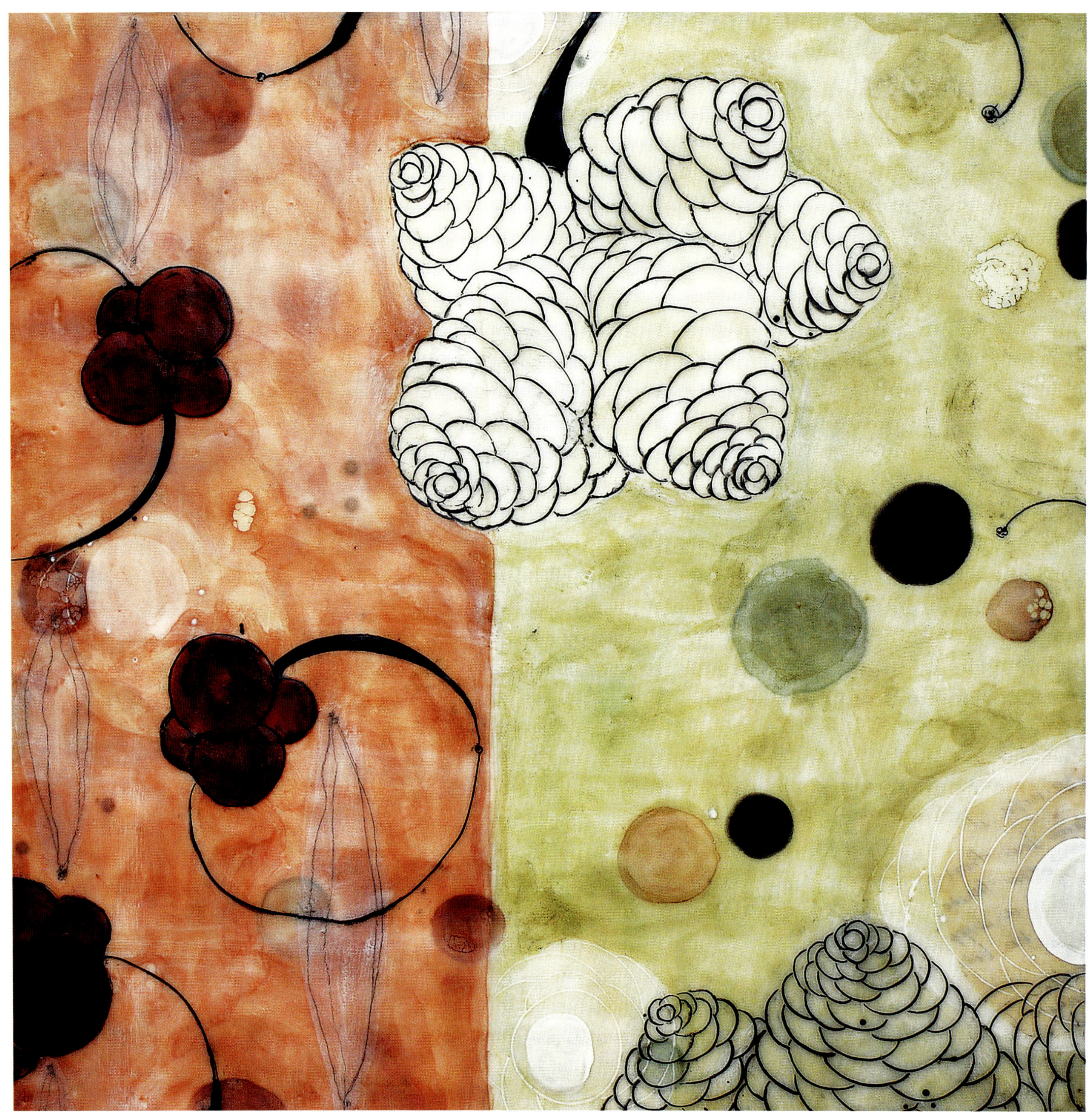

Stephanie Hargrave, *Anemone 4*, 2008. Encaustic, 60.9 x 60.9 cm.

Lesson 8: Incised lines

1. To create incised lines, start by applying a background with at least four layers of wax. You need to create a thick enough surface to scrape into without hitting the background substrate. Fuse well between each layer and create a glossy smooth surface.

2. Use a tool to scrape thin lines or shapes into the wax. You can use wood carving tools, a razor blade, or any sharp pointed object. Get creative and try different tools. By varying the tools you use, you will create different line weights. Wipe away excess wax which comes up with a palette knife as you go.

4. Next fill the incised lines with oil sticks or oil paint. Use a rag to rub the oil paint into the cracks, or apply the oil sticks. Afterward wipe off the excess paint with paper towels. What remains will be only the color in the lines and whatever color you choose not to wipe away.

5. Fuse very lightly. Paint on a layer of clear medium over the top and fuse to seal. For variations, try using different tools or objects to create carved lines. You can use the sharp metal edge from a lid to create a circle, or experiment with cookie cutters. You can also use mixed media line drawings on paper or tissue, which you can fuse into layers of wax. Next incise lines into the same piece. The contrast in line styles can create an interesting contrast.

NOTE
An alternate way to create incised lines is by painting colored melted wax into the lines. Next scrape off the excess with a sharp tool such as a razor blade. All that will be left is the delicate line of wax remaining in the incision. This creates a similar effect, but is more time consuming than using oil paint or an oil stick.

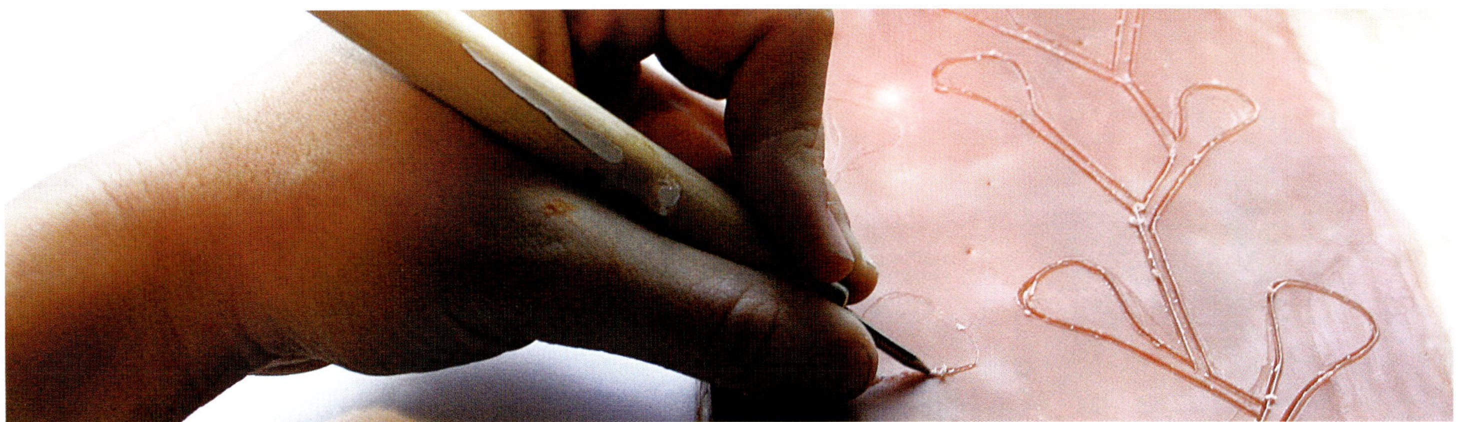

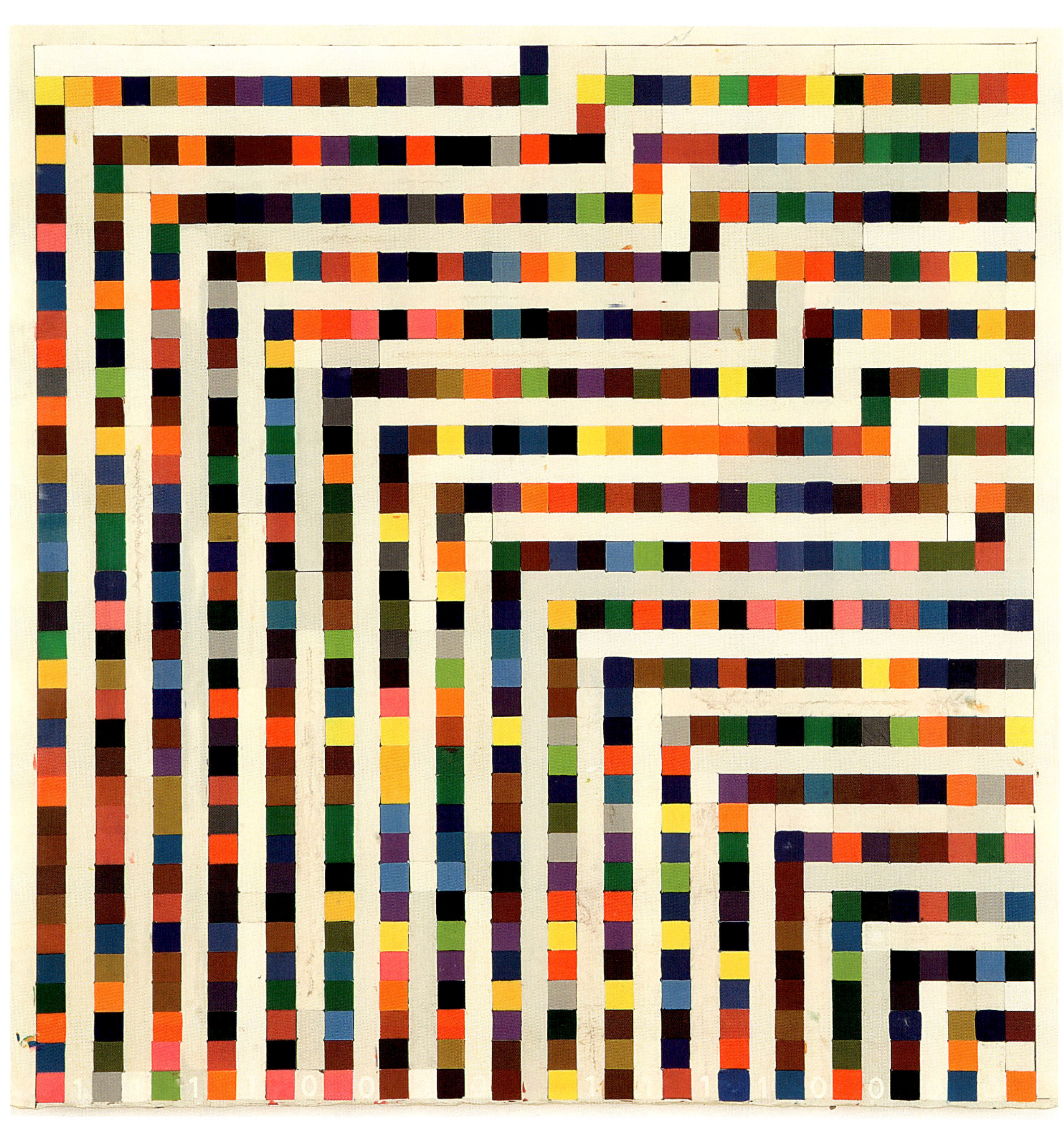

Richard Purdy, *230-240-250* (detail), 2004.
Encaustic on plywood, 10.6 x 40.6 cm.

Lesson 9: Scraping layers

1. Start by choosing a contrasting color palette. Decide which layers you would like to be revealed when you scrape back into your piece later. Next begin painting and fusing smooth layers of wax in your base color. Be sure to gently fuse in a circle to remove any air bubbles which may form.

2. Build up many layers of color to create an interesting look later. Add additional layers in different colors to reveal later.

3. Use a tool to scrape away sections of the wax. Experiment with different techniques and tools. You can use grouting tools, a razor blade, or a long knife edge.

4. You can also use wood cutting tools to carve interesting designs into your piece. Wipe away excess wax with a palette knife. When the piece is completely finished, lightly fuse to seal the wax.

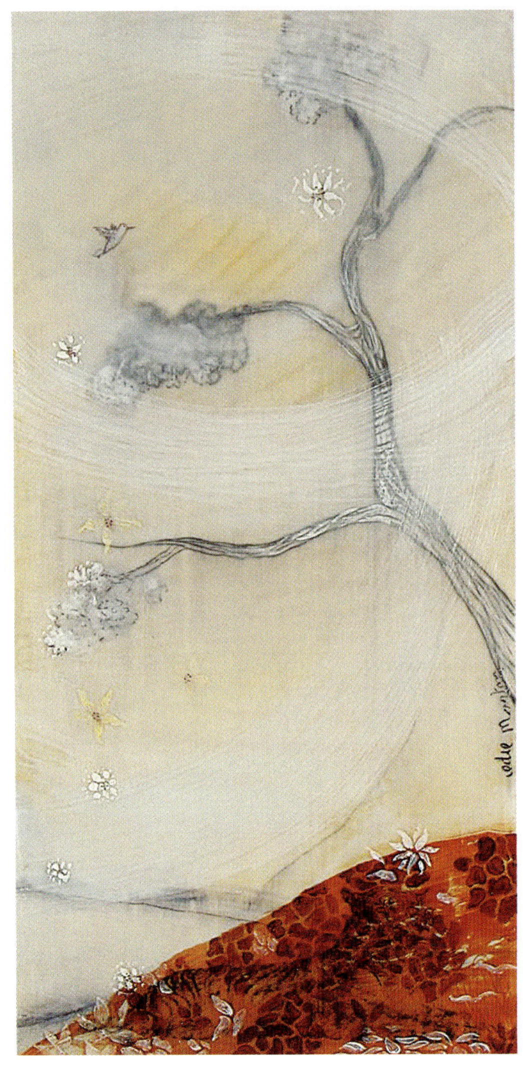

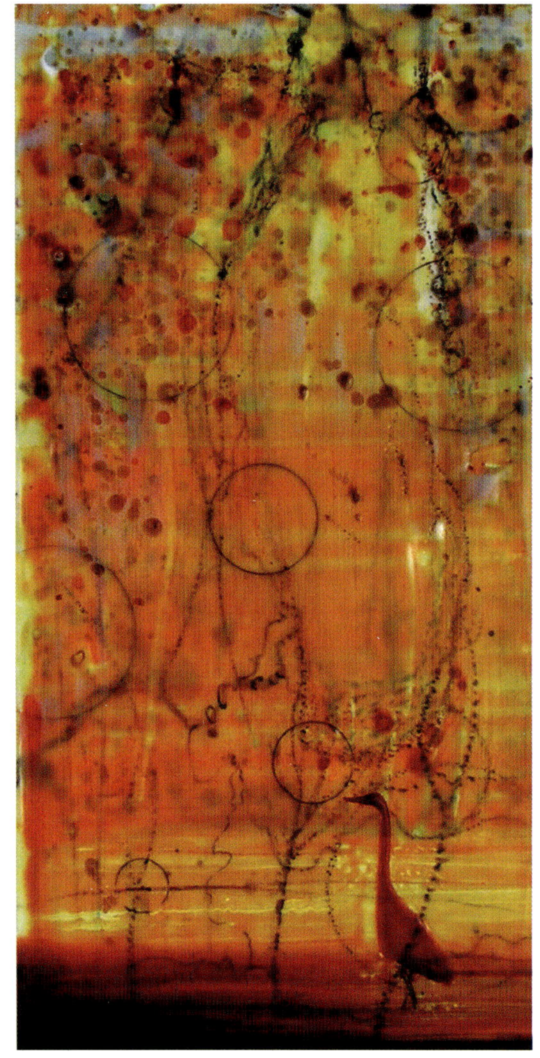

Edie Morton, *Lama*, 2007. Encaustic, 30.5 x 15.2 cm.

Edie Morton, *Summer Solstice*, 2008. Encaustic, 30.5 x 15.2 cm.

Lesson 10: Photo transfers

1. Paint at least three layers of tinted encaustic medium to create a base to work onto. Fuse well between each layer. A very smooth surface is required for a good photo transfer.

2. Choose an image to use. Either photocopy the image with a standard copy machine or print it on a laser printer. Inkjet printers will not work. Remember that the image will be mirrored and your final image will be a reverse of your original print.

3. Cut out the part of the image that you would like to use, and lay it face down on your surface. Next, use the back of a spoon to thouroughly burnish your image onto the painting. It is helpful to put down a layer of wax paper and burnish with the spoon through the paper in order to not move or tear the paper print.

4. Next, use a cotton ball or paper towels to apply acetate to your print. Nail polish remover also does the trick just as well. Apply acetate until you can see that the print is semi-translucent and fully wet. You will start to see the print and the paper will start to wrinkle when the paper has begun to separate from the toner.

5. Use your finger to rub along the paper, which will roll up and flake away. Continue to add acetate as needed to keep the paper moist. Rub gently until the paper has all flaked away and the toner remains. Do not worry if small pieces of paper remain. Fuse the piece lightly when finished, and small remaining pieces of paper will become translucent in the wax.

NOTE:
Another way to create a photo transfer is by printing with a laser printer directly onto wax paper. Next use the back of a spoon to firmly burnish the print onto your surface. Gently remove the wax, and what remains is the toner transfer. Give the toner time to dry, then later add a layer of clear medium and gently fuse.

"The dark lines are incised into the wax using a ceramic pin tool. It is sort of my drawing instrument and then I fill in the incised lines with oil stick. Beneath the hill in the foreground, is an ink transfer of a tiger. There are layers on top of that so it is kind of subtle."

Edie Morton - Interview Regarding "Lama" shown Left

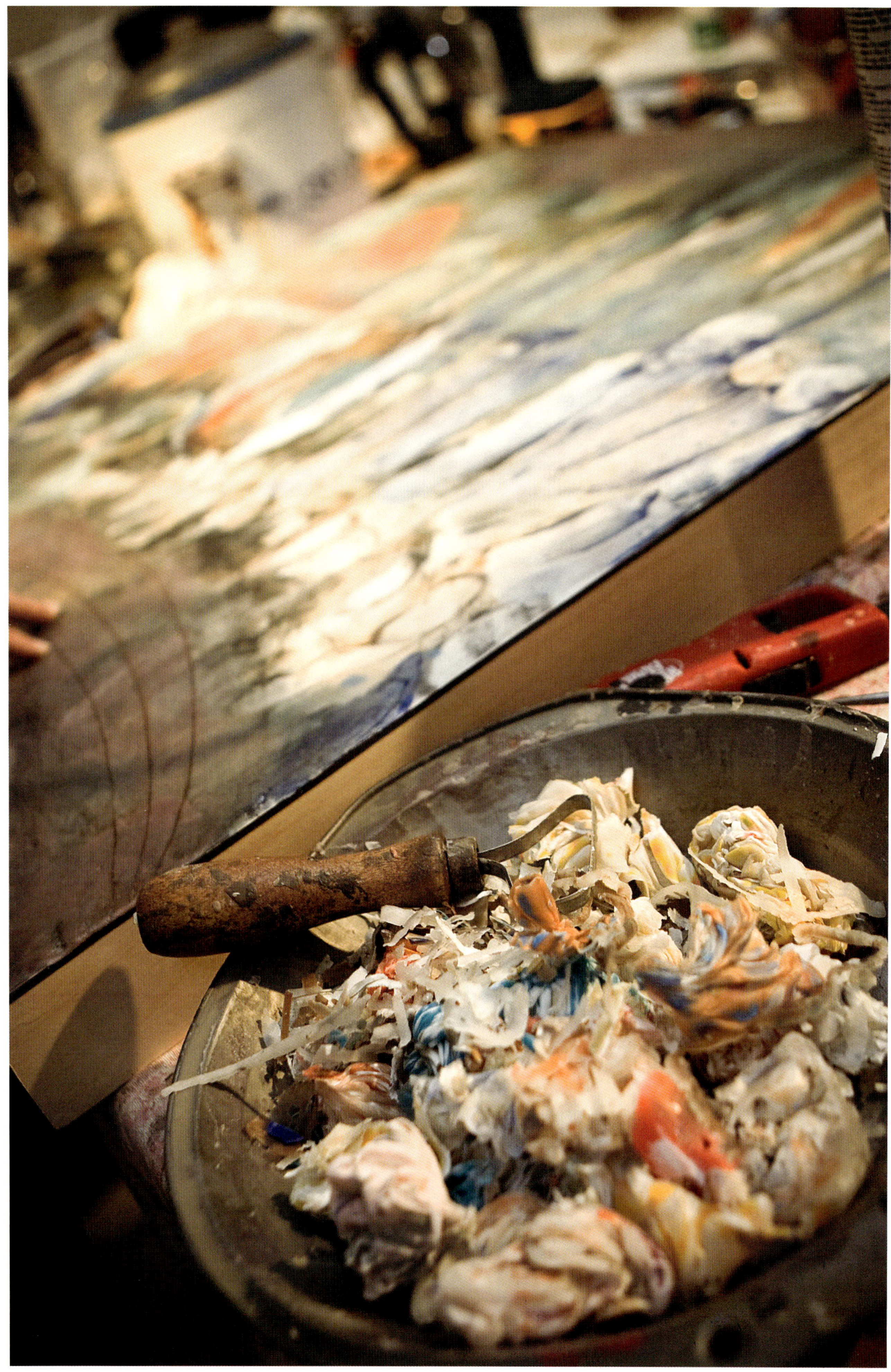

Safety precautions

VENTILATION

As with oil paint, you should only paint with encaustics in a well-ventilated studio environment. Use either an industrial ventilating system, or a fan in combination with open windows. You should have a window open to allow incoming airflow, and a fan near your work surface to blow air away from your and out the window. You can light a candle as a test and blow it out, then watch where the smoke blows; it should blow away from you and out the window.

SAFE TEMPERATURE RANGE

A safe working range for encaustic is between 150-175° Fahrenheit. Beeswax has a flash point of around 470° Fahrenheit, but at no point should you allow the wax to get close to this temperature. If you wax begins to smoke at any point, turn down the heat. Keep a fire extinguisher handy in your studio because water does not extinguish inflamed wax. If you use tools such as a griddle with encaustic painting, do not later use them for food preparation. Rather, use cheap materials from the thrift store and dedicate them solely to work with encaustics.

MIXING MATERIALS

Never use crayons for pigment when painting encaustics. Regular crayons are made with paraffin, which is too brittle and will fade over time.

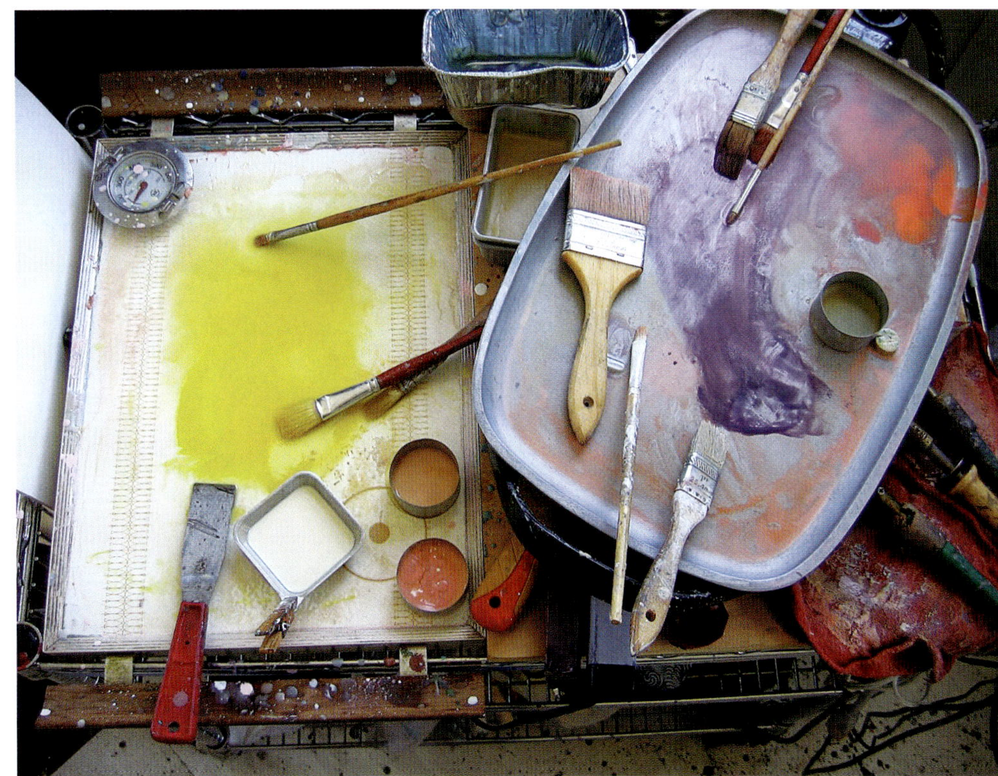

Amy Royce, Painting studio.

Adele Shaw, Studio detail.

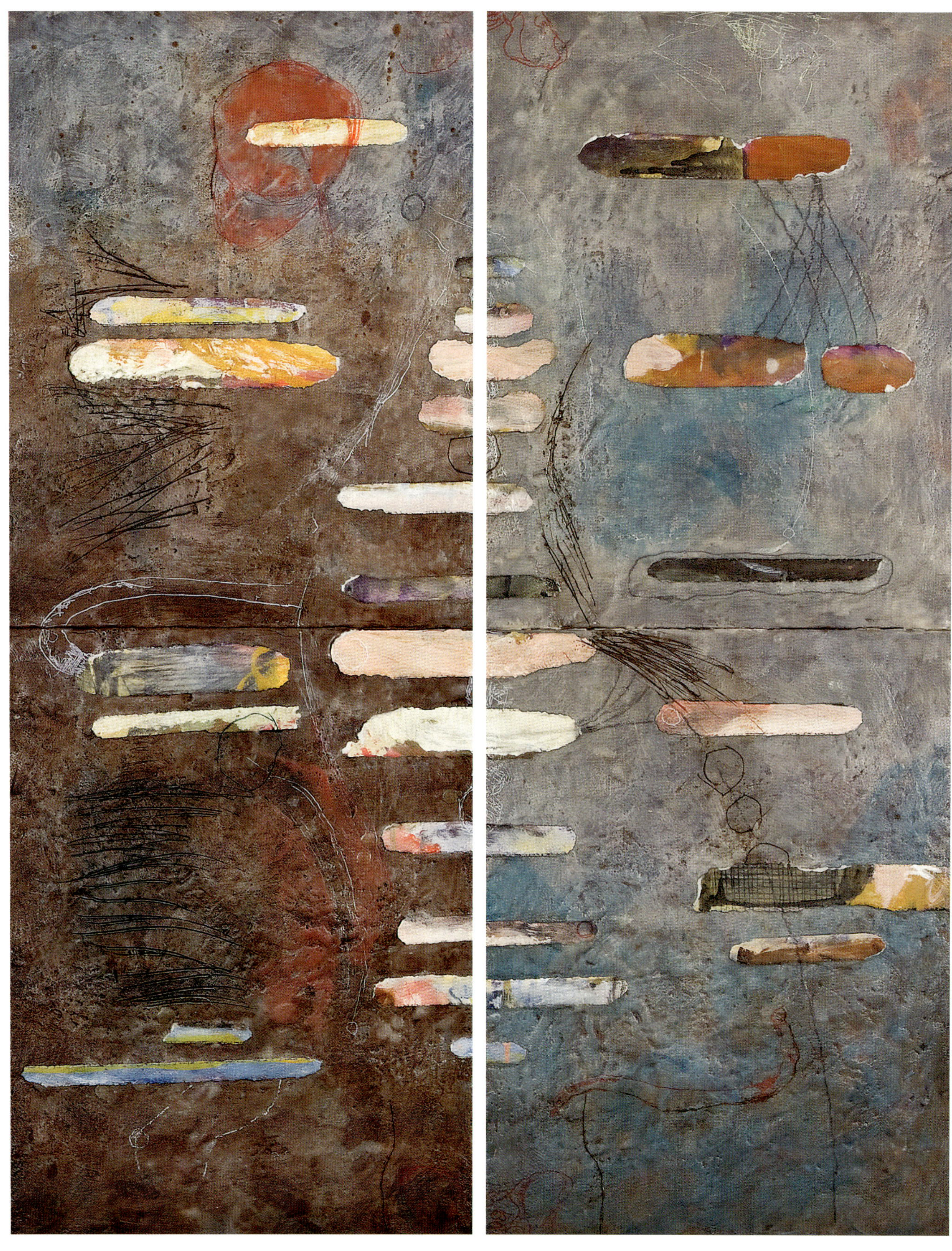

Amy Royce, *Sub-Blue*, 2008. Encaustic with mixed media on panel, 101.6 x 81.2 cm.

Artist Interviews

10 Artists Speak of their Ambitions, Inspirations, and Painting Techniques

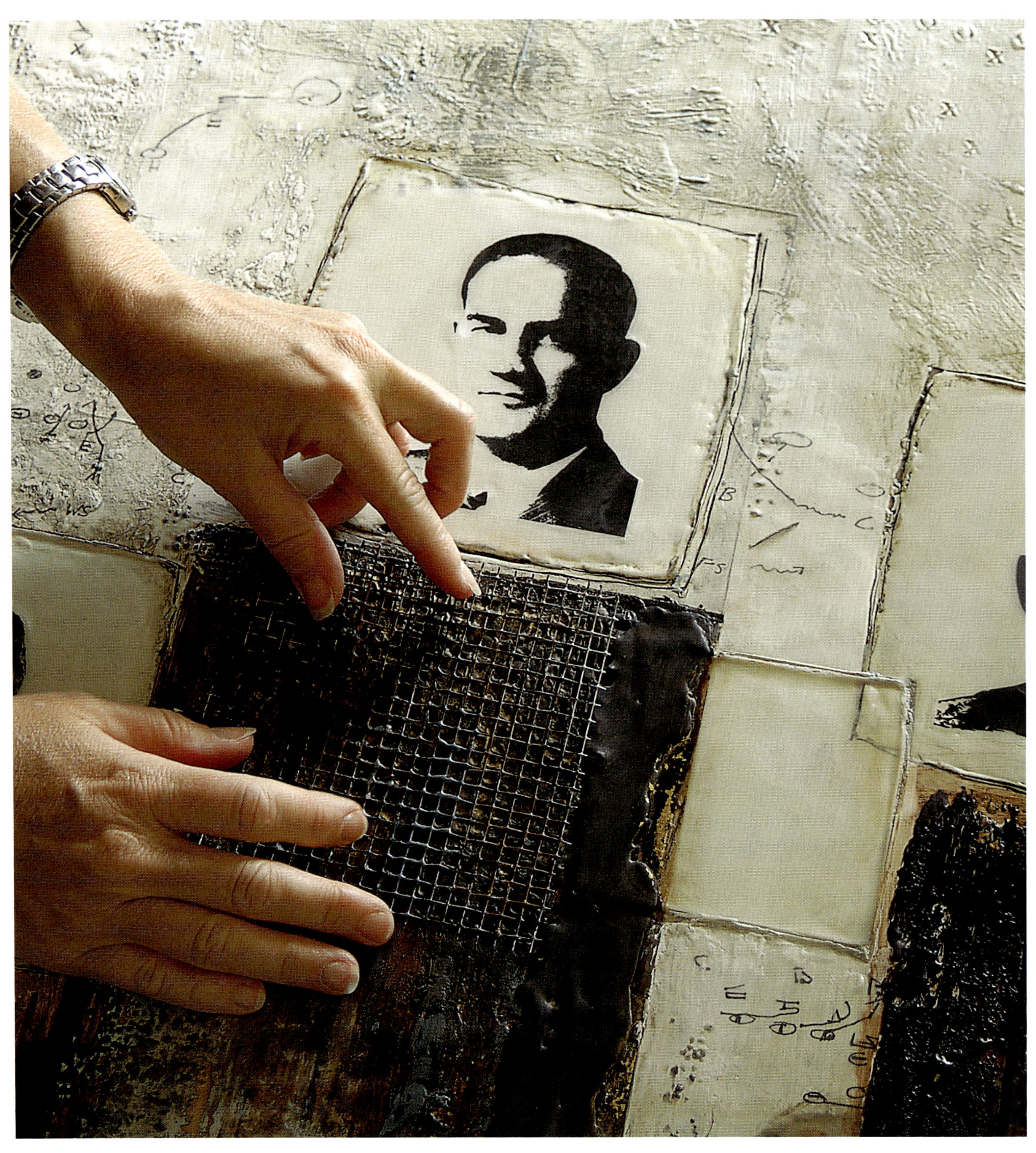

Kristy Battani, *Perseverance* (work in progess), 2010.
Encaustic with photo transfer, embedded wire, football pigskin, and multiple layers of etchings, 121.9 x 304.8 cm.

Kristy Battani

Kristy Darnell Battani's artwork and installations reflect her interest in environments and their effect on individual character. Battani enjoys working with encaustics because it allows her to literally embed part of the environment in the artwork. For example, the delicate environment of a Japanese lotus may be delineated with slivers of origami paper or the rough exterior of a prickly pear cactus with rusted detritus.

Battani herself is the product of a series of contrasting environments. As the only child of a college football coach, Battani's life was influenced by the very public world of collegiate athletics and many of her works in the *Gridiron* series are a reflection of the personalities and experiences of those days. Battani followed her undergraduate studies in communications and art, with a career in law, focusing on intellectual property protection. Battani returned for graduate studies in design, followed by teaching and ultimately gravitating back to an art studio practice. Battani currently resides in Austin, Texas and specializes in creating original artwork and installations for commercial and private collections. Battani also lectures and works with educational institutions and artists' groups on art business topics.

"Lately I have been using textures with stucco and concrete. But I have used wire and mesh, slate, pigskin, and leather. The possibilities are really just endless."

What do you find challenging and endearing about working with encaustics?
I think that, very often, something that we love can also be something that we hate, which I think is very true for encaustics. I love encaustics because they really have a mind of their own. There are serendipitous accidents which occur in this art form which are beautiful, and you really couldn't recreate them in any other medium. However, you cannot completely control encaustics and at any moment you could do something which would completely alter the piece. Of course, if you don't like the result, it can always be scraped or melted away, however, it can be frustrating at times.

What artists have influenced your work?
There are so many artists doing interesting and wonderful things with encaustics. I like Cari Hernandez, Laura Moriarty, and Eileen Goldenberg. I have a friend right here in Austin, Sharon Kyle Kuhn, who is fearless about experimenting with materials. Outside of that, I often enjoy going to the R&F paints website, and they recently updated their website so it is really quite nice. They feature a different encaustic artist each month. That has definitely introduced me to some interesting techniques that people are using out there.

What unconventional materials do you like to use in your work?
The best thing about working with encaustics is to experiment with different materials. Lately I have been using textures with stucco and concrete. But I have used wire and mesh, slate, pigskin, and leather. The possibilities are really just endless. For me, going to a hardware store is similar to going on safari, just going up and down the aisles; you never know what you are going to find in a little bin. It may be uncertain as to what it is really supposed to be used for, but you look at it more for both the texture and the shape of it. It is not the intended finished product, and you know that if you ask a sales associate for help you will certainly confuse them. But that is the fun of it, the joy of finding the unexpected. But you do need to be mindful of, in encaustic art, the fact that there is some science involved and you have to be careful. Avoid adding materials to the wax which have properties comprising plastic and petroleum, and be sure that you really understand the relationship between the materials. If you get a product or material which you are not familiar with, be advised to read the ingredients or find out what it is made from. Sometimes I am happily surprised that it is a natural element, but sometimes it is actually a chemical or a plastic, and you really shouldn't be trying to mix both.

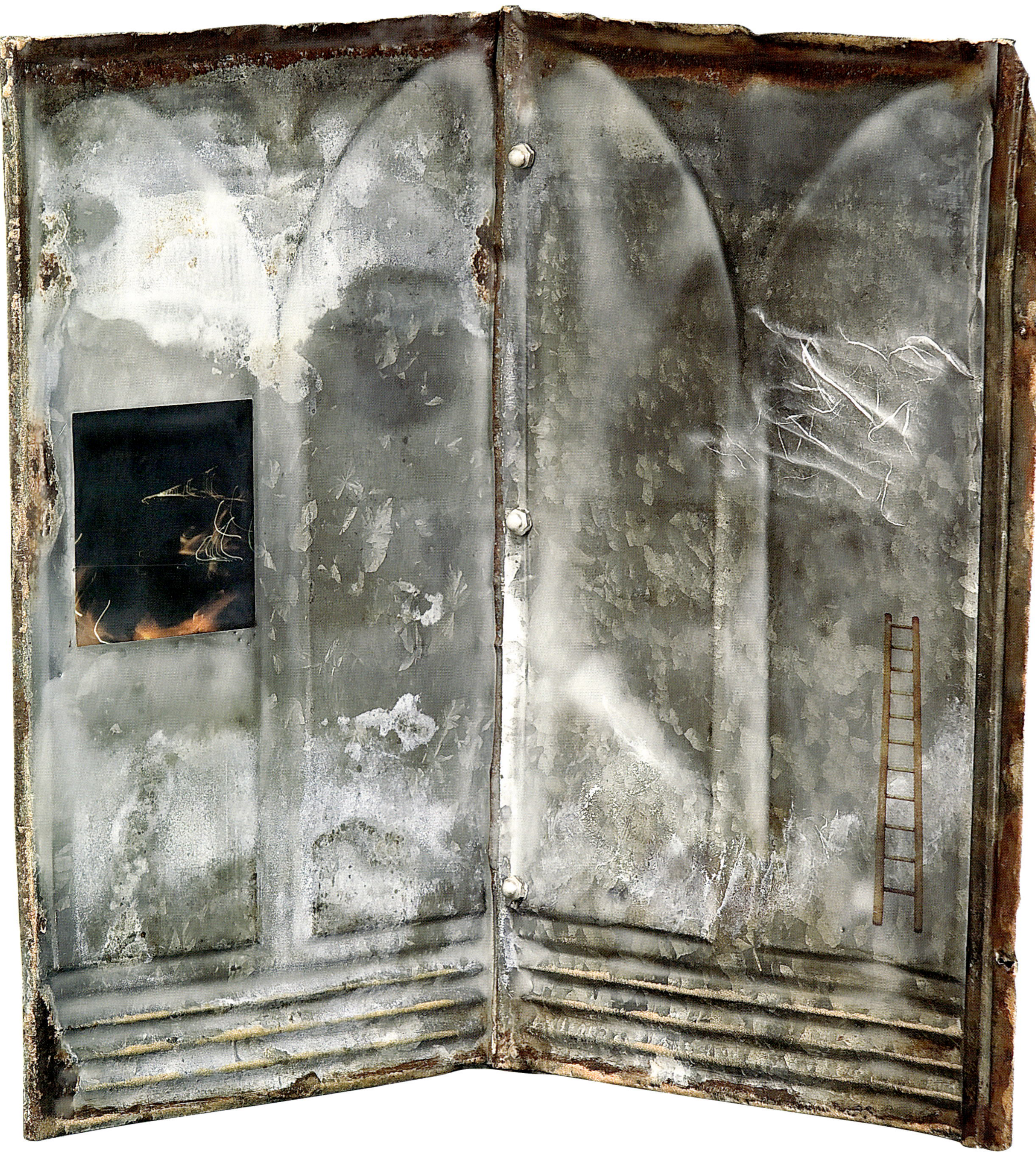

Brandy Eiger

Fascinated by our spiritual relationship with the universe, I make mixed media work to explore inner states of being and the seemingly contradictory feelings that coexist within us. We feel private, yet exposed; we feel energized, yet we possess an inner stillness; we constantly question, yet feel sure. We can be one thing on the surface and something altogether different within.

Rather than discarding or denying these contradictions, I feel they are what make us complex and interesting. In both life and in my work, even the most flawed or imperfect elements become an essential part of the process of becoming whole, or more fully who we are. Finding beauty in unexpected places, I integrate recycled elements with more typical artist materials like oil paint, photographs, and encaustic made from beeswax, resin, and colored pigments. I often incorporate elements that are normally discarded such as rusted metal, old wood, hair from the stylist's floor, scraps of old newspaper or burlap, or thrift store markdowns.

It isn't essential to me that the viewer recognizes the materials that make up a finished piece, but the transformation that occurs is intrinsic to my artistic process. An abandoned cart axle becomes a mystical temple, a rusted roof tile becomes a prayer book, and a photographic image submerged in wax and paint takes on new meaning.

"I allow the materials I use to become something more than they were before. Sometimes I direct the process, and sometimes I just step out of the way."

- Brandy Eiger

Brandy Eiger, *Devotion I*, 2010.
Encaustic on mixed medium, 35.5 x 33 x 17.7 cm.

How long have you been working with encaustics?

I have been a sculptor and painter my whole life, and became an encaustic painter about three years ago because I love the textures and the layering effects that it allows me to build. I love that it allows me to build in both an additive and reductive way.

What inspires your paintings?

I am fascinated by our spiritual relationship with the universe. How we define that relationship, how we try to measure it, and how we interact with it or influence it. My work is about our state of being and dealing with the contradictory feelings within us. Like when we feel private or exposed, when we feel energized, yet we might have an inner stillness. We are constantly questioning, yet we feel sure. We could be one thing, but something altogether different a layer below. Rather than discarding or denying those contradictions, I find those contradictions interesting, and that is what inspires my work.

What advice do you have for encaustic artists who want to take their work to the next level?

I think that ninety percent is simply showing up. You need to have a consistent work ethic where you go to the studio every day and practice your craft, or if you have a day job, then nights or weekends work just as well. But the goal should be about your own visual language and communicating consistently. I think it really helps to work in a series where you are doing a similar thing in each work and you can watch yourself improve. I think it is also helpful to create a trusted group of artist friends where you can critique each other's work and that way you can find out if your work is communicating what you have intended. In terms of a prettier technique, I think classes and demos are really helpful. Particularly with encaustic, because I think it is not an easy medium to learn. You can save a lot of time and frustration by learning from more experienced artists. There is a really great yearly encaustic conference in June. It is put on by Joanne Mattera. If you go to this you can network, meet other artists, learn how to market yourself, and see incredible demos of techniques. On the West Coast, there is a yearly retreat as well. I really recommend joining the International Encaustic Association, because it can put you in touch with a lot of classes and opportunities in your area.

What materials do you like to use with your encaustics?

Well, I love to use unusual materials. Particularly things that are normally discarded, and that most people have thought have outlived their usefulness. So, some examples of things I use are rusted metal, old wood, hair from the stylist's floor, old newspaper, or burlap. Then I also use my own photographs, or more typical materials such as encaustic, oil paint, glass, and I love pastels and things like that.

What steps do you take when you start an encaustic painting?

Well, basically I take the edge of my encaustic board, and then I paint on several layers of gesso which is specifically made for encaustic. Sometimes I might sand it lightly for a smoother surface. Then I add layers of medium, either clear medium or a background color for the last layer before I start.

How do you frame your pieces, or give them hardware on the back so they are ready to be hung?

Well, because I work on cradled board and I paint the edges, the pieces do not need to be framed because they have a really nice surface and I put wire in the back for hanging. If the piece really needs a frame and a frame would really help the piece, I use a float frame. That gives it a slight reveal around the piece so that you can see the edges, and there is no glass.

In the floating frame that you mentioned, do you buy that premade or make it yourself?

No, I go to a framer and have them do it. Actually, a great resource is Chris Paschke, she is an encaustic artist and a framer. She will explain and give demos about how to do it yourself if you want to, or she will sell you the materials, or she will do the whole thing for you if you want. That is a really great resource, and she goes to the conferences and retreats, that is how I met her.

Can you tell us about your series called *Urban Nightscape*?

Yeah, that series came out of a series of night photographs that I took. Most of my photographs are of light at night, which to me represents the energy of urban life. I decided to do this series of light in black and white, just to emphasize the light and the energy I captured.

Brandy Eiger, *Devotion VI*, 2010.
Encaustic on mixed medium, 35.5 x 36.8 x 13.9 cm.

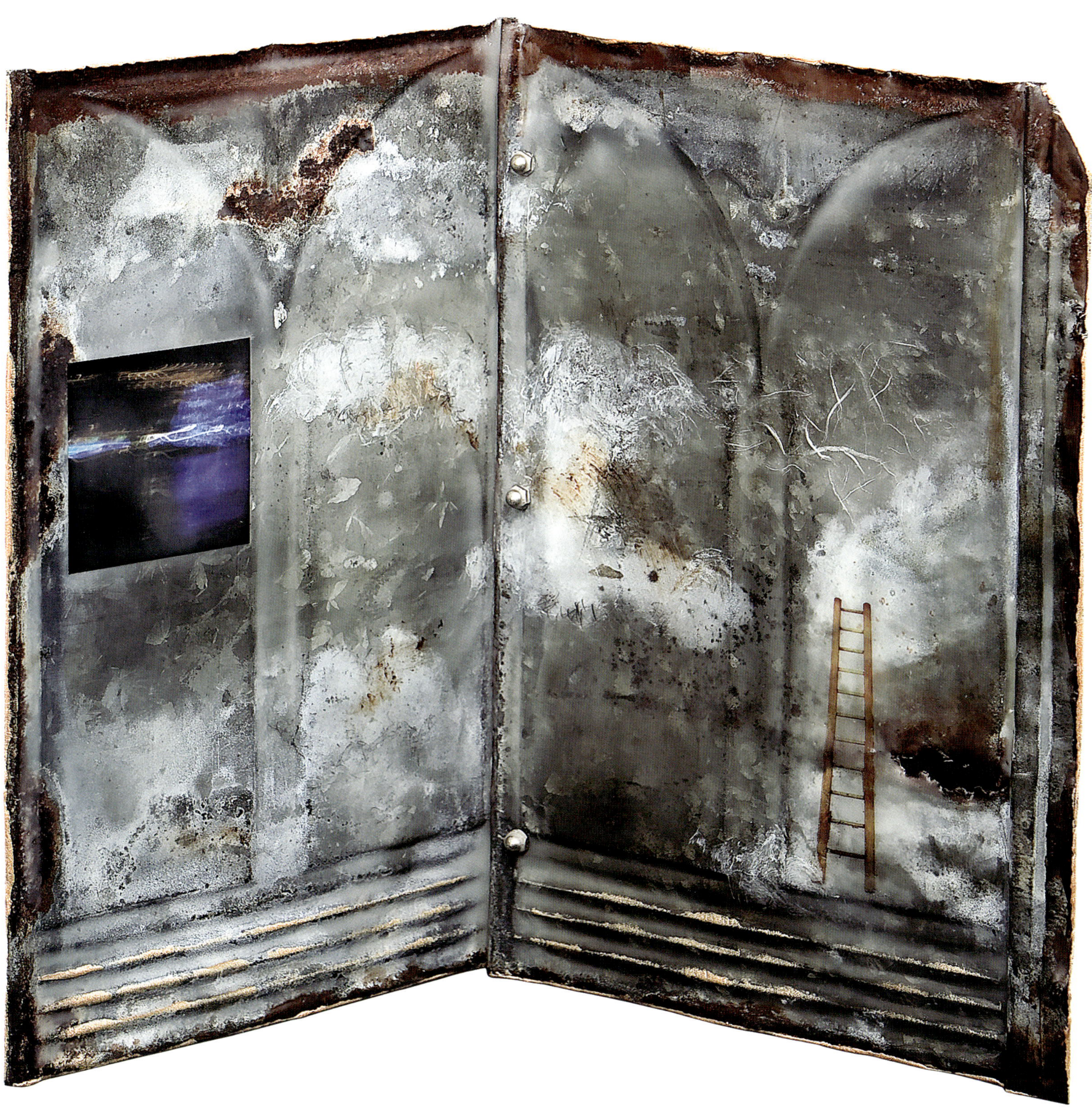

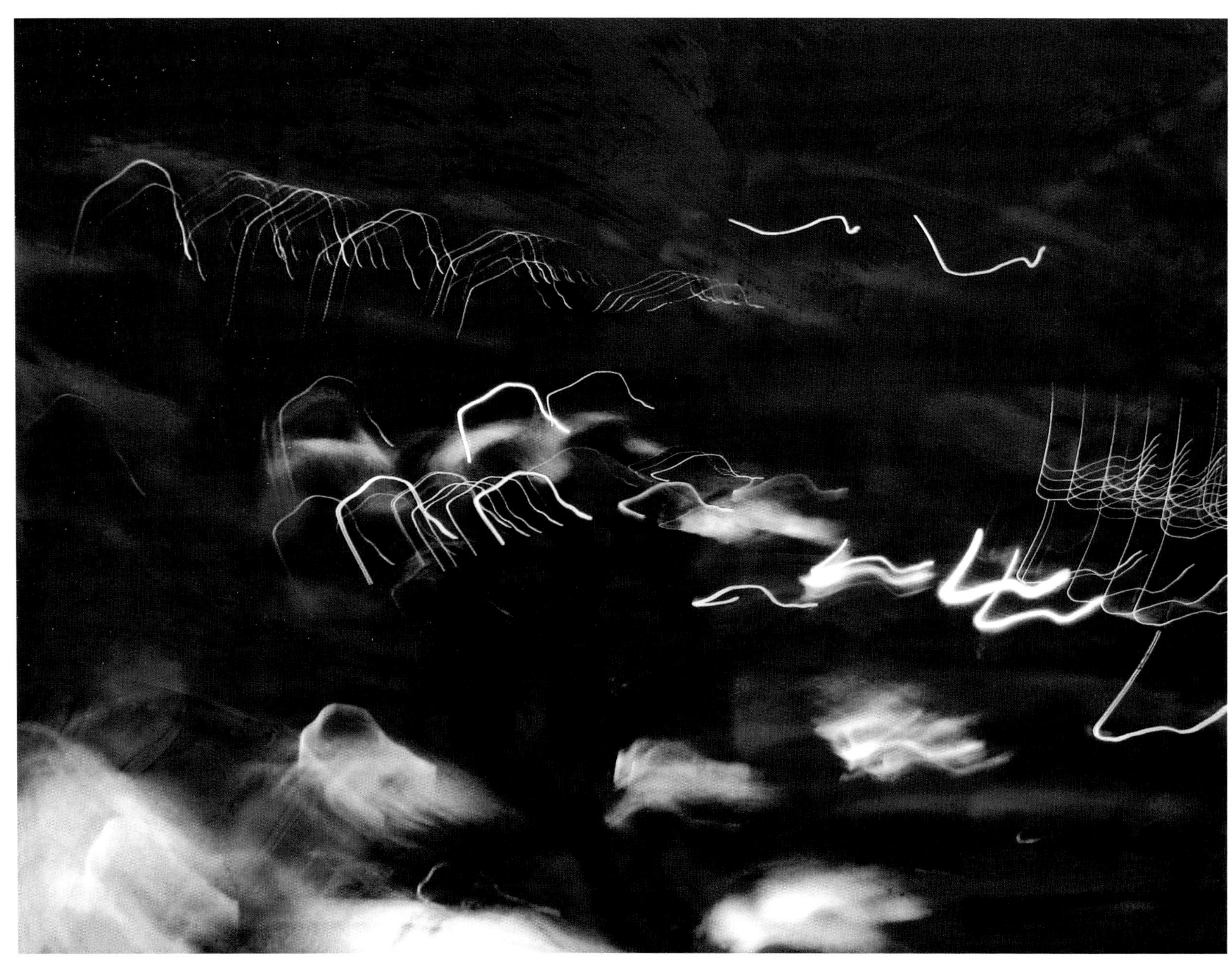

Brandy Eiger, *Energy Emerges*, 2008. Encaustic on mixed medium, 30.5 x 40.6 cm.

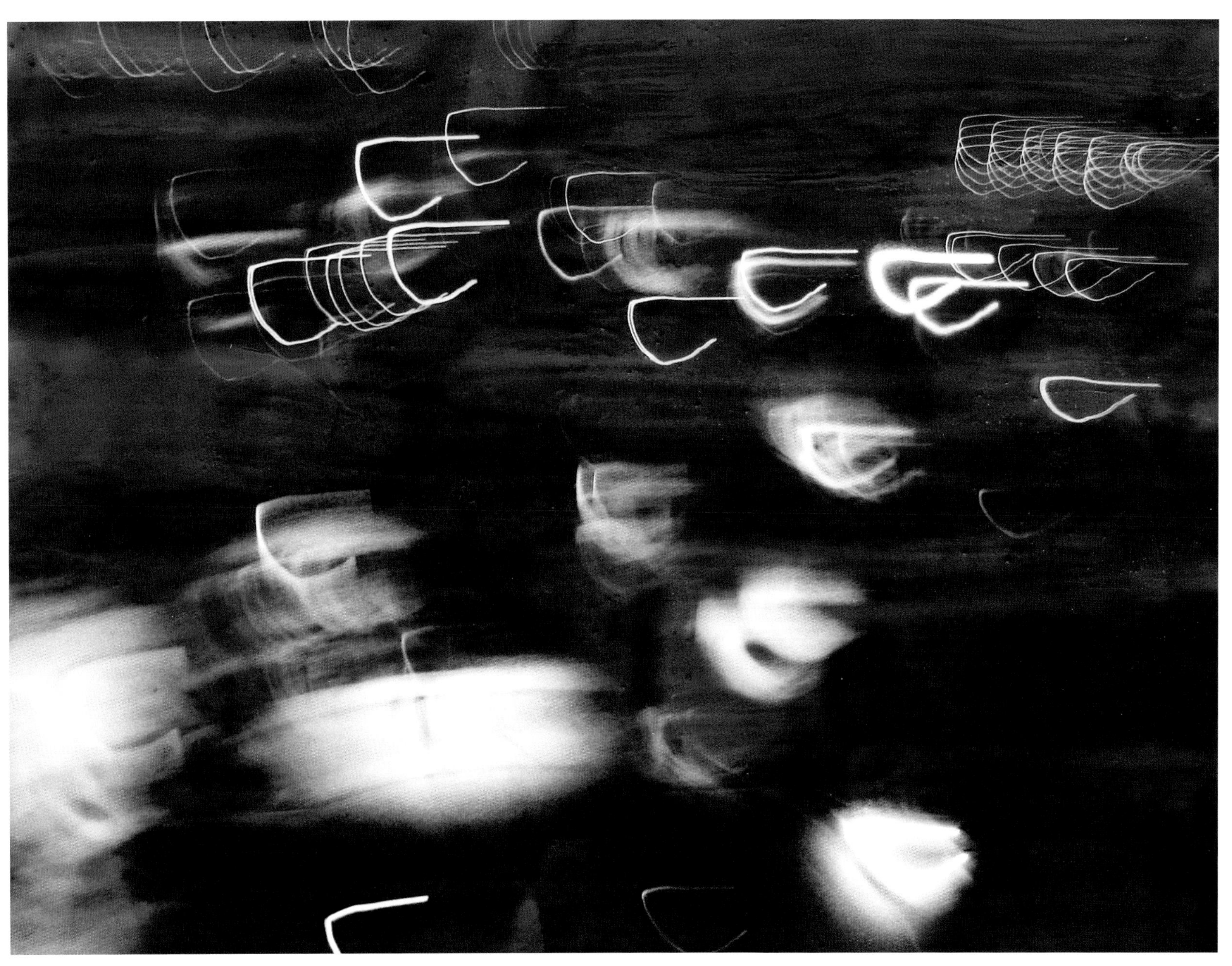

Brandy Eiger, *Pulsing Exuberance*, 2008. Encaustic on mixed medium, 30.5 x 40.6 cm.

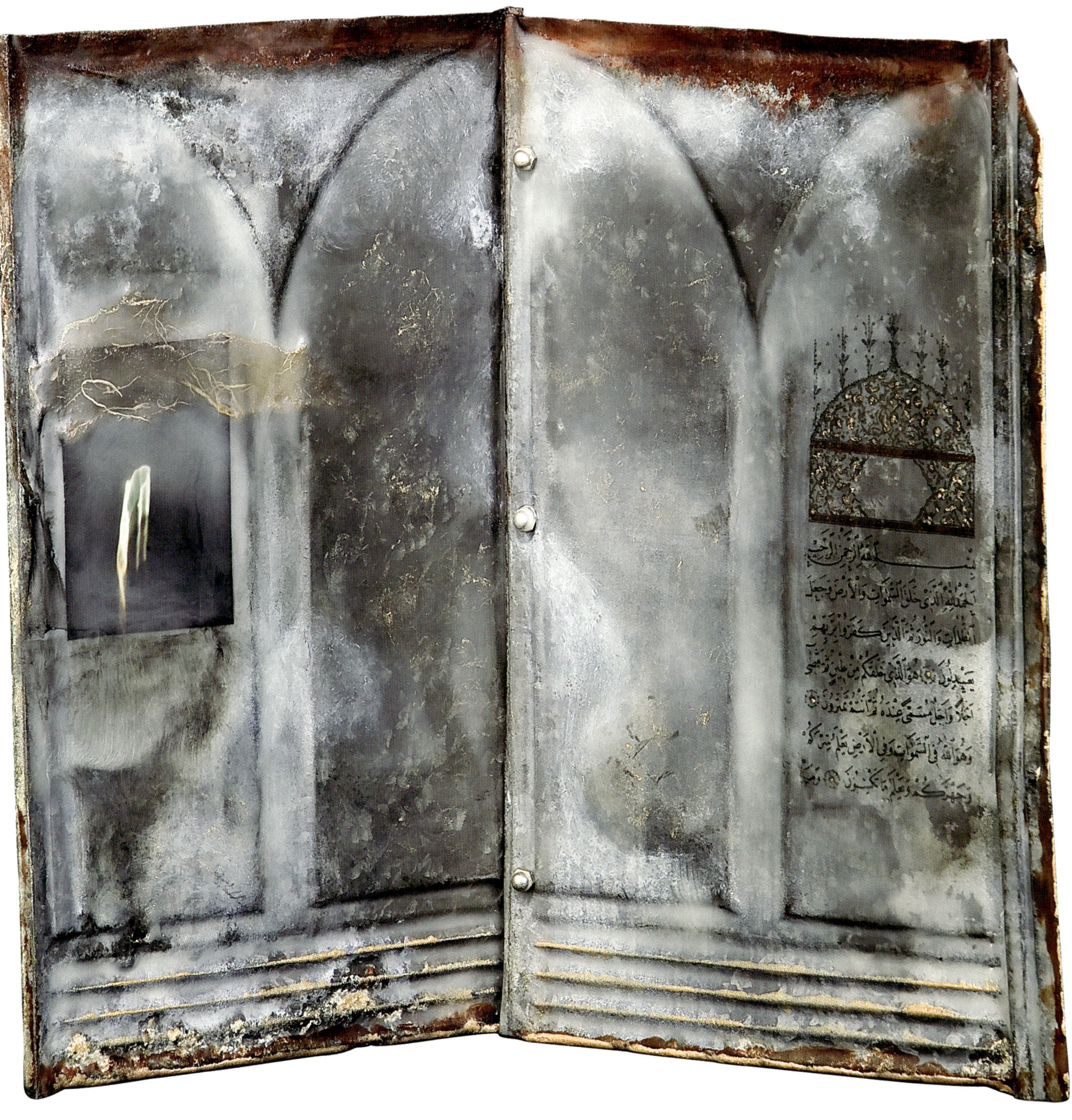

بسم الله الرحمن الرحيم
الحمد لله الذي خلق السموات والأرض وجعل
الظلمات والنور ثم الذين كفروا بربهم
يعدلون هو الذي خلقكم من طين ثم قضى
أجلا وأجل مسمى عنده ثم أنتم تمترون
وهو الله في السموات وفي الأرض يعلم سركم
وجهركم ويعلم ما تكسبون وما

Can you tell us about what technique you used when you created *Pulsing Exuberance*?

I sometimes do photo transfers, but in this case, I printed my photographs on uncoated watercolor paper and I used a custom profile I created to get crystal blacks. This is because when you are using paper which is not designed to accept photographic ink, you need to have a custom profile; the encaustic might not adhere as well to coated photo papers. So, what I did was, I glued down my photos to a cradled board, and I used archival neutral PDA glue. I weighed it overnight simply by piling books on top of it. Then I painted it in mostly layers of encaustic and graphite in monochromatic colors.

Can you tell us about the inspiration behind your *Unknown Territory* series?

The *Unknown Territory* series started after a trip to Europe where I went to the Biennale in Venice. After I was viewing all of this inspiring art, I was exhausted. So I went outside to take a break and took out my camera, and my photos were all abstract images taken at really close range. Then when I got back home and looked at them, I realized that I got this feeling of traveling through unknown landscapes. I didn't have my own studio at the time; I was working in borrowed studios in various cities. The series of paintings that came out of that are about finding home wherever we are. Mapping our territories and creating pathways through the unfamiliar.

What techniques did you use for these pieces, such as the textured and abstract piece *Passages II*?

Passages II and for most of that series, I used a photograph for the bottom layer. Then I used encaustic and I drew on the wax with wax crayons and oil stick. *Passages II* has a very smooth surface of medium on the surface, although it appears very textured from all of the layers and detail in it, but some of the other paintings in the *Unknown Territories* series have much more texture on the surfaces which are carved into. Some of the dark lines are from the original photograph and some of them I drew on with wax crayon. You can draw directly onto the wax with oil pastels and wax crayons, then coat it with a layer of medium on top of that. You just have to be very careful not to heat it too quickly or you will melt it and lose the detail.

You also have a series of very interesting monotypes. Can you tell us about how you came up with the idea for them?

Yes, there are other artists doing encaustic monotypes, and I have never taken a class. I didn't have an expensive hot box, which is what is usually used. It is a beautiful, smooth aluminum surface which is used specifically for encaustic monotype. But I didn't have one, I just had an ordinary palette, the kind that many people have. It is used for grilling, or pancake making, etc. Unlike regular palettes, I wanted to work quickly and gesturally on paper, so I just invented my own technique. When I would put the paper down on the palette, I would dip it in the palette and move it over several passes, usually of one color at a time. I think about various movements to get the effect that I want, but there is always a level of spontaneity and I can't completely control the process. Right after I did that, I saw a wonderful demo on monotypes by Paula Roland, who is one of the most well-known encaustic artists working in monotype. She has several different techniques. But usually the artists melt it in the hot box in a specific way to make the design, and then the paper is pressed down on the hot box and held in place while the back is rubbed with a tool. Stencils can also be used on the hot box to control where the paint goes. She teaches lots of wonderful classes.

Can you tell us about the parchment transfers that you use with your encaustic painting?

Last fall at the encaustic retreat that I went to in Carmel, there was an artist named Gretchen Papka who taught us a new technique for transfers using parchment paper. The way we used to use it was with laser copiers, and it took a really long time. But with this process, you basically print your image onto parchment paper using a laser printer. It doesn't work especially well with an inkjet printer; it works best with a laser printer. In fact, the parchment paper is actually the type of parchment paper that is used for baking so that your baked goods don't stick to the pan. The type that a lot of people like to use is called Bake-O-Matic. So you just print your image right on the parchment paper, and you take that image and put it face down on the wax and rub. It takes no longer than five minutes. There is nothing to remove, the transfer comes up immediately. The only difference is that it

Brandy Eiger, *Devotion V*, 2010.
Encaustic on mixed medium, 35.5 x 36.8 x 13.9 cm.

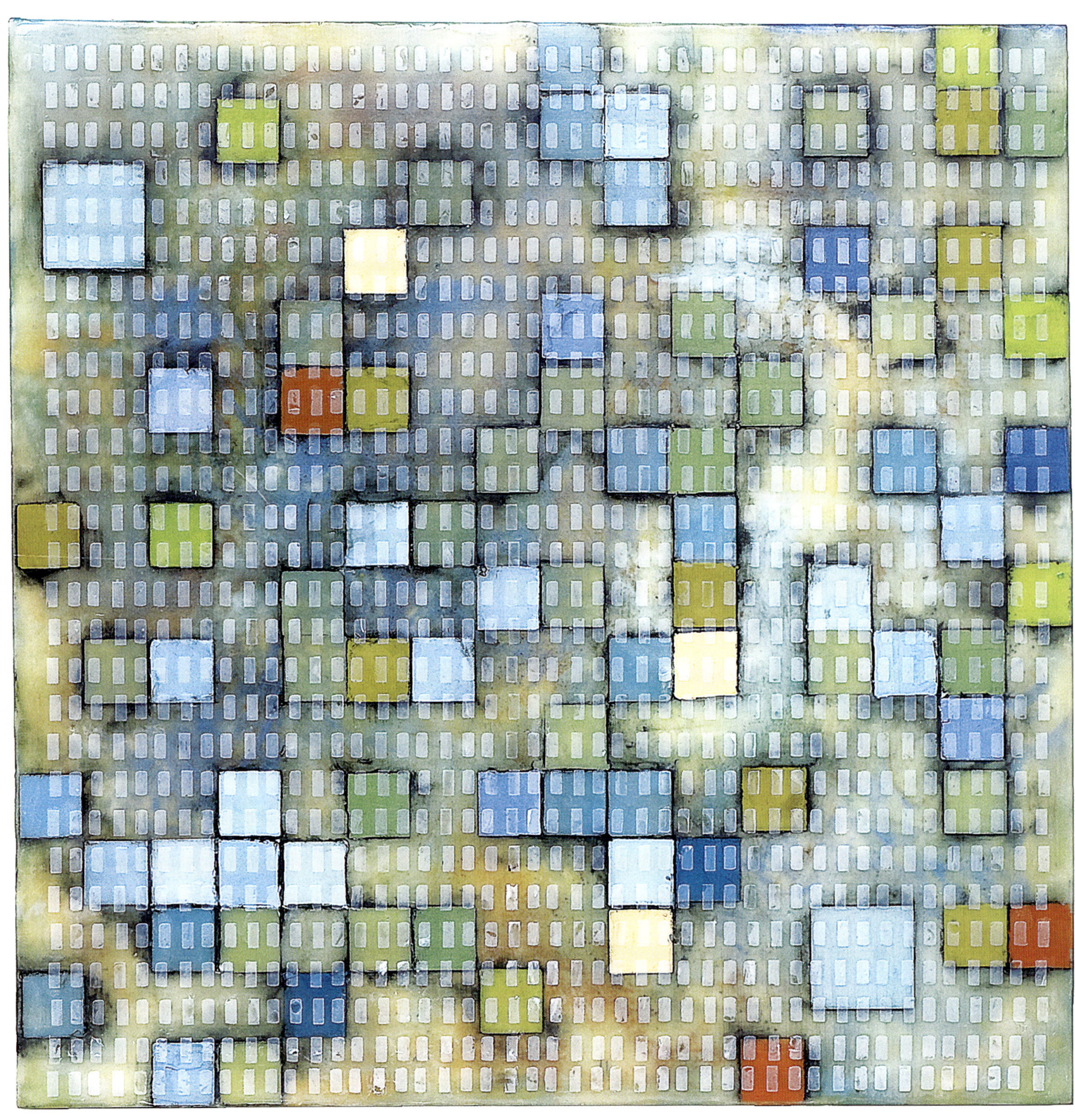

Karen Freedman, *Veiled Tranquility*, 2009. Encaustic and cold wax on wood panel, 30.5 x 30.5 x 4.4 cm.

Karen Freedman

Order and Repetition. No matter how many alternate paths my work takes, I always seem to return to order and repetition. These twin elements are with me as an underlying touchstone of inspiration.

In my current series, I take this concept of order and repetition and introduce a semblance of disarray without ever really abandoning the grid-like structure. The use of colors may seem arbitrary, yet they are chosen and arranged to give structure and movement to the randomness I have imposed on the grid. The use of encaustic enhances the effects that I can create with texture and color. I am drawn to its warmth, to its tactile quality. I love the physical demands of working with wax and I am challenged by its constraints.

"Order and Repetition. No matter how many alternate paths my work takes, I always seem to return to order and repetition."
- Karen Freedman

Which artists have been influences for you?
Well I end up going back to my originals (influences) from college, who were Klee and Kandinsky, mostly because of color, form, (and) movement. And then I switch over to quilts, which I have always been intrigued by.

These evoke geometry, which I like, and color play, and I am always so amazed that the quilts are created by women who have very little or no formal training, and yet have made these masterpieces.

Other than that, I try not to think about it too much and try not to be too influenced by others, otherwise it starts showing up in my work and I want to stick to my own voice.

Can you tell us about the order and repetition that you incorporate into your work?
Well, I think that harks back to geometry. Every time I seem to get away from geometry, I come right back to it. What I like to do with my work is take geometry and find ways to bend it, alter it, and to create movement by using depth or color, or a combination of the two.

I try to find a way to get geometry to dance by stepping outside of the order that might be naturally expected; I take contrasting elements to create harmony within certain contexts I am creating.

What unconventional materials do you like to use?
I don't think that in encaustic there is such a thing as unconventional anymore. I see everything done and I think that is the beauty and attraction of this medium. I was drawn to it because of that. I am a tool junky and it allows me to play around with different tools. Whether I invent them by finding them in a hardware store and repurposing them, or a kitchen store, it really allows me to do that.

I like to get sculptural, to dig and get sculptural with it. But that being said, I consider myself to be fairly conventional as, other than using certain tools, I am would call myself a purist and my work does not have a lot of mixed media, if any, in it. The most unconventional, if even that, would be my use of stencils, and those I design myself.

What do you like to cut your stencils out of?
I design them in Illustrator on my computer and I have discovered through trial and error that printing them out on overhead projector film that is designed for an inkjet printer will allow me to reuse them. It handles the heat really well, rather than printing them out on a piece of paper or using a stencil that you might find in a hobby store.

They can handle the heat from the gun or any other heat source, and this way I can use them. I can clean them and reuse them, they are excellent. Eventually they get somewhat warped, but they have saved me a lot of time in the long run.

How do you deal with framing and hanging your work?
Generally at this point, I tend to purchase teak cradles, about one and a half to two inches deep. I leave the sides unfinished and just wire the back. If I have work that is of lesser depth, I put them in floater frames just to set the work off. But I prefer to stay away from that now at this point.

What steps do you take when you start a painting?
Well, there is the mechanical step of putting gesso on my panels. I prefer to gesso them and I like to do five or six at a time, because I like to work on a few paintings at a time.

Then it is pretty much choosing my color palette and that is based sometimes on photos that I might have taken in the past, I do take a lot of photographs of abstractions. Things that I see, then I abstract it and further abstract it for color and composition and that can be an inspiration. Sometimes I am just in a certain color mood and I start playing with those colors. Once I am into the piece, it is a matter of what kind of odd colors I can throw in that might break a rule. That might be a surprise, but also may happen to pull the whole element together.

That leads us to our next question: what influences the color palette that you use for a piece?
It really comes down to gut. As I referred to in the beginning, I try not to think too much because it really ruins things. I tend to over-analyze and it may ruin the painting if you take it too farm and then you have lost it.

I try to reconnect, clear my head, and just go with what is working or is not working. That, and being very careful to keep my colors clean and crisp, influences my color choices.

What was your inspiration for your *Abacus* series?
I don't know if I can actually refer to it as inspiration, but I did one of my first paintings when I was playing with the concept of stencils. It was a six by six that had that type of imagery which originally was very difficult, more difficult than usual to do, and I abandoned it.

But later, a couple of years later, I ended up coming back to it. The point was to try to take a static image and see how I could alter it from painting to painting by changing colors with

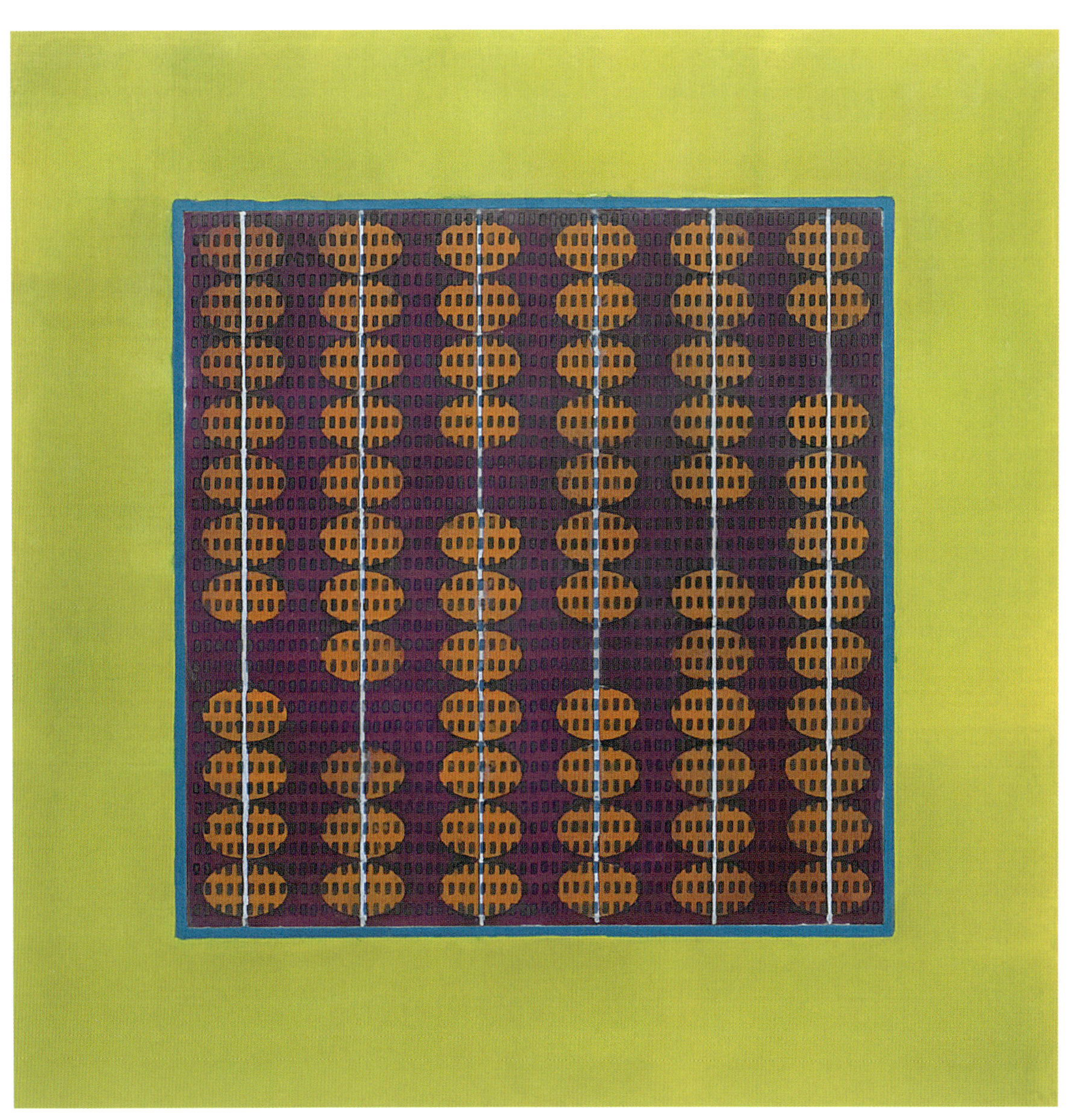

Karen Freedman, *Abacus: It Doesn't Count*, 2009. Encaustic and cold wax on wood panel, 30.5 x 30.5 x 4.4 cm.

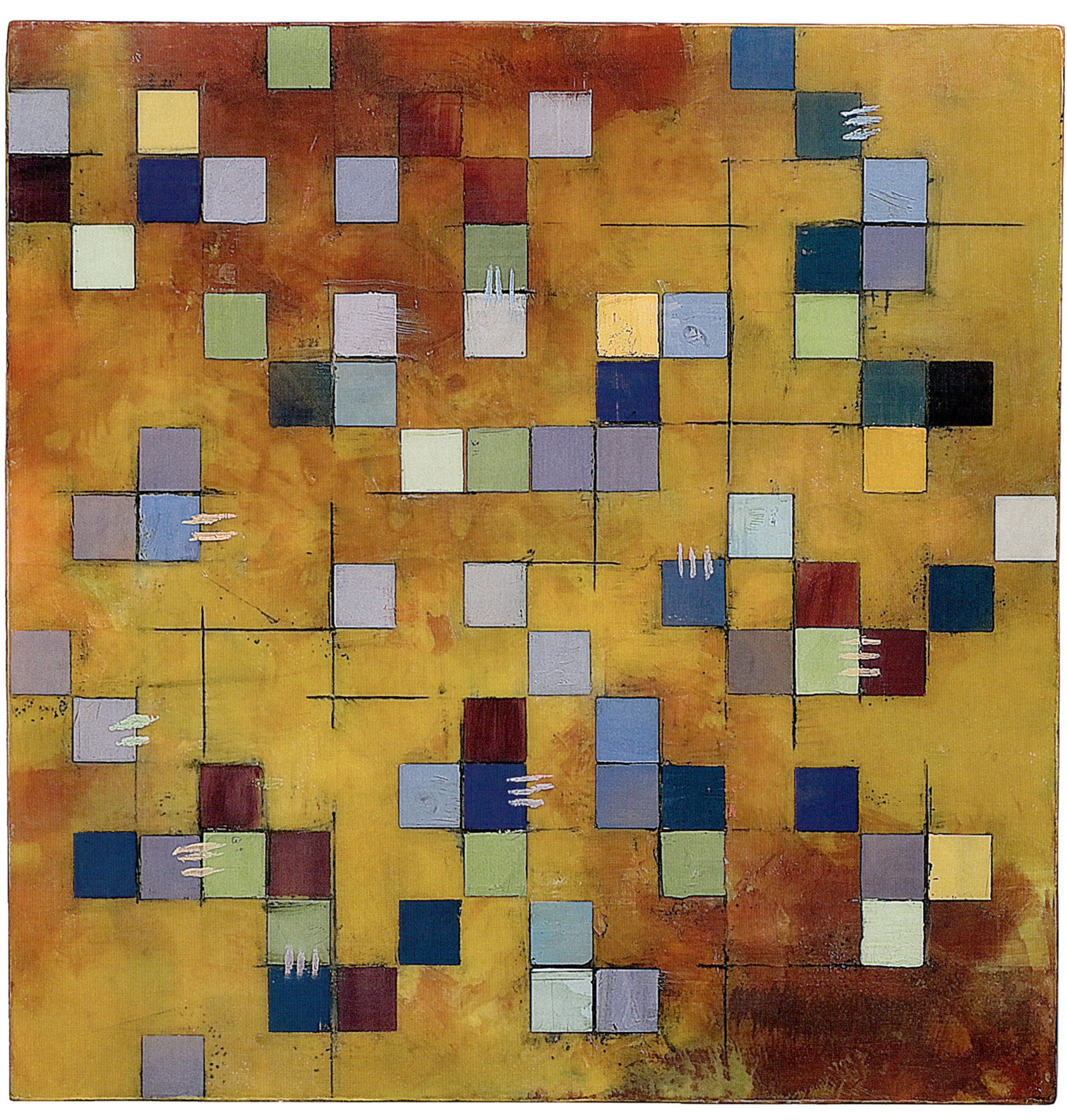

Karen Freedman, *Reclamation: Cooling the Flames*, 2008. Encaustic on wood panel, 30.5 x 30.5 x 4.4 cm.

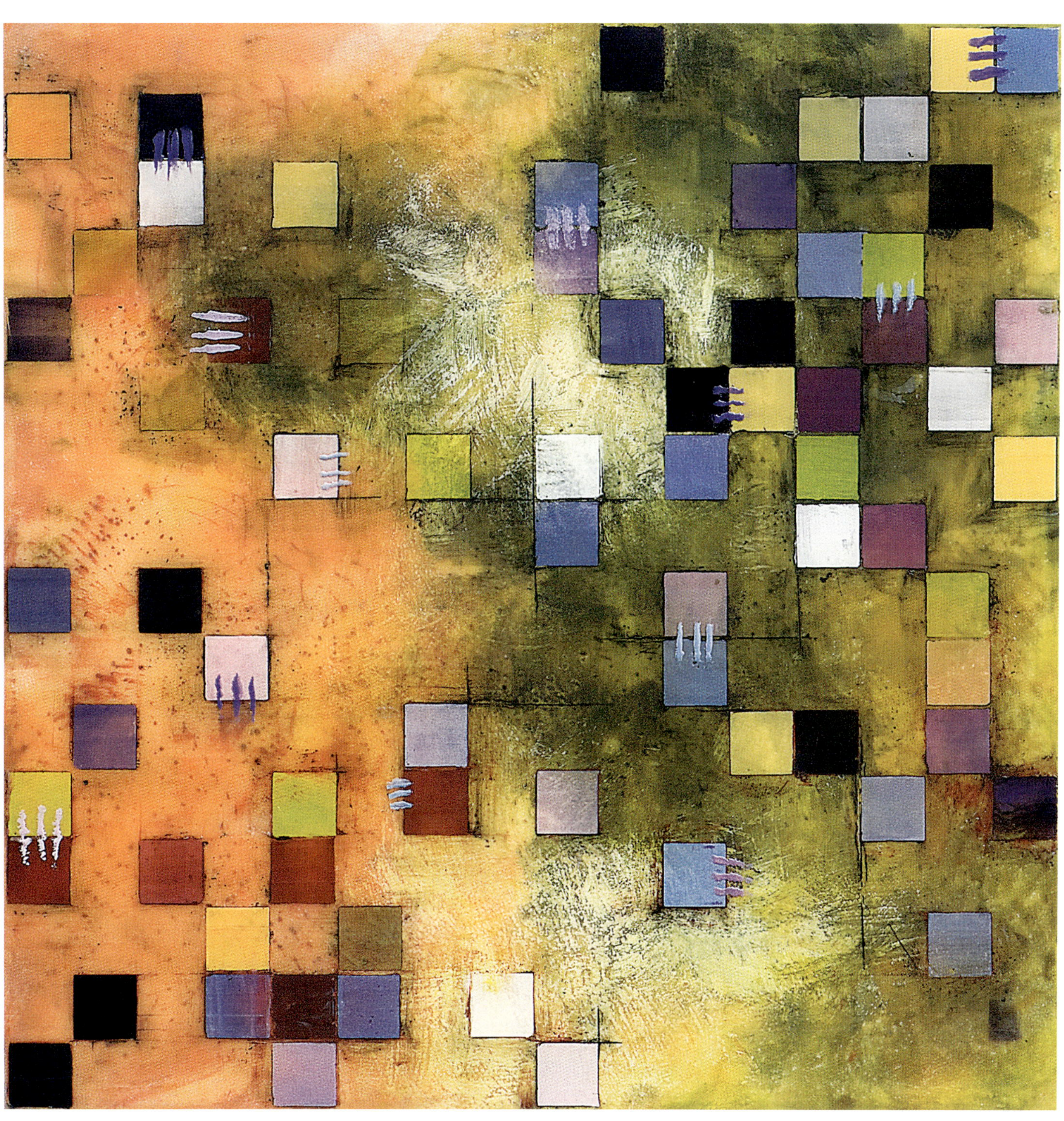

Karen Freedman, *Reclamation: Peachy Green*, 2008. Encaustic on wood panel, 30.5 x 30.5 x 4.4 cm.

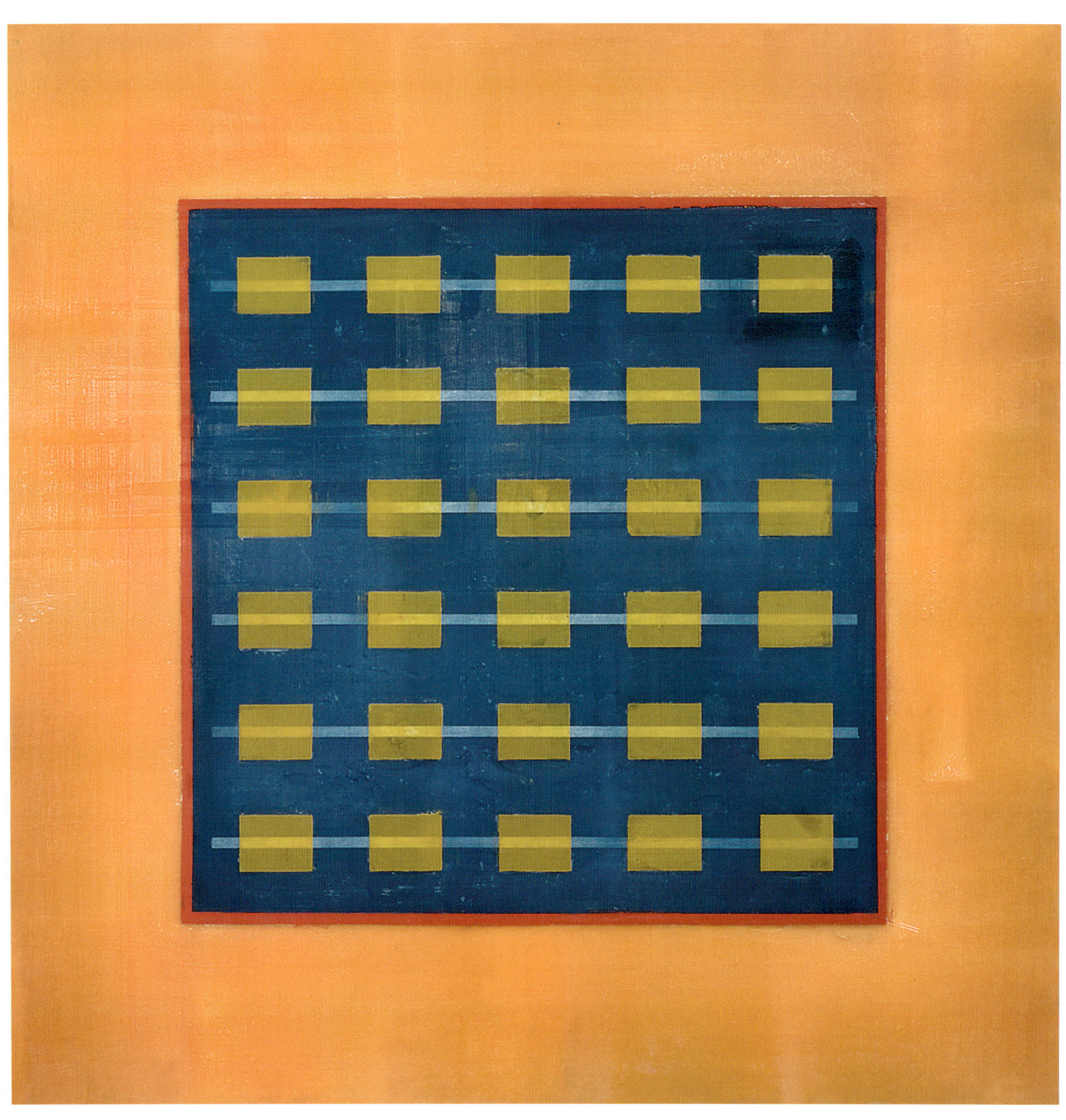

Karen Freedman, *Repatterning*, 2008. Encaustic on wood panel, 30.5 x 30.5 x 4.4 cm.

translucency, by layering and layering translucent colors and see what it did.

I also wanted a series that complemented the *Reclamation* series, because my paintings are twelve by twelve. They are very good to hang in groups, but sometimes too many *Reclamation* paintings together are too much.

I wanted to give the eye somewhere to rest from the *Reclamation* and to contrast and complement that series.

Can you tell us about your process while creating *Abacus Summation*?

First, I was inspired by a color that I mixed from re-melted scrap wax. I am a real hoarder of the scraped off wax that I have left over and I end up putting it into little tins of color groupings, then re-melt, sift, and clean it. I came up with a couple of really beautiful colors that I was in love with. So I chose them to make this piece.

Along the way I chose a few additional colors to complement those. The process of making it is pretty straightforward but very tedious in that I already know what the composition is going to look like and I use about four different stencils to create that.

The first thing I have to do is to lay down my center section which I create by masking with tape. I have to be very careful about mixing, and this is true for all of the *Abacus* paintings because if anyone has worked with encaustics, they know how difficult it is to lay down a smooth unblemished color field. So I make sure to premix a lot of whichever colors I am going to be using and to stir them really well before I lay them down, and that helps me lay down these clean fields.

Once the background is laid down I have to scrape that back smooth and level. Then I will apply a stencil and I will lay down the ovals. That is usually a couple of layers. I scrape those back then go in with either a clear medium or tinted medium. I fill in those elements up until it covers the ovals that were made.

When I do that, first I will go and outline each of the ovals with a very fine brush so that I will hold my edges and I will minimize the tendency to create air bubbles. So, it is a lot of gentle fusing and laying down of very, very thin layers of wax.

Once I have that laid down I have to let the wax cool off, because if I just start scraping, the wax is too soft and I will ruin all of the work that I have just done.

Once that whole center section is complete and cooled, I will mask that section to expose the sides. I then follow that process of laying down multiple layers of one color and fusing them back and forth until that comes to meet, or usually is a little higher than, the original center section.

I then unmask that section, making sure that there are no sections that have not been filled in, and then start scraping all over again until it is level. There is a lot of scraping going on.

What tool do you use for the scraping?

I usually start out with a wallpaper spreader. It is about twelve or fourteen inches long and that way I can put even pressure across my whole piece.

Then I usually take it down to a razor that is useful in getting a finer finish and more gloss on the surface.

What inspired your series *Reclamation*, which features abstract squares and beautiful balanced colors?

Well, I have always been motivated by color: strong color. But then I went through a period in my life where I was going through a divorce after twenty-four years, and I could not paint. But when the process of my divorce was a little clearer, I couldn't get them out of my head and the only thing that I could do was to paint them. I just had to paint them.

It was a different imagery than anything I had ever really come up with. Once I started, it was the basis of the whole series that I am still continuing with. I also came to realize after I was done, that maybe the process of painting symbolized putting my life in order. It has movement; it is sort of a contrast of the organic and control, which is pretty much how life is. It is my way of controlling elements.

How did you create such precise lines in the shapes featured in your *Reclamation* series?

Again, I used the stencils for that. But unlike the *Abacus* series, these are picked up and moved over and over again. I could not make a stencil with grids that close together.

There is also the element of color change; I have to allow the colors to cool before I can go back in and place a different color next to it. So I end up moving it around a lot, but it still comes back to the stencil.

Can you tell us about the technique you used to create *Reclamation: After the Storm* and primarily in the background you have some beautiful color variances as well?

That is my play time. It is when I get to play and loosen up; I just start laying colors down haphazardly, scraping back, seeing how they are working, and building up the layers until I feel

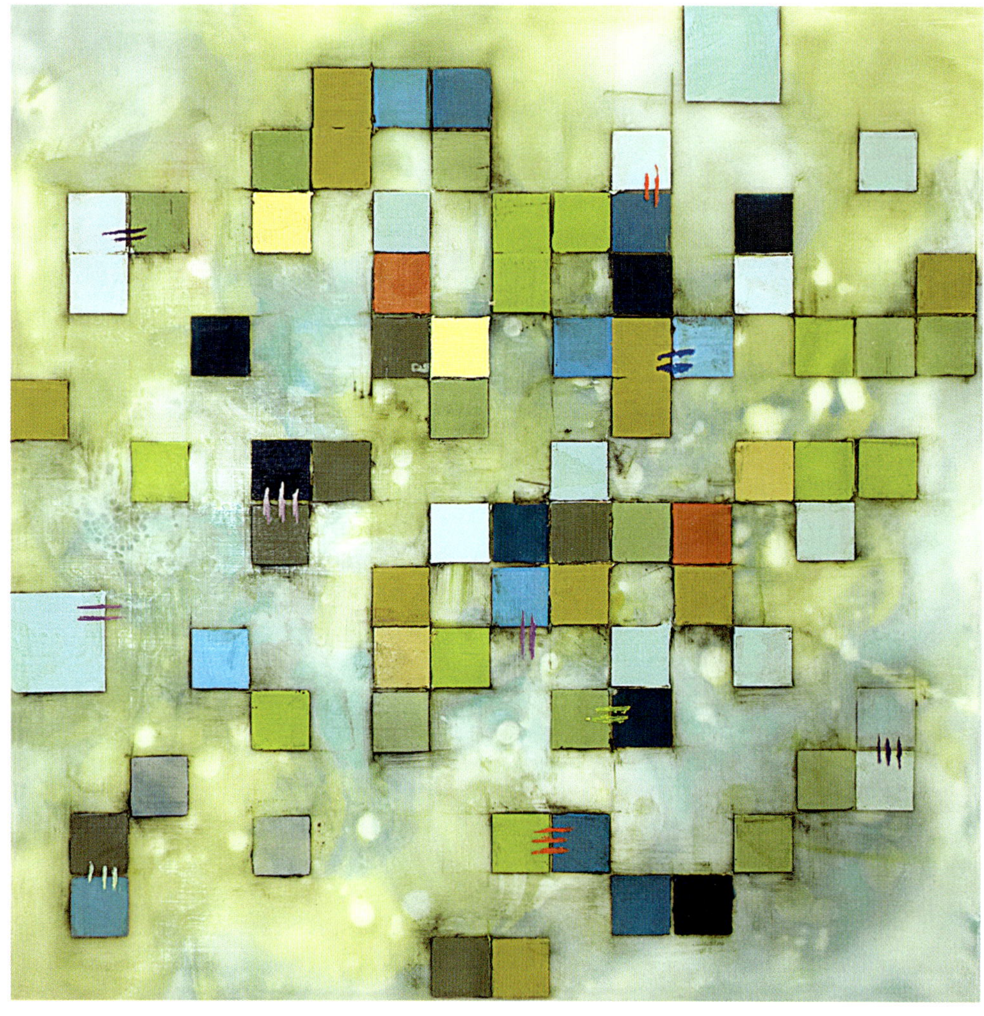

Karen Freedman, *Reclamation: After the Storm*, 2009. Encaustic on wood panel, 30.5 x 30.5 x 4.4 cm.

that I have achieved what I want, and again that gets scraped back until it is smooth. So there is not a lot of thought or science put into that part.

Occasionally, I will create texture by perhaps pounding the surface with various types of textural devices. I will then take that down until it is a smooth level surface.

After this stage I start to work on the placement of the squares. It is really important with any of the stencil work that I do to get that first base coat perfectly level, so that when I am ready to put the stencil down there will be no room for seepage.

When I first started doing these, I would pick up and move the stencils all around until I made a color decision, until I came up with a faster way of getting to that end.

I took a series of color aids and cut them up into the same size squares, and so now I sketch with these little color aid squares which I have created. So I can lay out the initial color placement before I even start laying down wax.

Then I mix colors to match my color aid squares; I make sure that I have all of them ready. Then I go back and replace each of those color aid squares with stencils and start painting over it with encaustic.

There comes a point when I have replaced all my squares. I have to place it on a wall somewhere and take a look at it, because you start staring at it from one perspective with only one focal point, and it doesn't look the same. So I make sure to put it far away from me, work on another painting, glance up and take a look every once in a while, make sure it is working.

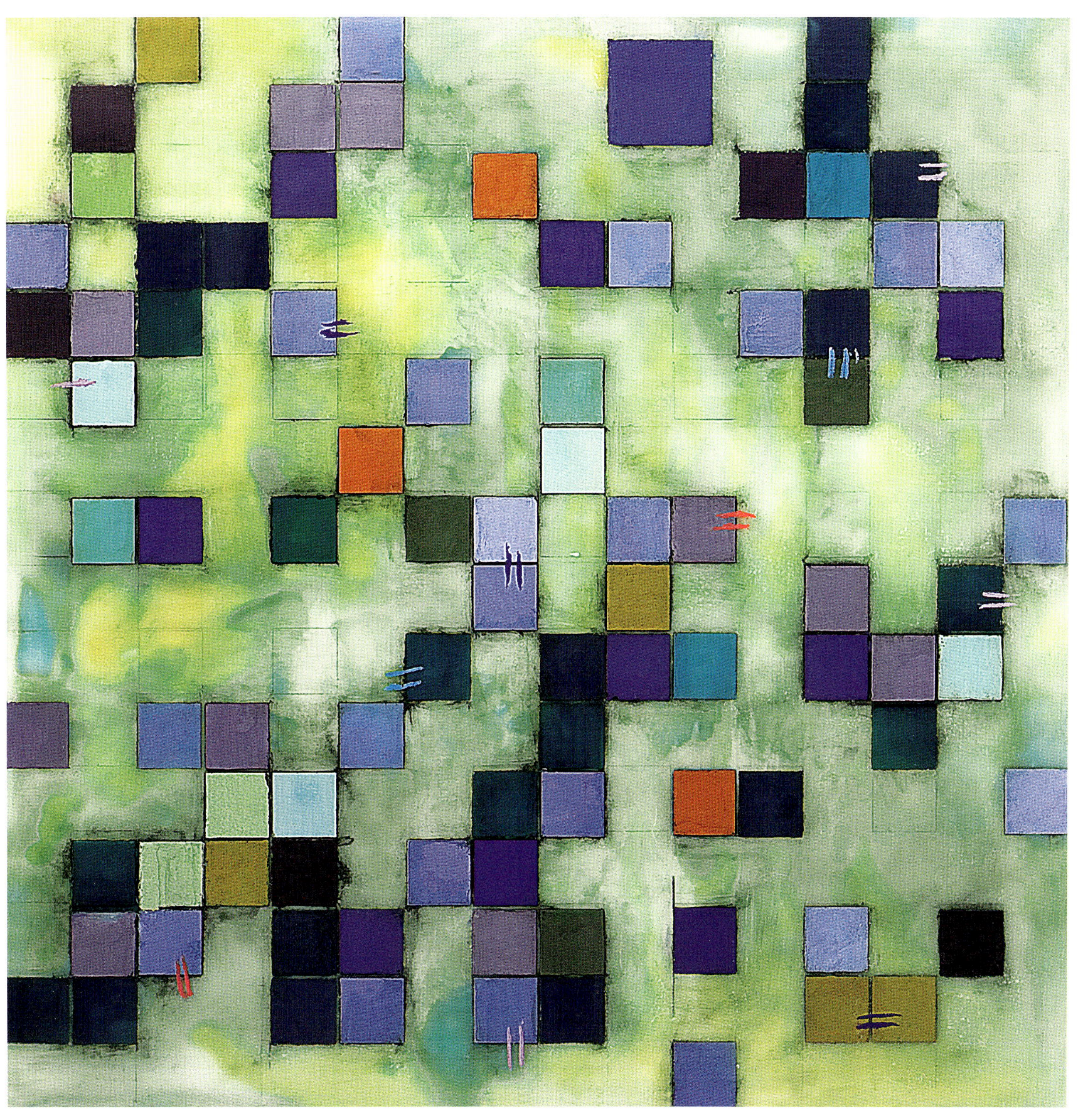

Karen Freedman, *Reclamation: Smiles of a Fool*, 2009. Encaustic on wood panel, 30.5 x 30.5 x 4.4 cm.

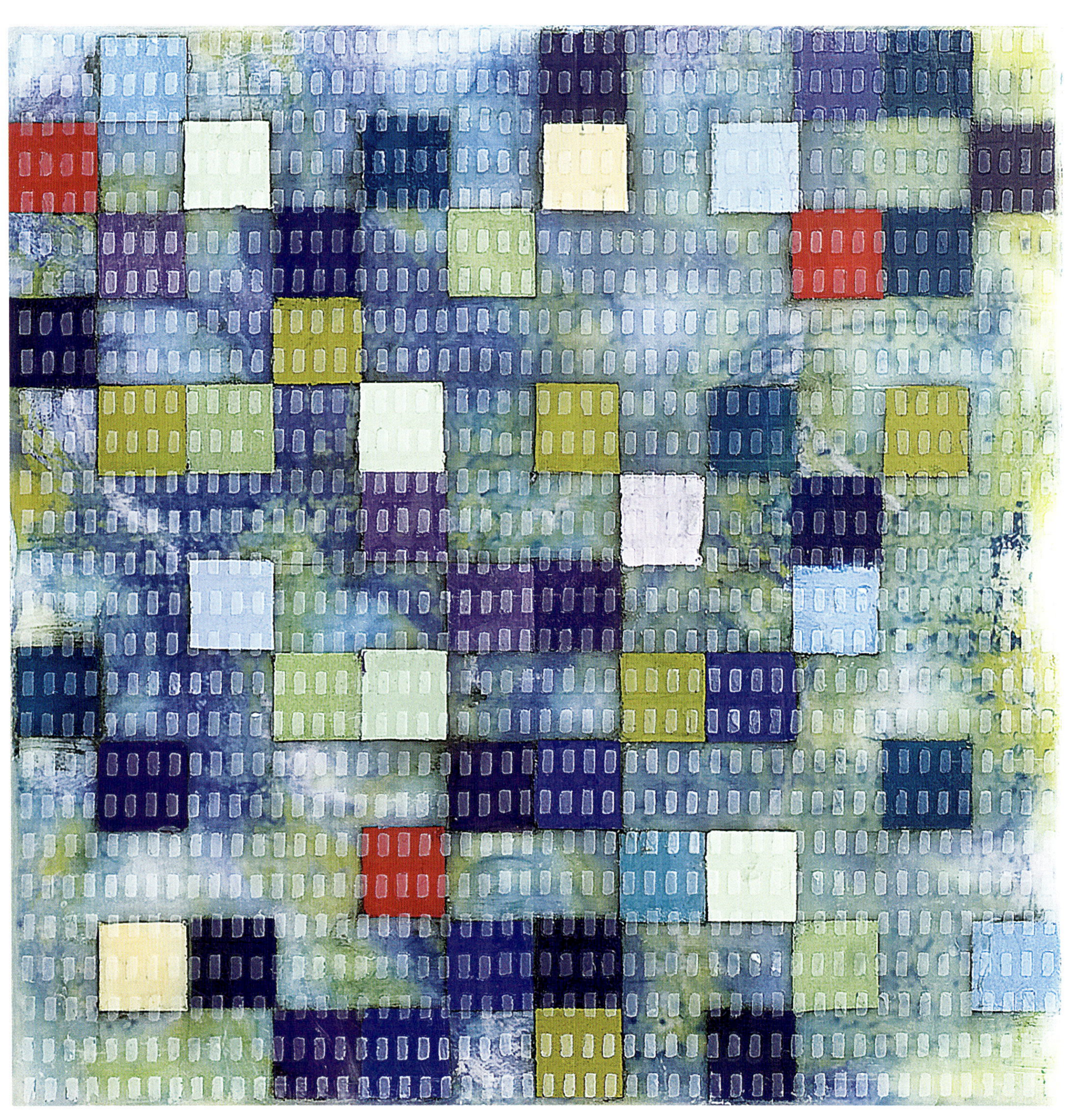

Karen Freedman, *Reclamation: Veiled Gift*, 2009. Encaustic on wood panel, 15.2 x 15.2 x 5.1 cm.

Sometimes colors have to be removed, sometimes other colors go in.

At that point, when I am ready and feel like the colors are in the right places, I take the painting back and start working with an oil stick. With the oil stick, I will outline each of those little squares and then I rub it all off again. It gives it depth and it softens the edges a little. It softens the painting, which without that, would not be there, and I also think that it helps separate it from the negative space of the background.

Once that is completed and I am sure the oil stick has dried enough, because if it hasn't it can prevent good bonding, I will go in again with medium. I will outline each of the little squares again with thin layers of medium and build it up until it pretty much covers all of the squares, and I scrape it all back again until those squares start coming through again and the whole area is smooth.

Often, a lot of air bubbles appear, which means a lot of filling in and bringing those air bubbles back up to the surface. This is kind of the tedium of it, but is also the Zen of it. I get lost in the mechanical process and really enjoy it. Once I am happy with the lack of air bubbles, I make sure it is as smooth as possible.

Can you tell us about your piece *Veiled Tranquility* and the additional layer of translucent rectangles you have over the front of the piece?

I was looking to add another layer on top which was textured and something which was smaller. I was having a very difficult time getting it to work because when I tried a typical process of laying the stencil down, laying down encaustic and removing the stencils, a lot of them would pull up. They were not working well and were starting to ruin what was going on underneath.

But I wanted these marks to have that translucency; that milkiness to them. I tried using oil stick and rubbing that on top. It was oil stick which was mixed with a blender so it was also translucent, but I didn't get the smoothness that I was looking for.

Finally I came up with using cold wax, mixed with a touch of white oil paint and it worked. I got exactly what I wanted and that is how I made that layer.

Once I'm at the stage where I can remove the stencil without the encaustic pulling up, I let it dry and gently fuse it. I heat it enough so that it will fuse with the underlying surface because I don't want the cold wax to fall off.

How did you apply the wax while it was cold?

Cold wax is very pliable if it is warmed up. So I will lay my stencil down and I will take cold wax in its natural state, mixed with a little bit of the oil and rub it on with a palette knife.

While the stencil is still there, I scrape it back as fine as possible to get to the depth of a piece of paper. That is it; that is all that I do to it.

What have you learned in your experience teaching encaustics which may be helpful to artists new to encaustics?

Take classes. When I first started to paint encaustics I taught myself and I always prided myself in the ability to teach myself lots of things and I have been fairly successful at it. But then I went to take a course in teaching encaustics, and I suddenly realized how many things I had been doing wrong. I was really grateful for that and I can't emphasize enough how important it is.

After that, I would recommend to students to try and let go, because I see so many who want to take home a pretty, attractive, and great painting. It is a shame because what they are throwing away is this great time to master a technique in front of somebody who knows how to do it.

They will have all the time that they want once they get home, or once they get back to their own studio to work on that imagery. It really is so hard to do and it is so hard to let go, but the art will follow once the technique is mastered, once they have experimented to get to know that medium.

Even if they don't, I can't emphasize enough, even if you don't think you are going to use something, even if it is a technique that you don't like and you don't want to use, listen, learn, and store it away somewhere. You never know if you are going to want to use that technique at some point in the future or if it may inspire you to an avenue to use in your own way.

What advice do you have for artists to make their work stand out?

An artist needs to figure out what they want to do with their work. Everybody has different intentions. Some want to do it for themselves, some are more interested in being highly commercial, some are more interested in the art, the philosophical process. It is just as important to find your voice, and doing that may take time, so it is important to set aside that time to do it.

Try different things. Once you have gotten all of those ideas out of your head onto the paper, paint, or whatever

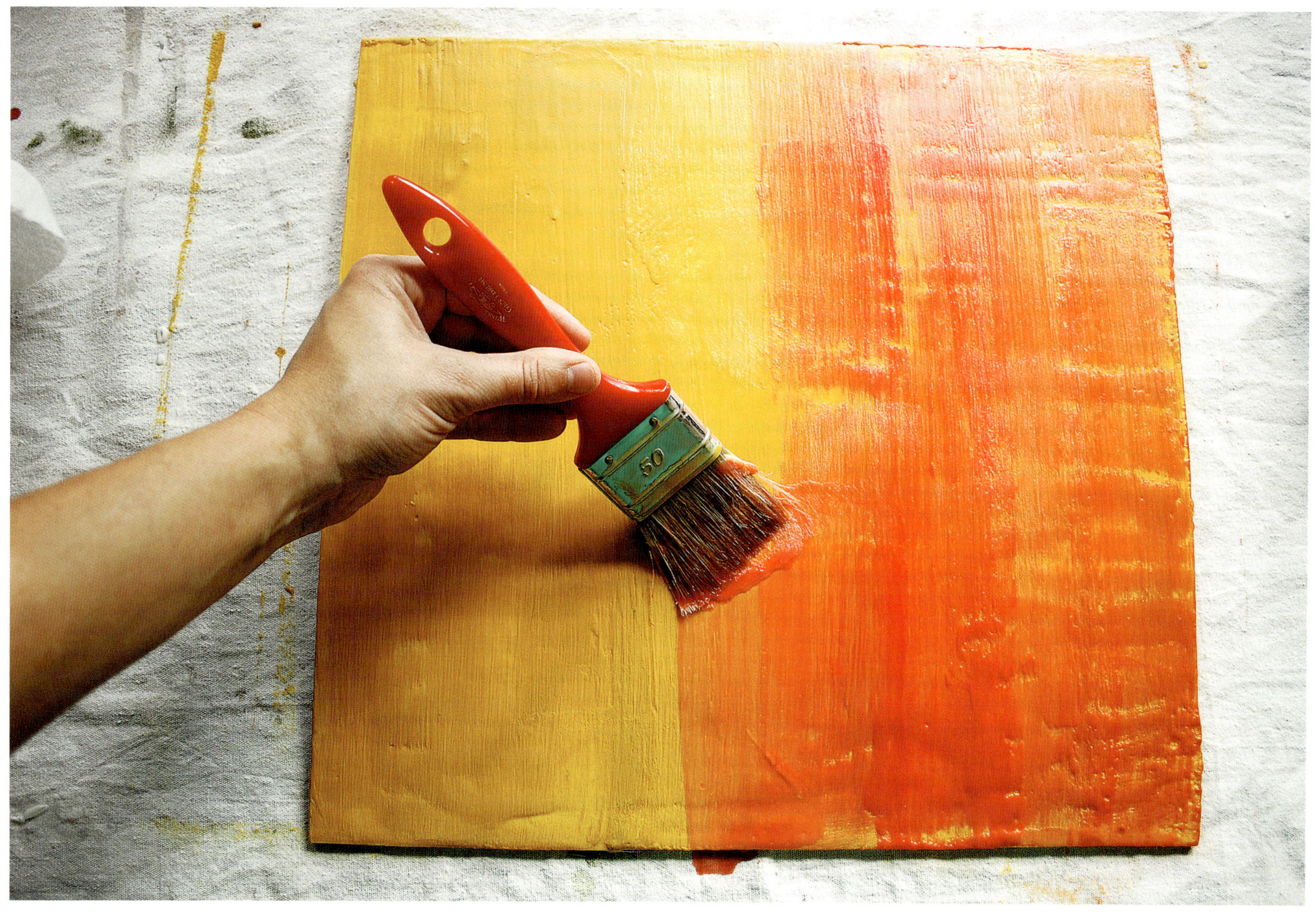

medium you are using, you are going to naturally come across your voice. Once you have done that, it is very important to define your intent. By that, I mean planning a series, because a series is your backbone: it is your jumping off point. It gives all of your work continuity. It gives you a point of departure and from there you can grow as an artist. With that being said, it is extremely important to trust yourself.

Try not to listen to others if it conflicts with your gut instinct. But it is also just as important to join a critique group. It is very helpful and will help you with several things that you may not have thought you needed help with, and it is a wonderful way to network.

Another thing which is more on the business side, along with networking, is making sure that you have made yourself as visible as possible by having a webpage, by blogging, by joining all of the networking sites, and also by joining as many competitions as you can to help build up your resume. Finally, if you choose to follow this as a professional pursuit, then it is important to realize that it is a business. It needs the respect that you would give any kind of business entity.

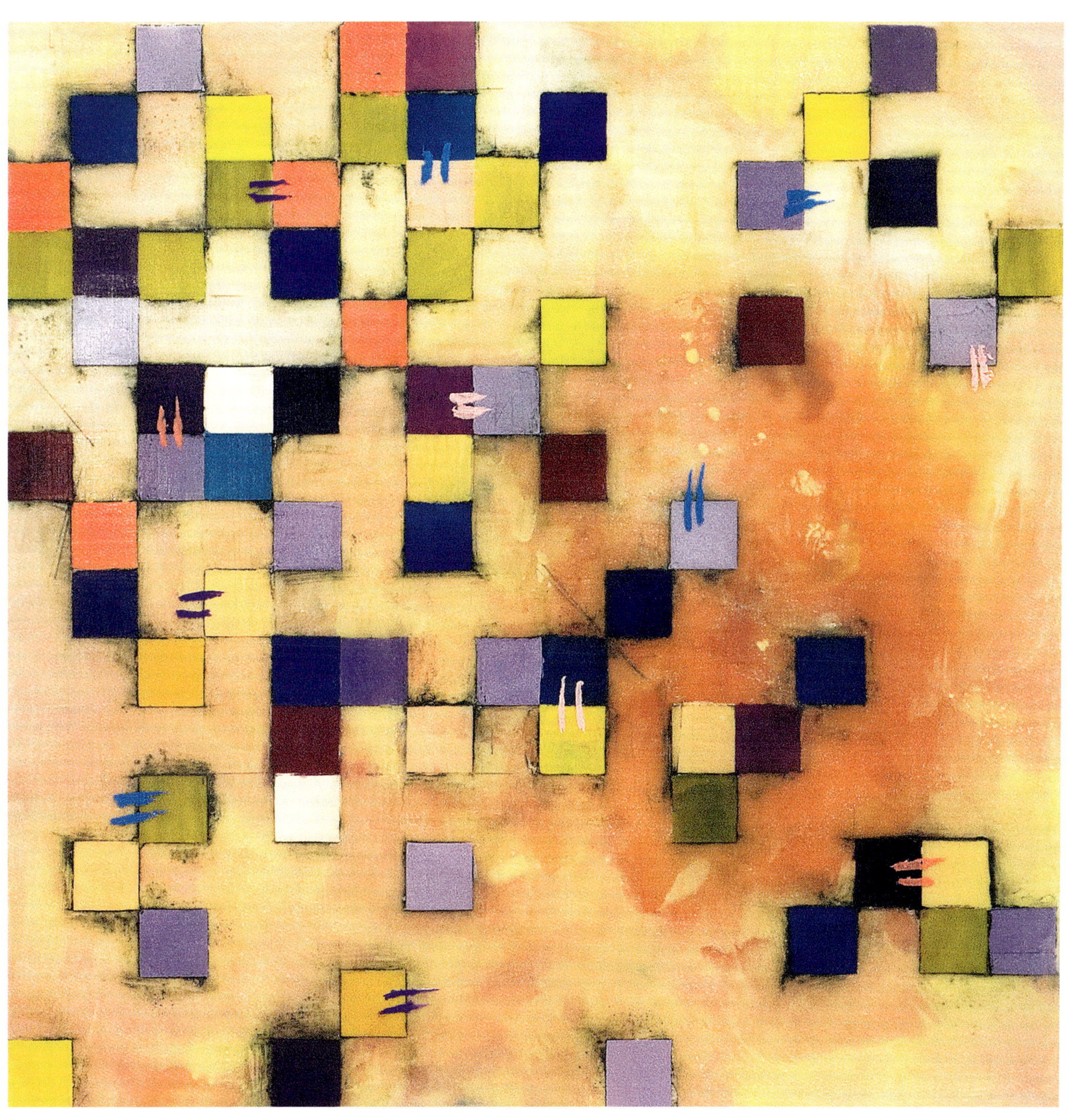

Karen Freedman, *Reclamation: Almost Dusk*, 2008. Encaustic on wood panel, 25.4 x 25.4 x 0.4 cm.

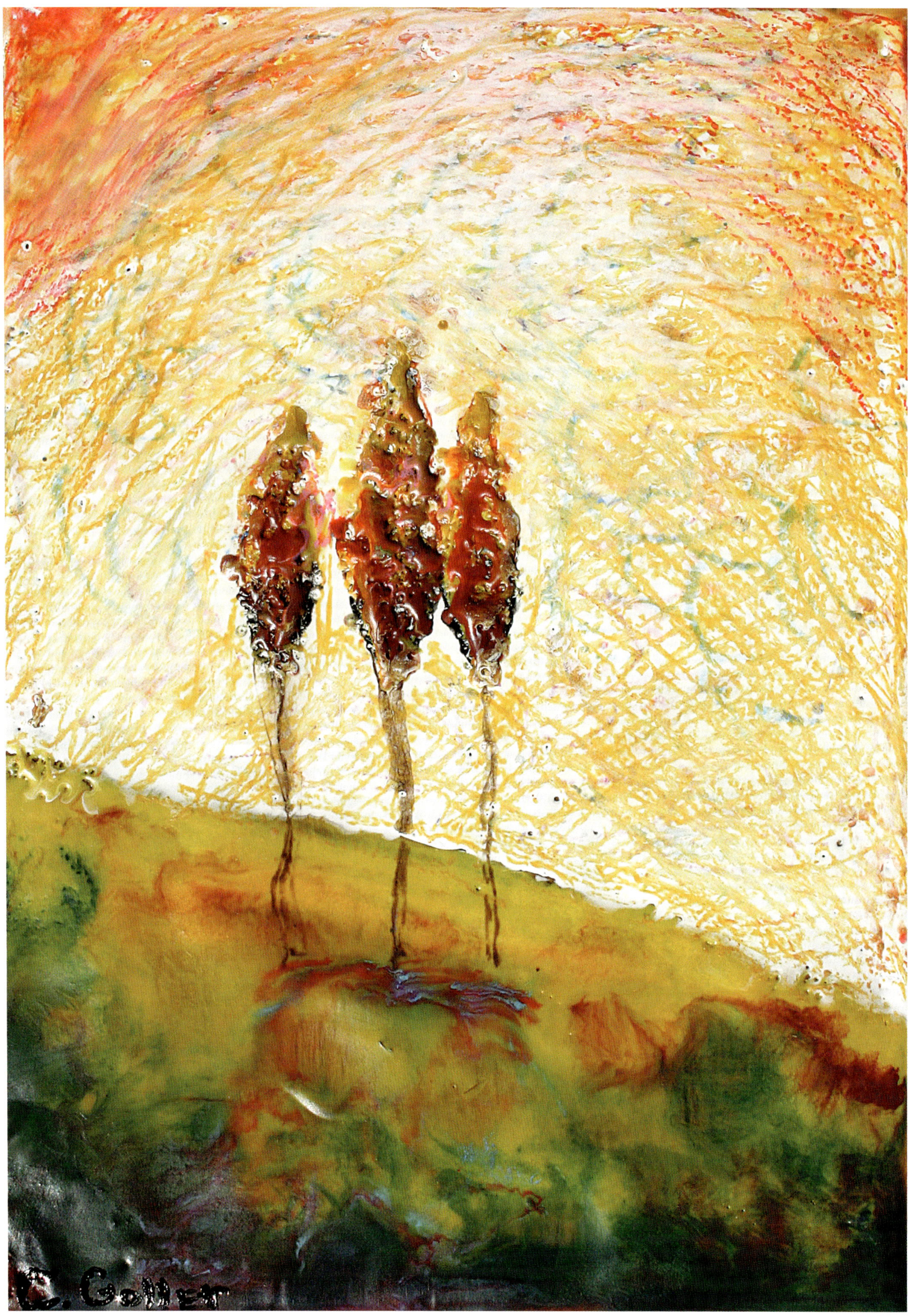

Carrie Goller

It was apparent from childhood on Washington's tiny Bainbridge Island that art would be a dominant force in Carrie Goller's life. After pursuing a Fine Arts degree, she spent many years focusing on other priorities until an illness provided the catalyst for her to reevaluate and more fully express creativity. Goller has work in international collections, as well as around the country. As many as nine galleries showcase her work. Her newest venture is the idyllic Rockwater Art Center; her exclusive gallery and a private retreat for intensive art instruction from some of the best art instructors available.

Art has become a necessity for me. It's both work and play – exhilarating yet restorative. It's where drama is safely indulged – and thus balance achieved. While absorbed in the creative process I lose track of time and feel all is well, content and confident in my creative ability.

Goller responds enthusiastically to color and is particularly lured by simple, yet sensual, organic forms and the intoxicating realm of vibrant colors, shapes, and textures found in nature.

She paints a wide variety of subject matter; mixing media keeps her endlessly inspired – oil, watercolor, pastel, charcoal, and especially encaustic – the ancient process of melting, applying, then fusing beeswax.

"I am a big fan of the golden mean. If I am doing something very detailed, I will actually measure it for .618 before I place my elements."
- Carrie Goller

Carrie Goller, *Hills IV.*
Encaustic on wood block, 12.7 x 17.7 x 5.1 cm.
Brenner Collection.

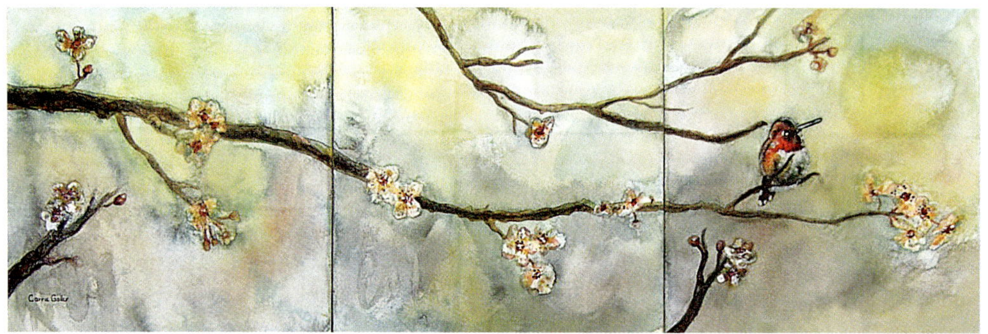

How long have you been working with encaustics?
About 5 or 6 years: I had a weak start. I was always told from childhood that I should be an artist, but I was also told that artists starve. It actually took a bout of cancer in 2002 for me to finally get serious about creating art. I am very excited to be an artist and I will be doing it for a long time.

What inspires your paintings?
Inspiration is wonderful when it arrives; but I am a professional artist, so I also realize that it is my job. I can't always count on inspiration. I just show up at my easel and paint every day. That being said, much of my work is inspired by daily life and the emotions I'm going through.

For instance, I did a superhero series and that was a tribute to my son's childhood. He was becoming a teenager and I coped with this transition by incorporating images and superhero costumes into my work. I also began an oil color series about nests, eggs, and birds at that point; which I felt protective of. They were hard to let go of.

Which artists have been inspirations to your work?
First of all I would like to thank Jasper Johns. He has really brought encaustic painting back from obscurity in the 1950s. Judith Kindler's work is fascinating to me. Tony Scherman's portraits are so intriguing.

Of course, for oil paints there are the Impressionists, European masters, and contemporary classical masters too; for example, Juliette Aristides, from right in Seattle. Klimt is my all-time favorite artist.

When you are painting encaustics, what materials do you like to use?
With encaustics, I mix my own medium from scratch. Sometimes I mix my own paint; but when I am buying paint, I prefer R&F. I've also used Enkaustikos products. I have custom light-weight cedar cradle board supports that are made by a local craftsman. I incorporate other mediums into my work; such as oil paint, mica powders, leaves, and whatever other organic material I can get hold of. Recently, I actually coated some lumber and driftwood pieces with encaustic to make them into sculptures. Sometimes I mix medium with imagery, incorporating photography.

Do you have any advice about doing encaustics without spending too much money?
Well I am a true junky, so I have numerous heat guns, irons, and heated tools. Some of them are specifically for encaustics, and some I have adapted from the hardware store, or kitchen and grocery stores. You can improvise simple household items as well. For instance, a simple household iron will work. However, anyone who is serious about encaustics will find out pretty quickly that a professional iron is preferred. Hardware store wood burning tools can be put on a heat regulator, otherwise they are too hot. You can use a large heated plug-in griddle, which is good for a palette. I like to collect cat food tins from my friends; you can mix colors in them, and you can't have too many of those. I buy my beeswax in bulk, and it is not uncommon for me to buy twenty-five to fifty pounds or more.

Carrie Goller, *Cherry Blossoms II.*
Encaustic and mixed media on wood box panels, triptych 25.4 x 25.4 x 5.1 cm. Parks Collection.

Carrie Goller, *Leaving I.*
Sculpted encaustic with iridescent minerals on two interchangeable wood box panels, diptych 60.9 x 76.2 x 5.1 cm. Private collection.

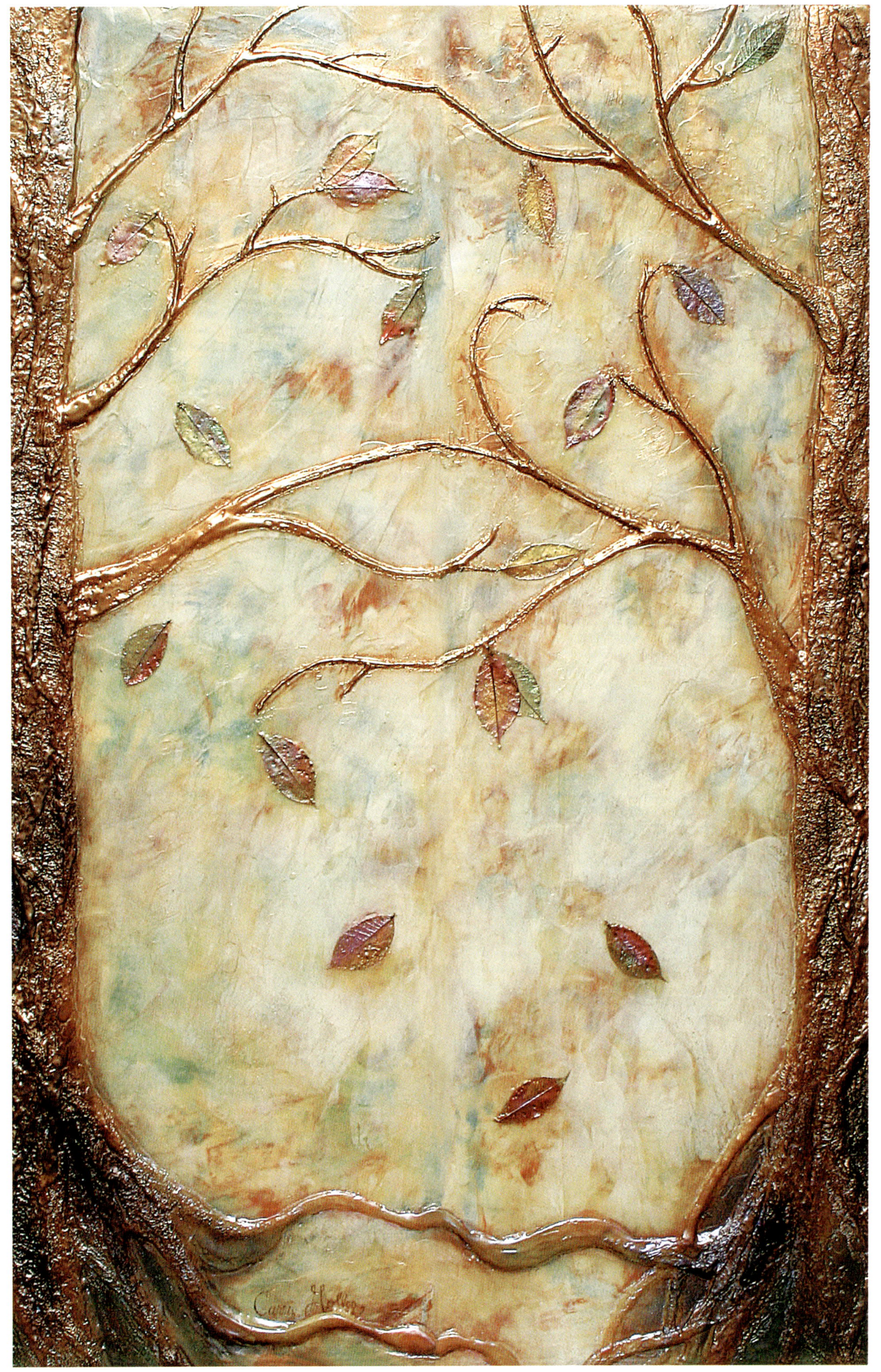

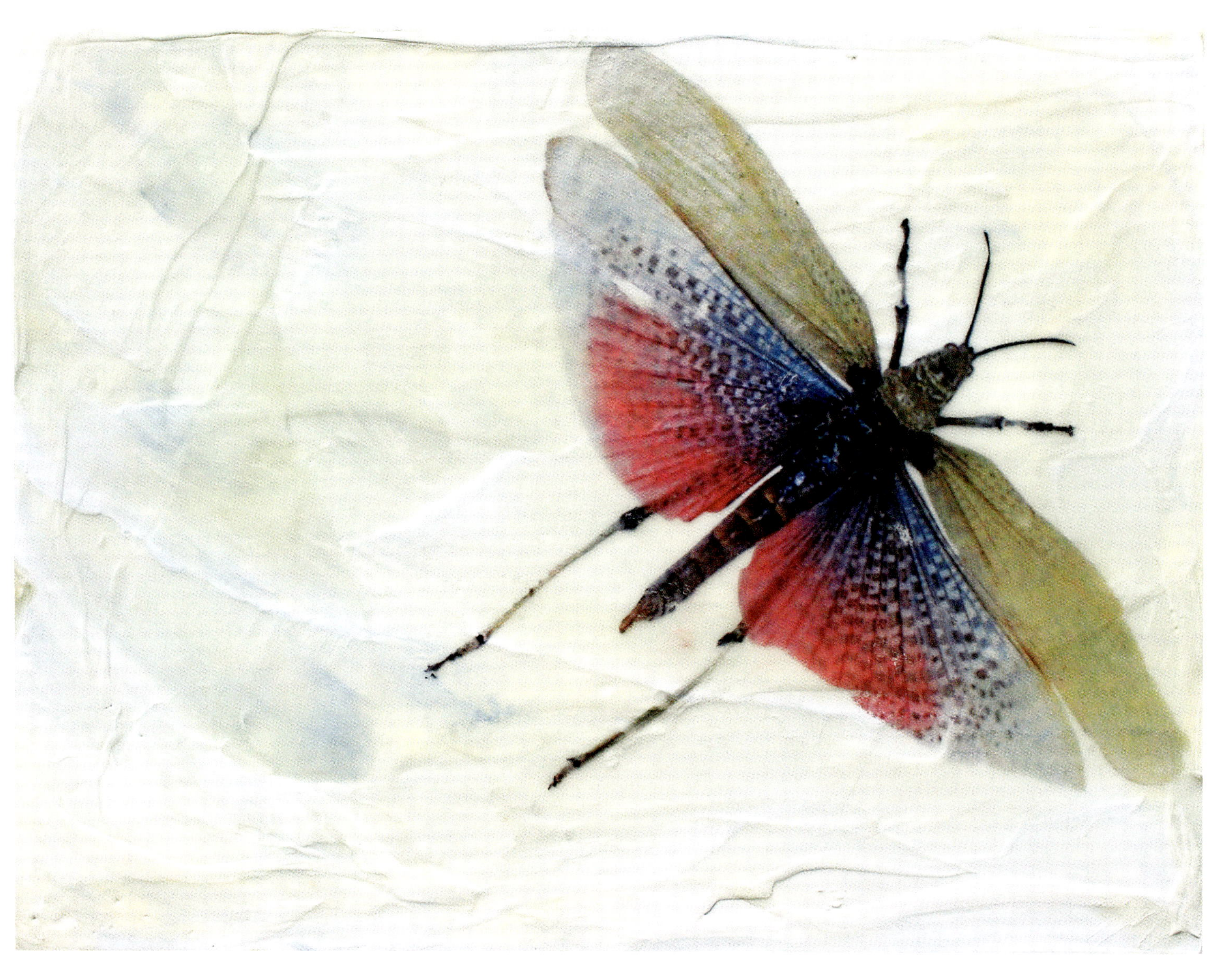

Carrie Goller, *Mothra.*
Encaustic and mixed media on wood block panel, 15.2 x 20.3 x 5.1 cm. Purbaugh Collection.

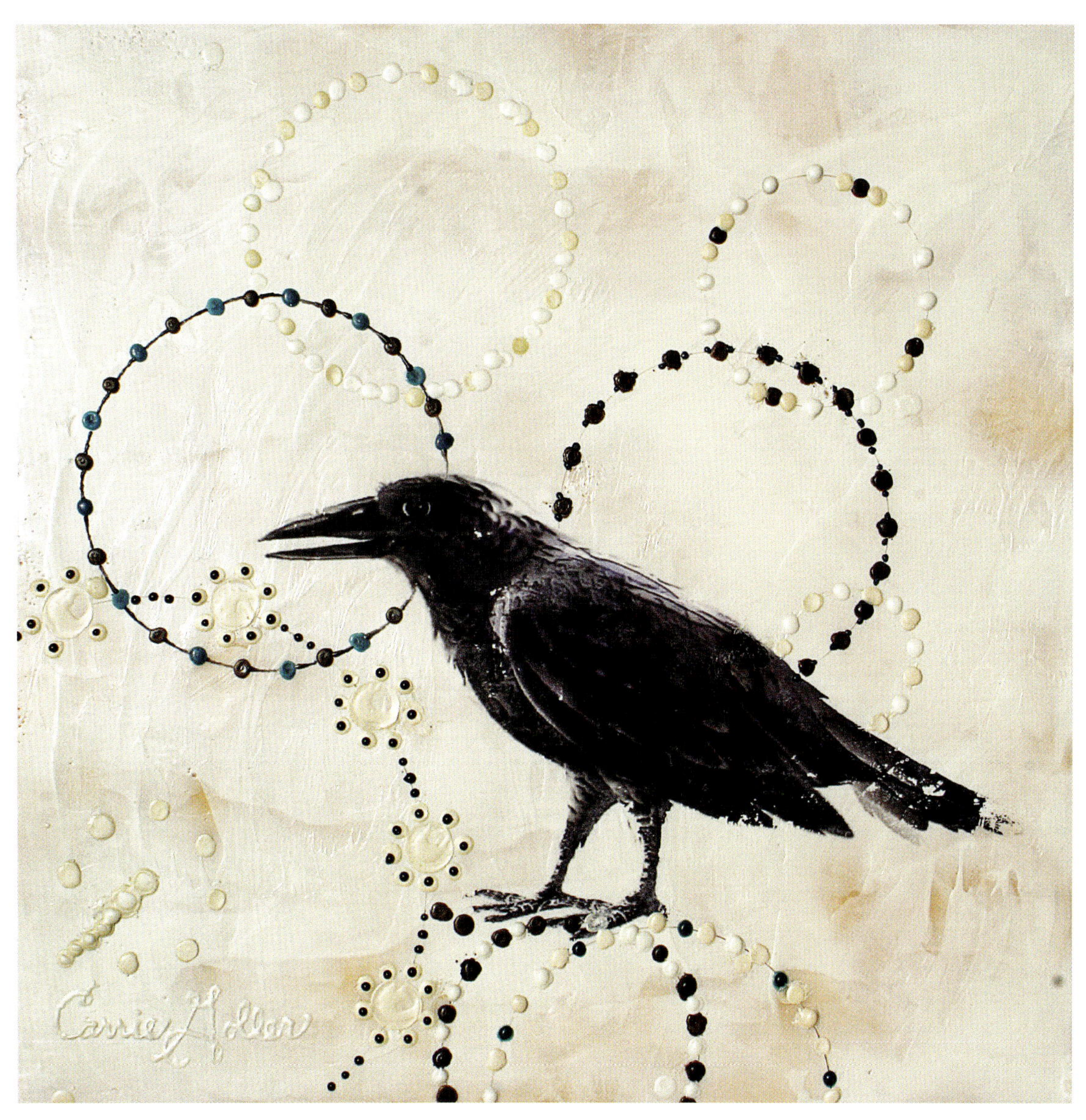

Carrie Goller, *Cuervo VI.*
Encaustic and mixed media on wood box panel, 45.7 x 45.7 x 5.1 cm.

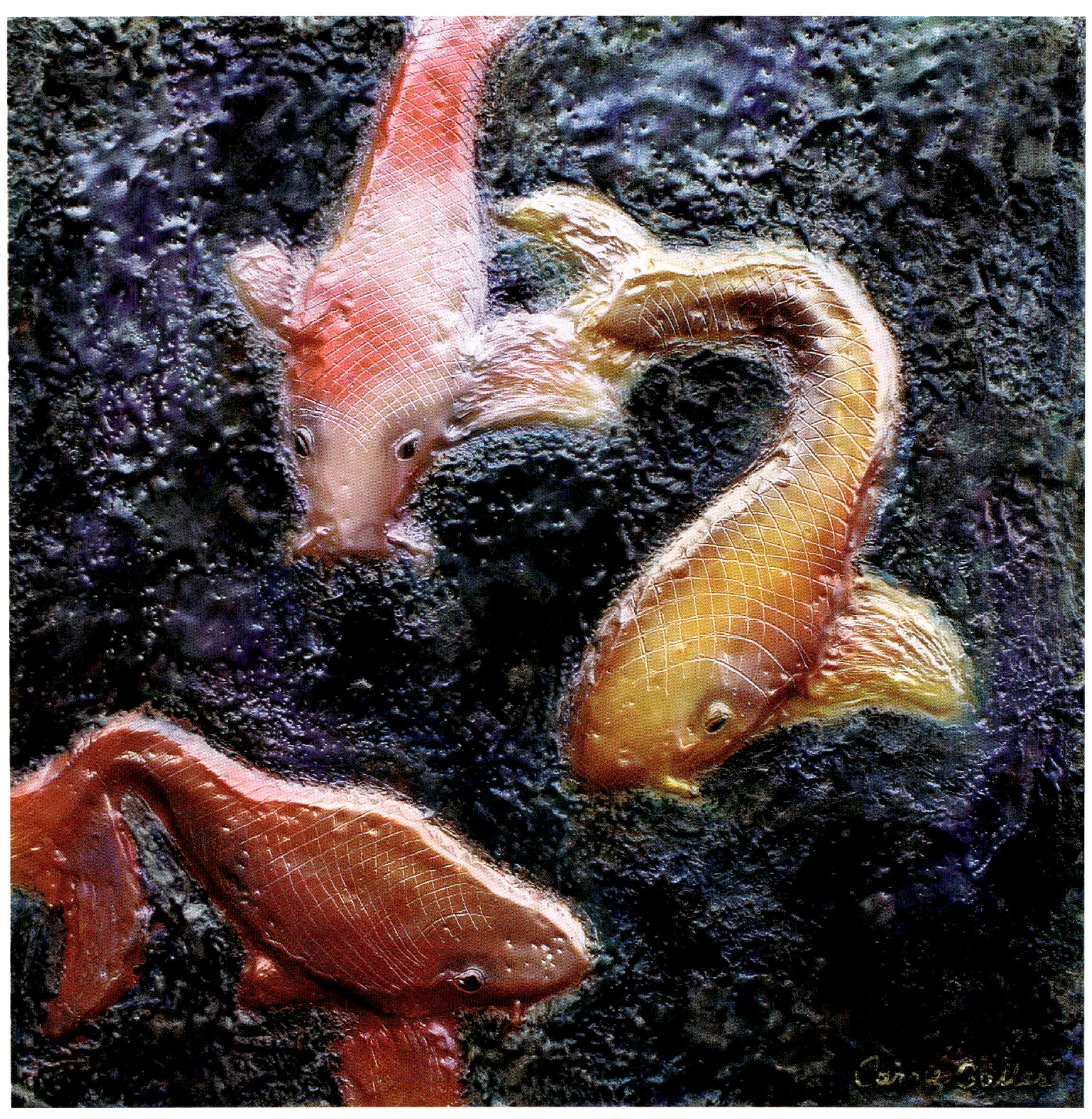

Carrie Goller, *Mahou (Magic) Koi V*.
Sculpted encaustic with iridescent minerals on wood box panel, 30.5 x 30.5 x 5.1 cm. For Art Sake Gallery.

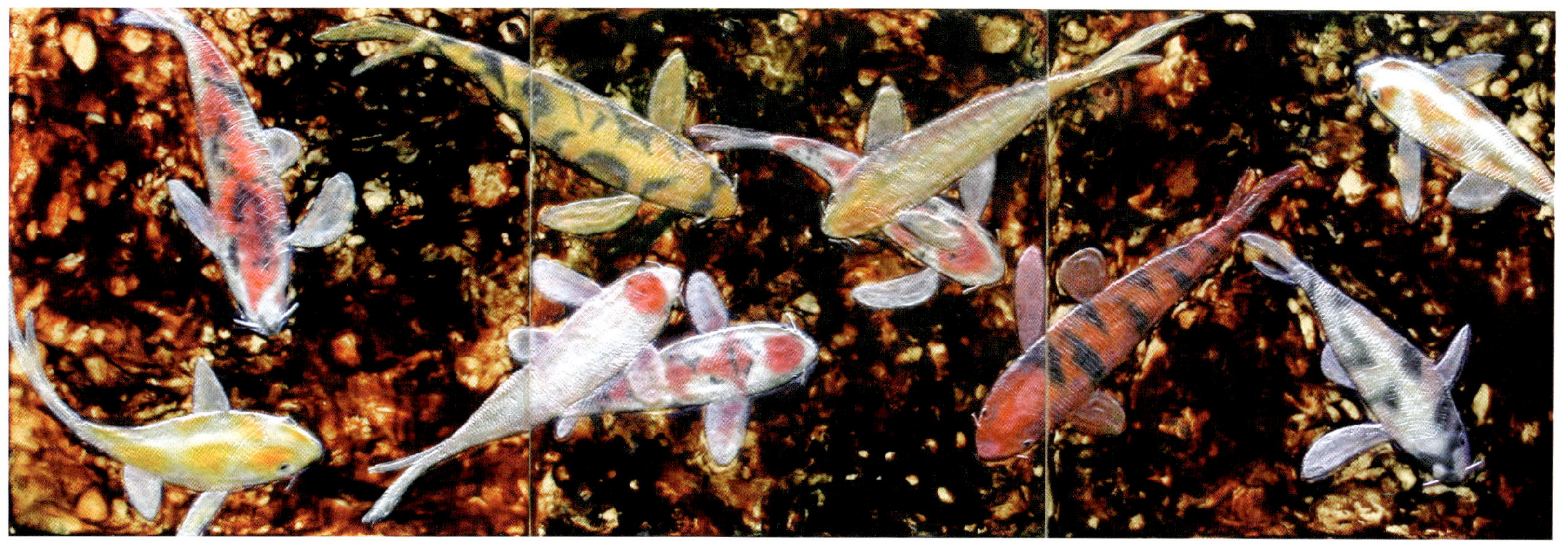

Carrie Goller, *Koi Takara (Treasure).*
Sculpted encaustic with iridescent minerals on three wood box panels, triptych 7.6 x 22.8 x 5.1 cm. Slattery Collection.

That helps me to save. I mix my own medium in disposable tin loaf pans from the grocery store; and I mix my own paints, sometimes with powdered pigments. I pour them into recycled muffin tins. I make two kinds of encaustic medium; this is probably the biggest money saver. I make natural beeswax encaustic medium, and I also make bleached muffin cake batches. I make sure that it is not chemically bleached, by the way. I reserve the most expensive bleached beeswax for the projects which I absolutely need it for. If I am going to paint color over the ground, I don't really need clear beeswax. I keep wax paper or tin foil under the work area so I can recycle some of the wax. Never skimp on safety equipment. You can use a respirator, but proper ventilation is really a must. My studio is equipped with a greenhouse fan system, but any way to get the fumes out is well-advised. Test by lighting a candle, blowing it out, and watching where the smoke goes. It should go out away from you and out of the studio. In case of fire, a big box of baking soda and a fire extinguisher on hand is really a must.

How do you create your paintings?

I usually plan my projects well before I begin. I like to think of what the size, shape, and dimension is going to be for the piece. I think about if it is a part of a series, will it be a triptych, (and) what kind of elements will I incorporate. I am very careful with composition and placement; unless I am experimenting. I am a big fan of the golden mean. If I am doing something very detailed, I will actually measure it for .618 before I place my elements. I am a colorist, so color is really a key decision for me. I feel like a mad scientist! There is a feel of mad scientist when I am mixing color in my encaustic studio, it is pretty fun. I preach about this by the way, the first grounding coat needs to be thoroughly heated into the support. You can use an iron, a heat gun, or a blow torch. Every subsequent layer needs to be heat sealed as well, if only briefly, or it may not be archival.

Do you frame your pieces or give them hardware in the back so they will be ready for hanging later?

The immediacy of having this work available to touch and enjoy is one of the amazing things about this medium. I rarely frame because I want to see it all. For smaller work, if I am using wood blocks, I finish the edges smooth with wax or paint. But for anything one foot square or over, I generally prefer a white profile finished edge. I use clear cedar trimmed pieces that are wrapped around my supports to make a box. I have hanging grips which are cut into the trim, or hardware attached to the back. So, everything is very tiny and ready to hang. On larger work I double wire and give it a yank test. I don't want anything to fall off the wall, and it can get rather heavy. Encaustic is very delicate and easy to damage, so I have a system. I buy foam rubber plumbing tubes at the hardware store, cut out the middles, and they make excellent protective bumpers. However, there is still sometimes repair work, so you should be prepared for that.

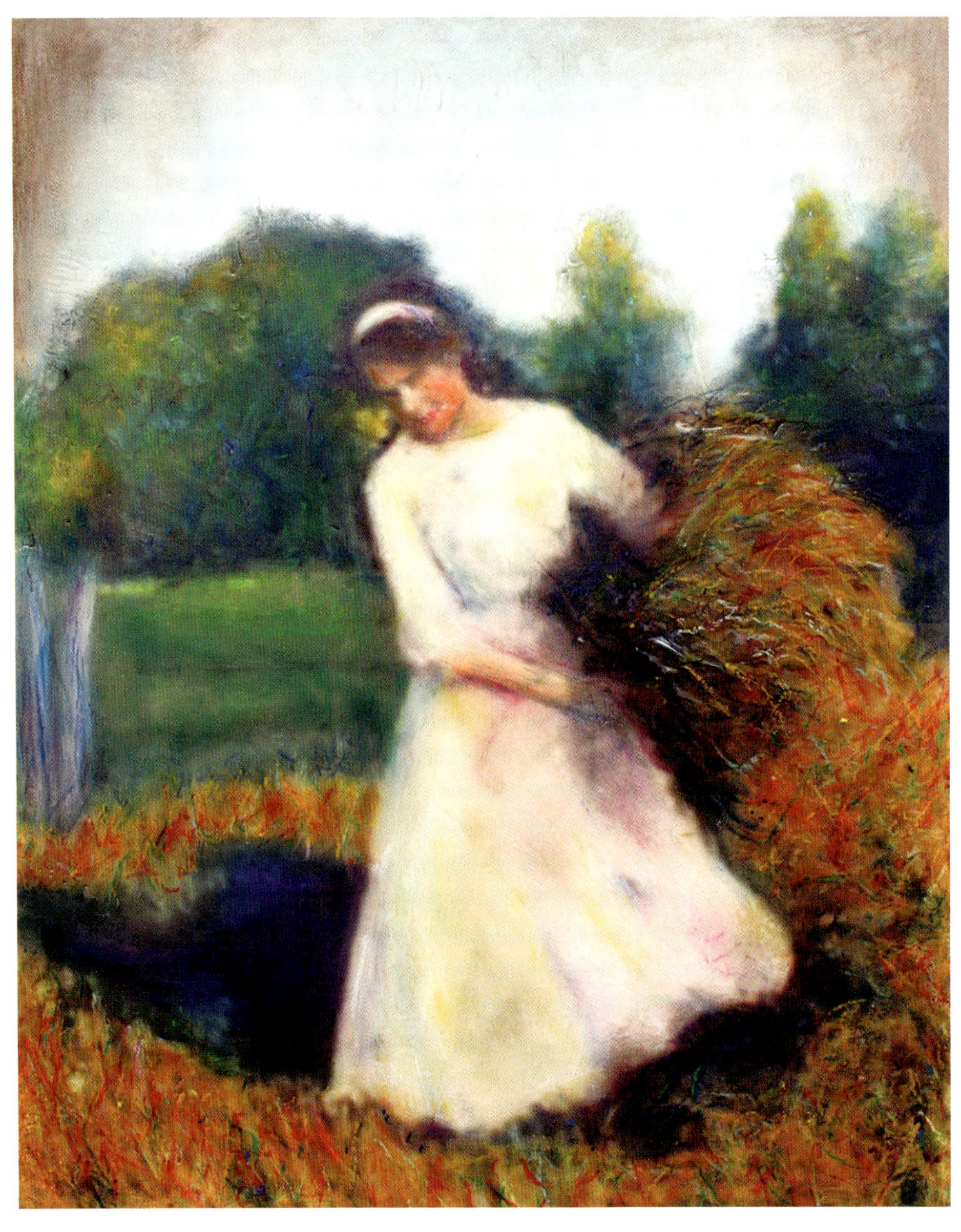

Carrie Goller, *Bringing in the Sheaves.*
Encaustic with mixed media, 25.4 x 20.3 cm. Obergottsberger.

Carrie Goller, *Autumn Cabin II.*
Encaustic on wood box panel, 30.5 x 30.5 x 5.1 cm.

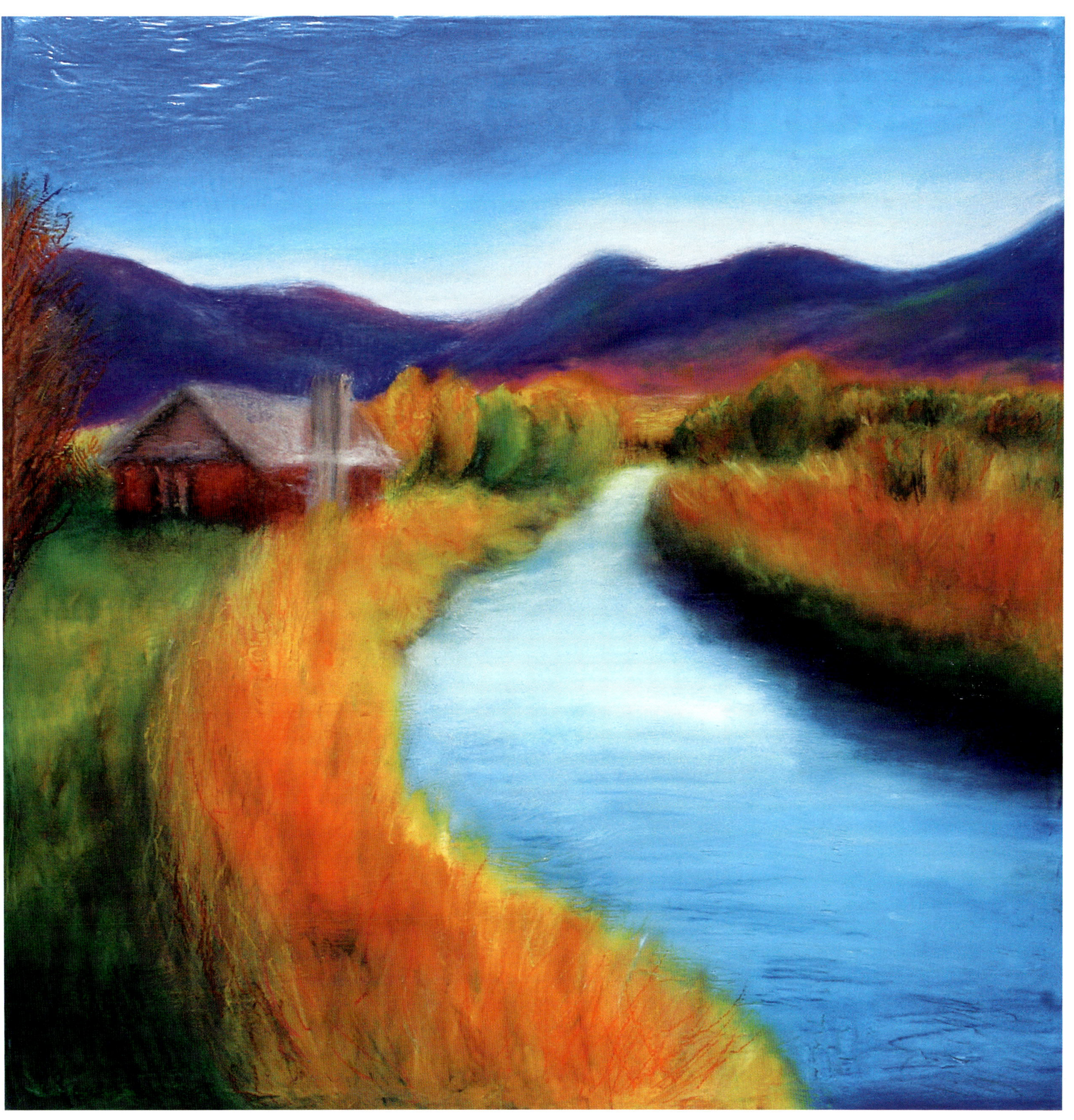

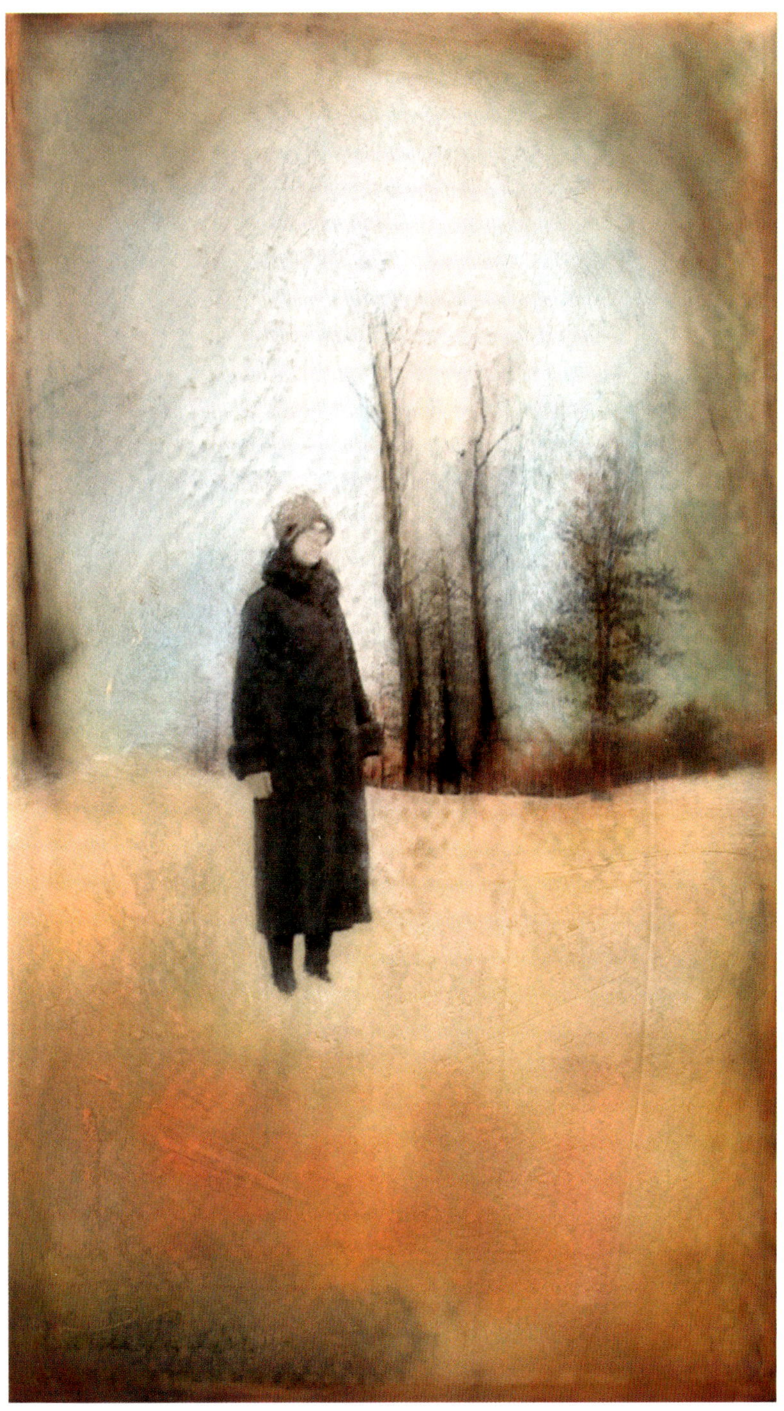

Can you tell us about your encaustic *Trees* series?

First, I created a number of mixed media diptychs involving watercolor tree paintings with salt patterns on them. Then, I fixed them to supports and put clear encaustic over that. After that, I sculpted over the trees, adding the iridescent mica powders and some metal leaf. A gallery asked me to create some more, and it evolved from there. The trees became even more sculpted and (then) the actual leaves were incorporated. More iridescent mica powders were applied. It is a series that I hope to expand upon. I envision many panels that are exchangeable, in a modular pattern. I have so many ideas and not enough time.

What techniques and iridescent materials did you use when you created *Leaving II*?

For the larger tree areas, I built up layers while heat sealing every layer, using hog bristle brushes. For smaller branches, I used a wire brush of heated tool with a stylus on the end. For texture I simply brush the wax on and allow it to stay textured, or sculpt it with a brush or heated tool. I am careful with each heat sealing not to melt the texture. For iridescence, I usually use mica powders which I build up in many layers. It is messy and there is sometimes cleanup with a damp cloth before heat sealing; or I leave it messy if I like.

Your *Koi* series is also very interesting; can you tell us more about it?

The *Koi* work is very technical, each piece is very different, but the nine foot triptych entitled *Koi Takara* especially took months to complete. First of all I laid my ground with several layers of colorless encaustic medium by, burning in the first layer thoroughly and heat sealing each additional layer. I then applied the transparent colors for the negative space, leaving some of the under layers showing through for a glazed effect. Then I drew in the Koi fish; and began the tedious process of applying many, many layers of clear encaustic wax with a brush, to build the fish into sculptural elements. Next, I scored the scales and other details into the wax with a sharp clay needle. Then, I removed any Stabilo Tone crayon drawing marks that remained. Then, I applied several layers of iridescent mica powders while meticulously cleaning up the excess with a damp rag; and again heat sealing each layer. This was a really tricky process because I only wanted to heat seal enough for archival quality and to sink the powder into the wax without destroying the lines I had sculpted in. I am pleased with the results; but as with all encaustic pieces, this one translates much better in person than in a photograph.

What techniques did you use to create the textures and lines in the background and on the Koi in the piece *Mahou*, which means magic?

This piece was like *Koi Takara*, the large piece, except this piece was even more textural. I used a hog bristle brush to pound and manipulate the background texture, then applied darker cool-colored mica powders to the negative space.

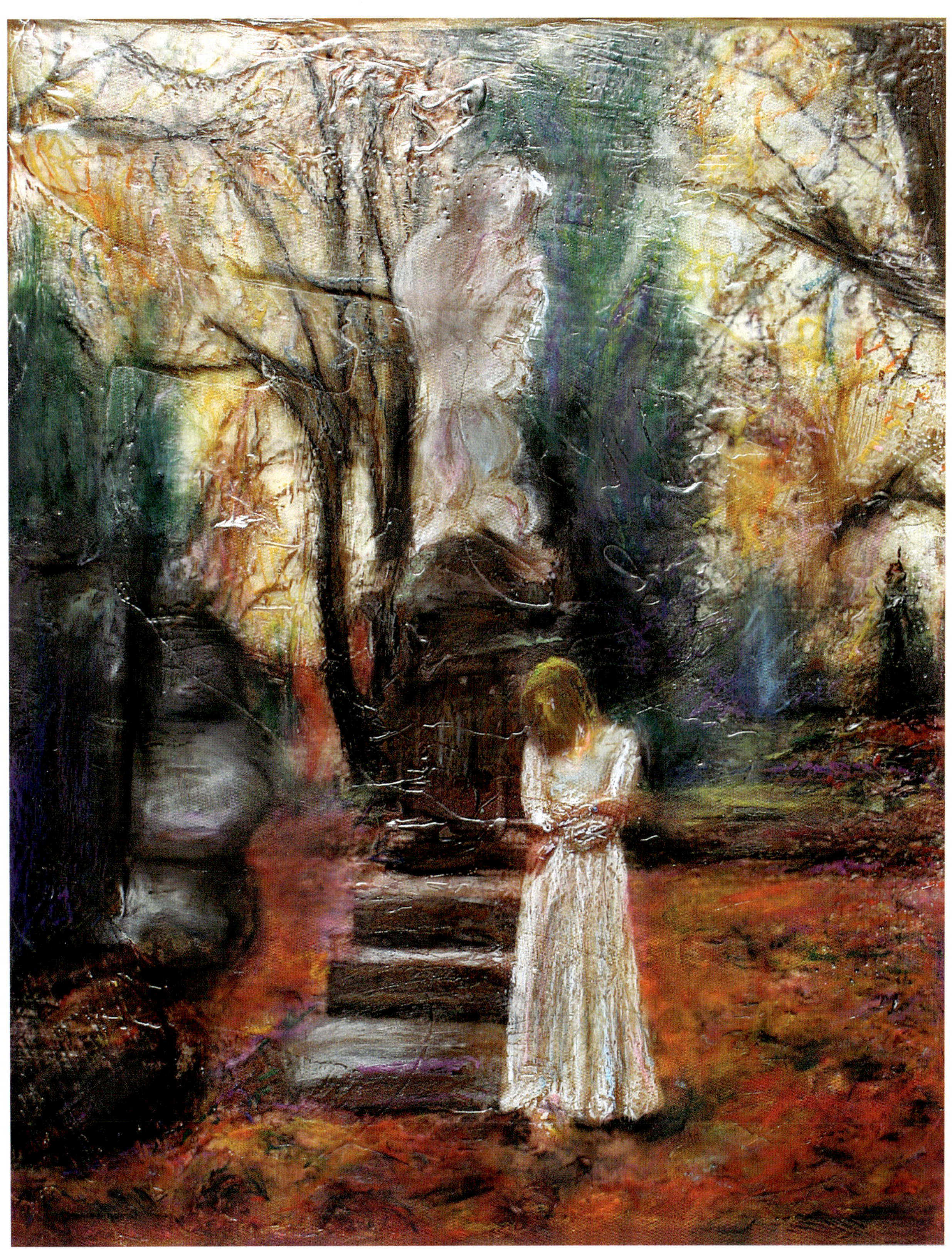

Carrie Goller, *Lost.*
Encaustic with mixed media, 20.3 x 11.4 cm.
Pagosa Springs Art Gallery.

Carrie Goller, *Portal.*
Encaustic with mixed media, from photo by Bryna Hoffmeister,
25.4 x 45.7 cm. Sweeney Collection.

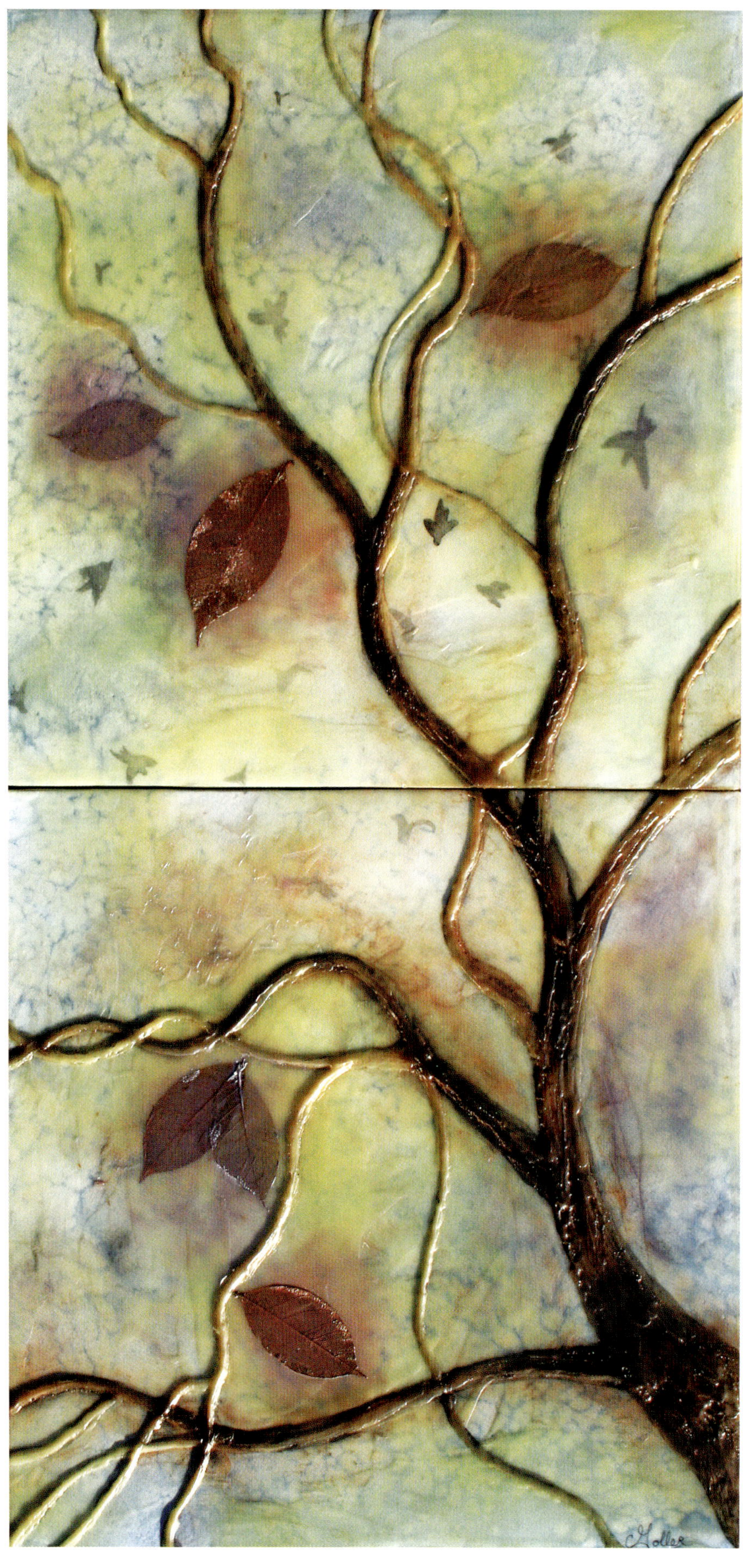

What mixed media did you incorporate into your piece *Mothra*?

I transferred a laser print of it by spoon rubbing it face down onto the still warm wax. Incidentally, I am very careful about getting permission of use from photographers, using copyright free images, or taking my own photos. I have had some problems with my own work being copied. I saw a reversed copy of one of my pieces featured on the front of a magazine.

Can you tell us about *Hills IV*; and the techniques you used to create the textural contrast between the soft foreground, textured trees, and sky?

Well, to lay my ground of encaustic medium, I applied several layers of off-white wax, sealing them smooth with an iron. Then, I applied brush-loads of yellow, green, brown, and magenta. I glazed in the layers for the hill, and then I used a hog bristle brush to apply the colors for the trees. I heat sealed the under layers and added the textures with my heat tool, using a small wire brush attachment. There is no need to seal in wax applied with a heat tool. I then used sable tones; drawing the tree trunks using cross hatch patterns and also embellishing the other elements of the piece, and then heat sealing the crayons into the wax as it cooled. I smeared some of the wax with my finger as it cooled to soften the lines.

What are you working on now?

I am probably most excited about a new venture, Rockwater Art Center. It is in an idyllic farmhouse setting and we actually lived there until recently. It is in a quaint little Norwegian Village of Poulsbo, Washington. It sits on a beautifully landscaped area with four water features, with outdoor fireplaces, a mini lavender farm, and prune orchards. It is just beautiful and it houses my old gallery.

It is also a private retreat for extensive art instruction from some amazing artists. My encaustic studio is there and it is just twenty minutes from my home and oil studio on hood canal. The director there is trying to talk me into giving lessons, but I'm very busy right now. As far as specific art projects, I'm very excited about a new encaustic mixed media series. It is vintage figurative work from cool images from the 1920s through to the 1970s, mostly of families. My uncle's mother and aunt were opera singers, so there are some great photos of Aunt Lorie. She was actually the lead in Madame Butterfly in the Vienna Opera House. There are also a lot of pictures of my family camping: my red-headed mom looking glamorous while wading in Lake Chelan in her turquoise bathing suit with a cigarette in hand and we children paddling on air mattresses. There are AirTran trailers, cool vintage cars, flappers, and picnics. I'm really enjoying the process, because I'm in love with the images. They are really comforting, and it's a bygone era. In addition, I'm planning to complete the *Leaving* series, which are the modular diptychs and triptychs of sculpted iridescent trees. I have also just returned from Wyoming and Montana, and I have made quite a few trips there lately. I have been inspired to create a large piece called *Buffalo Jump*, which is actually in process and quite abstract. I am trying something new; a collaboration with a great photographer.

It is for a joint exhibit. Plus, there are a couple of coachings I agreed to and I need to get going on. I am also looking for the right metal artist to collaborate with on some large museum pieces with encaustics. It has been very busy and it is going to be a hectic year, because I'm trying to keep eight or nine galleries supplied, which alone is rather tough. There are also a number of nights when I have more than one exhibit at once and I have to have lots of help; domestic help, office, and intern help. Thank you everyone, you know who you are.

What advice do you have for encaustic artists who want to take their work to the next level?

Trial and error are essential for growth because encaustic is a pretty tricky medium. Research and learn all you can. Don't be afraid to try new methods. Just make sure you follow the safety precautions. I just read an article in a major art magazine which encouraged the use of turpentine with encaustics. Turpentine emits toxic fumes when it is heated: that is not safe. Work specifically for sale should be archival, or state otherwise if it is not. For instance, when using oil pastels with encaustics work there is no guarantee for archival quality, since the pastels never fully dry. I really love having this medium in my arsenal. Sometimes when I am about to start an oil painting, I stop and think, how would this translate in encaustics? Then I go for it.

Carrie Goller, *Arashi Ki II (Storm Tree II).*
Sculpted encaustic with gold leaf and iridescent minerals on two wood box panels, diptych 30.5 x 60.9 x 5.1 cm.

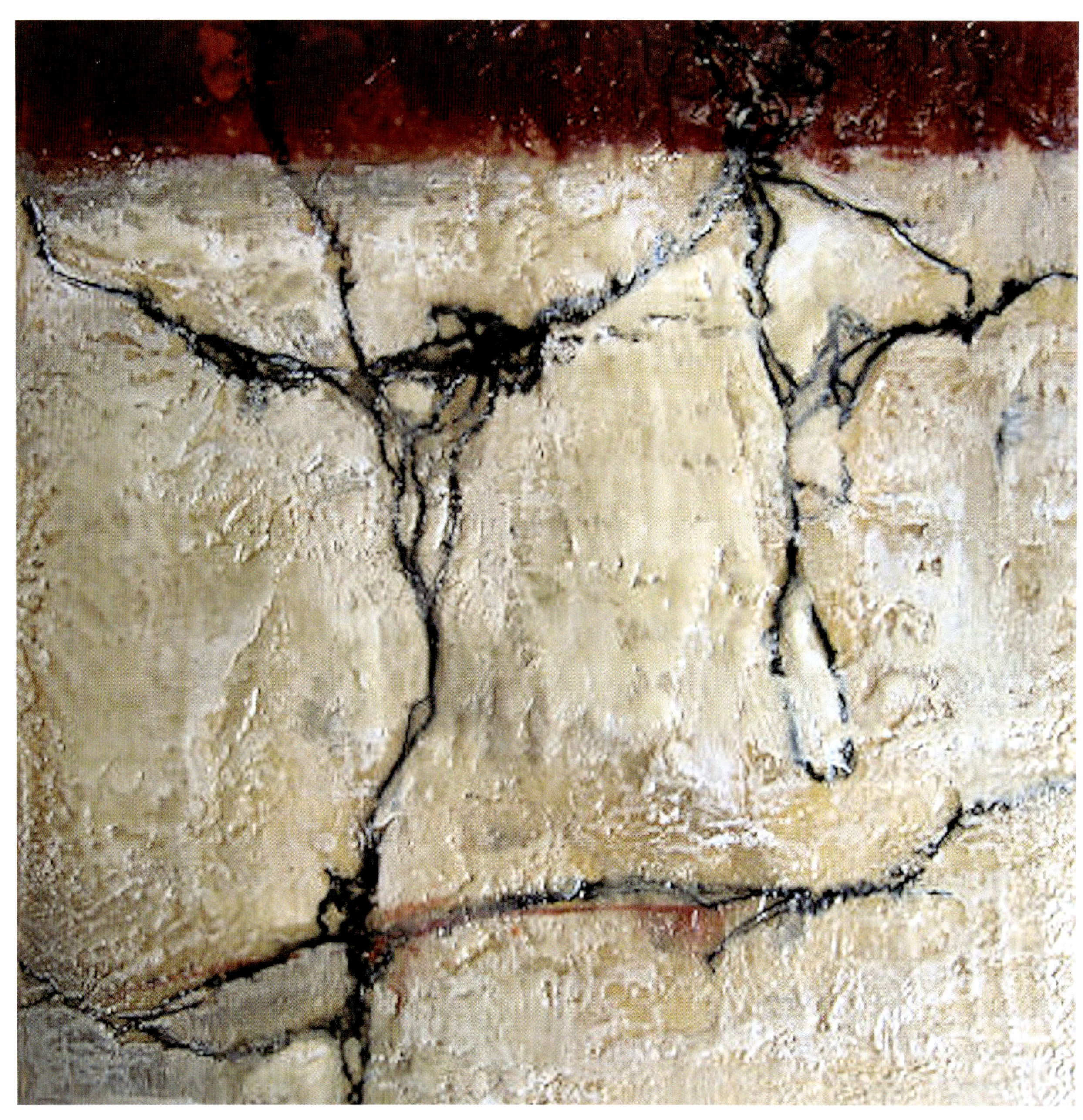

Cheryl D. McClure, *Fences* (detail), 2010. Encaustic on wood panel, 25.4 x 25.4 x 5.1 cm.

Cheryl D. McClure

I'm influenced heavily by nature and the land. Living on a ranch in northeastern Texas, this influence creeps into my work whether I plan for it or not.

I respond to the world on an emotional and intuitive level. My work continues to evolve in both style and form. In my paintings, each brush stroke, mark, and color is part of a story, expressing emotion I didn't know was there until the painting process drew it out. I rarely begin a painting with a goal in mind. I would much rather allow it to develop on its own. Once it reveals itself, the paint and I start our conversation, which results in the final painting. I enjoy the process of experimentation with techniques and materials; it affords me the opportunity to explore the expressive potential of abstract painting.

I have no formal art education other than my own time spent in the studio and viewing work of interest in galleries and museums. I have been painting for more than thirty years which is my education.

"I really just think you need to be true to yourself. If you work hard all the time and you do what you love to do, you will develop a style."
- Cheryl D. McClure

How long have you been working with encaustics?
It has been about three years. I started researching all of the technical questions that I had and watched some of my friends earlier who painted with encaustics. I spent a lot of time on the forum on R&F paints; they have a wonderful forum there for learning if you really scour it.

What are the inspirations behind your paintings?
I live in the country. I haven't always lived in the country, but we live in a rural area with small towns. So I guess you might say nature or the moods and feeling that I get from living in a place. We have a couple of hundred acres here, so I look out over pastures and see a lot of trees. This is probably the major influence for my paintings. But other than that, I don't really start with anything in mind. It is really more the formal aspects of painting that I am interested in. I don't know if you can call that an inspiration or not. I just think it is fun to paint, I enjoy painting.

Which artists have inspired your work?
That would depend, there are so many. In fact, sometimes I can't think of who all they are. I have been painting for thirty years and I just took up encaustic. The definition is not really encaustic artists, and I hate to say encaustic artists. I really think it is artist, and you happen to use encaustic, acrylic, or whatever medium that you like. In the past, Diebenkorn was a great influence on me because I am really interested in the design of one of his paintings and Rothko, Motherwell, and Franz Kline. People like that have such wonderful gesture, some have texture, as can be seen with Joan Mitchell, with her gestural paintings and Robert Rauschenberg or Hans Hofmann. I am very interested in collage, so artists like Kurt Schwitters and Joseph Cornell. I really respect their work and have learned a lot by just looking at their work.

What materials do you like to use for your encaustic paintings?
Actually, you were talking about books and I bought Joanne Mattera's book first. I just thought "there are so many different ways you can work with this, I think I will just try all of them to see what works best for me." Because you can start any kind of painting from a hundred different points, I just started working from a lot of the different ways to start in her book; and I have discovered, I think, my favorite way is to start out with paper. Or you can mount a heavy paper. It has to be a heavy enough paper that the medium underneath it doesn't seep through. Also, you can use something called an encaustic gesso. The kind that I use is called Holy Grail, by Evans Encaustics. I think there are some other companies that use it now, and they call it

encaustic gesso. It makes a white surface just like gesso would on another kind of panel, only you can use your wax over it. I like to start with that. I think it is my favorite way at the moment, but it could change next month. When I do that, I can then start using charcoal to draw. I have to have somewhere to start and I like to make marks. So if I start with a texture, I like to start making marks. I like oil paint; I haven't used oil paint directly, apart from one time. I use oil sticks, oil pastels, and collage papers; that sort of thing. Then of course, I buy encaustic paints and I also make mine with oil paints and medium.

One of the ways that I worked on a couple of pieces was to stretch some canvas that did not have any medium in it, just the clean unprimed canvas on a board. But I found that I did not really care to do that very much, it just took a lot of medium soaking into that canvas before you could even really get started. Now there might be a reason you would want to do it, and I tried it. Then, I decided that was a big waste and I would work directly on the board. The next thing I tried was working on the board, and the next thing I tried was working on the paper. I had a lot of watercolor paper around and decided to use acrylic medium and glue it to the board, and made sure I didn't get any of the acrylic medium on the top. It has to be a heavy paper so it won't bleed through. Then you let it dry and work on that. I really like that surface because I had something to put marks on before I started putting down the medium; and I only work on the plain boards. If you know you are going to be painting something darker, you might just want to start with a board, period.

What tips do you have for saving money on materials?

Encaustic is pretty expensive, but it depends on how you work. You can probably save a lot of money on materials if you do a lot of salvage type work or work where you use a lot of recycled pieces. I don't do a lot of that, so I just use plain boards. But, I do like to use several types of papers. Some of them are papers that I have found and some of them are purchased papers or papers that I have. There are not a lot of ways to save money other than learning to make your own boards, your own paint, (or) your own medium.

How do you start your paintings?

I still paint with acrylic probably more than anything. I paint with encaustic about half the year because it is hot here. Before encaustic, I would usually add texture and tone to my canvases; and this is something where you need a lot of modeling paste etc., but that is really heavy. You can't do this with encaustic and I don't need to do it with encaustic because I can make texture more readily. I start out using gesso, or glue down the heavy white paper like I said, or I just use a plain board, and then I make marks. I don't draw any particular design because I don't paint subjects. I am really an abstract painter, sometimes totally nonobjective. Every once in a while I have noticed that over the past few years a little more realism is creeping in. That is because I am surrounded by trees, but I have always had a thing for trees. I don't start out with anything in mind that I am going to do. When I say marks, I mean that I just want to put marks on the board. It is good to mess it up before you get started so that it is not a precious thing, and these marks help me determine sometimes if I am dividing up my space like I would like to. It keeps me in line later on if I like what I did because then I don't get away from the design that I decided I like.

Do you frame your pieces when you finish?

At the moment I only frame a few. I framed those two that had the canvas over them because I made those panels, and put the canvas over it because it was going to hide my carpentry skills, which are not really good. But if I have a really nice panel and it goes with what I am painting, I just leave the sides as they are. I am not fond of taping the sides though, so I sometimes have a bit of a mess, and I have to scrape that off. In fact, in the studio today I decided to paint the sides of the painting I have on the front of my website, which is a diptych.

Can you tell us about your piece *Almost Winter*?

You were asking earlier about saving money. On this particular one, I later got to thinking that I saved money because it is two twenty-four by forty-eight inch panels. My brother salvaged them from a neighbor who was throwing them away. I was

Cheryl D. McClure, *Almost Winter*, 2009.
Encaustic and paper on wood panels, diptych 121.9 x 121.9 x 12.7 cm.

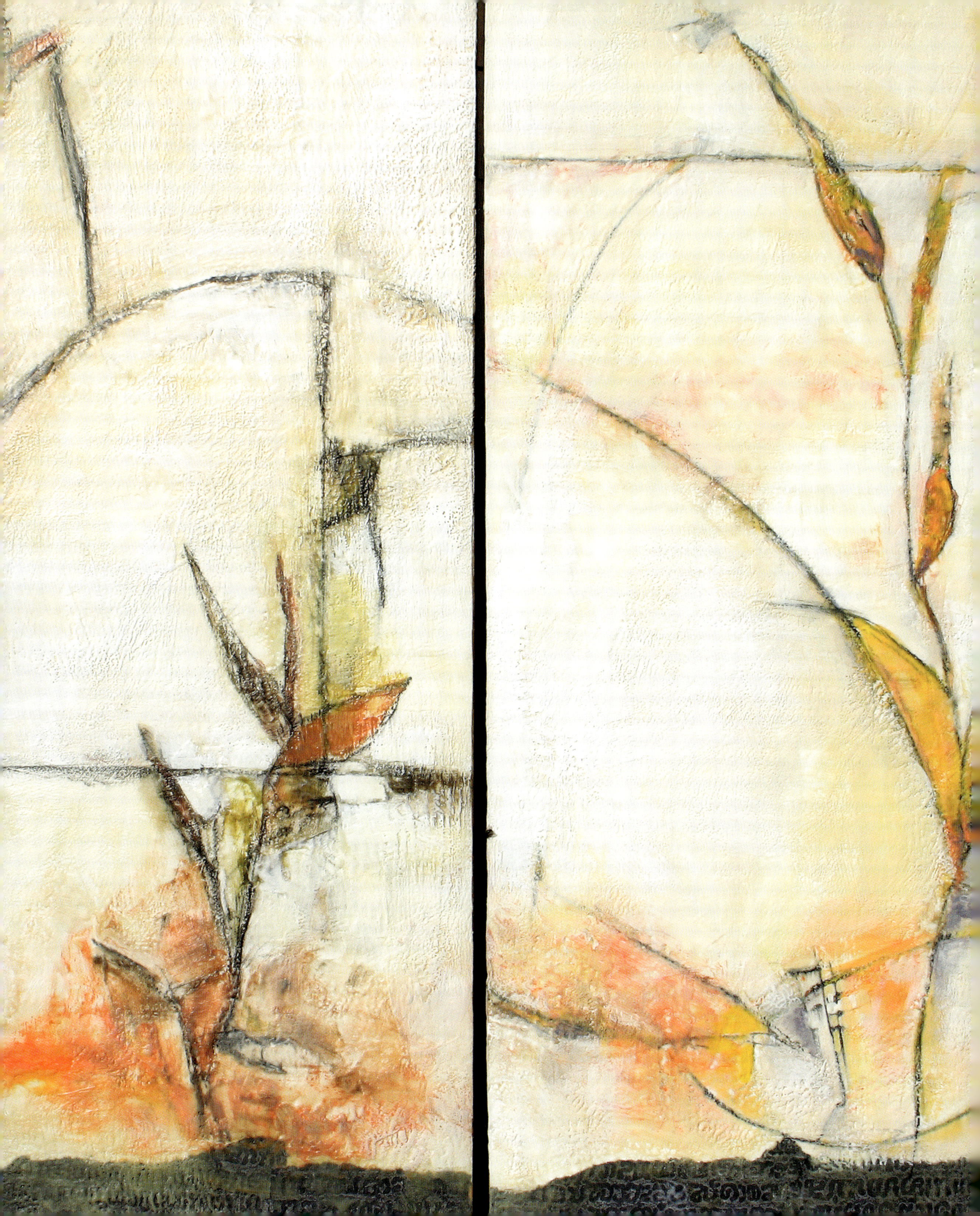

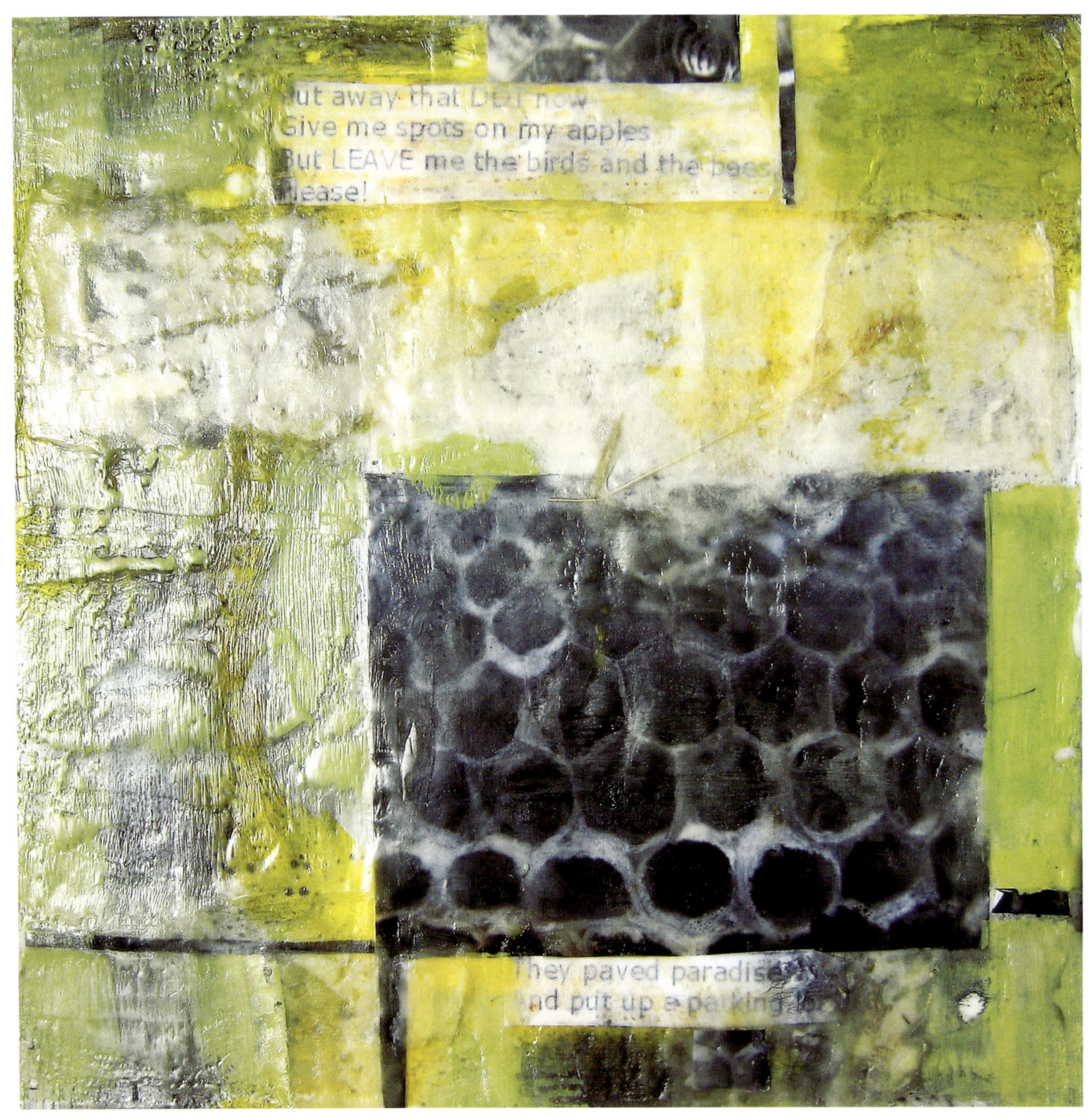

Cheryl D. McClure, *They Paved Paradise I*, 2009.
Encaustic and mixed media on wood panel, 30.5 x 30.5 x 5.1 cm.

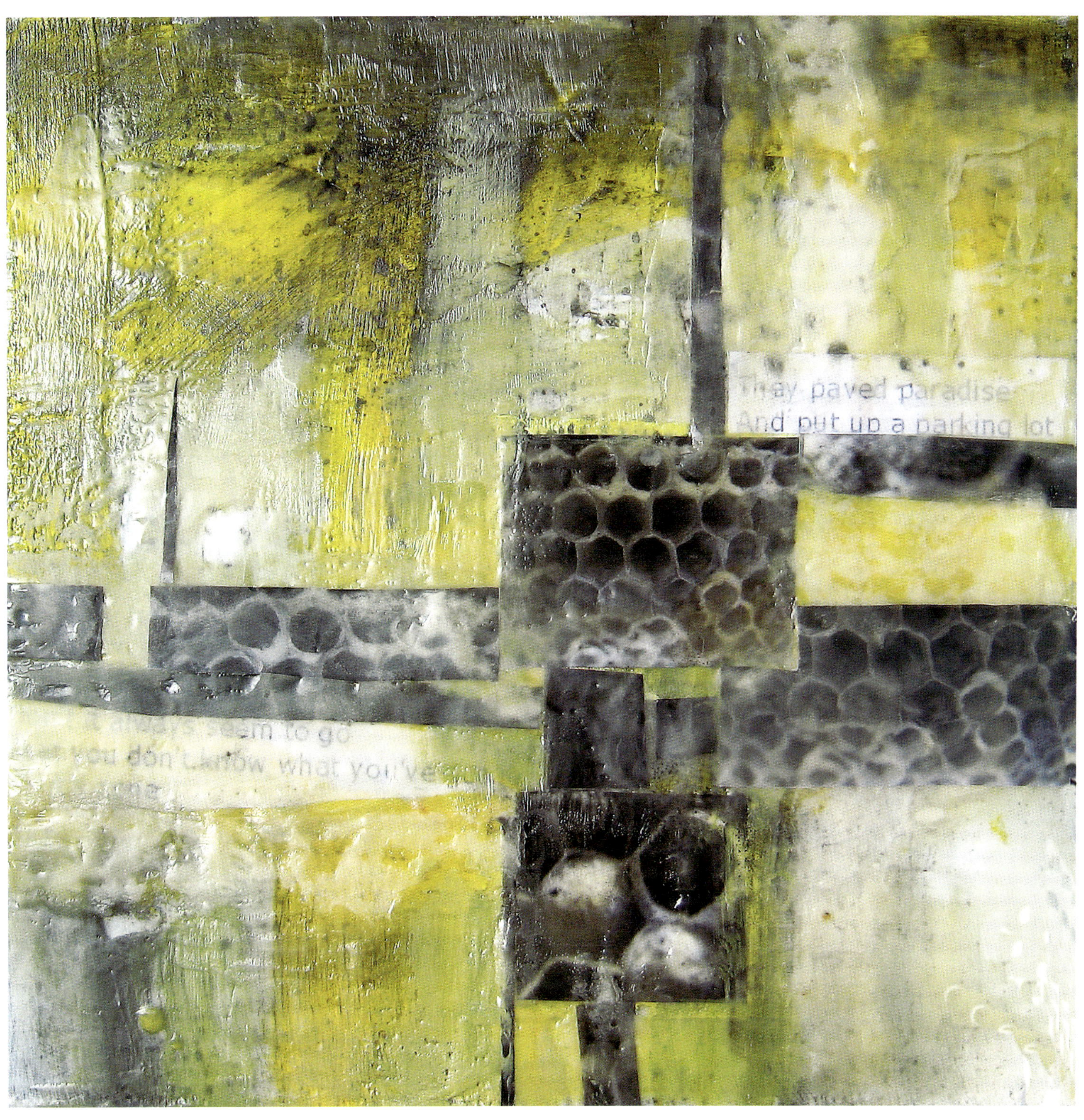

Cheryl D. McClure, *They Paved Paradise II*, 2009.
Encaustic and mixed media on wood panel, 30.5 x 30.5 x 5.1 cm.

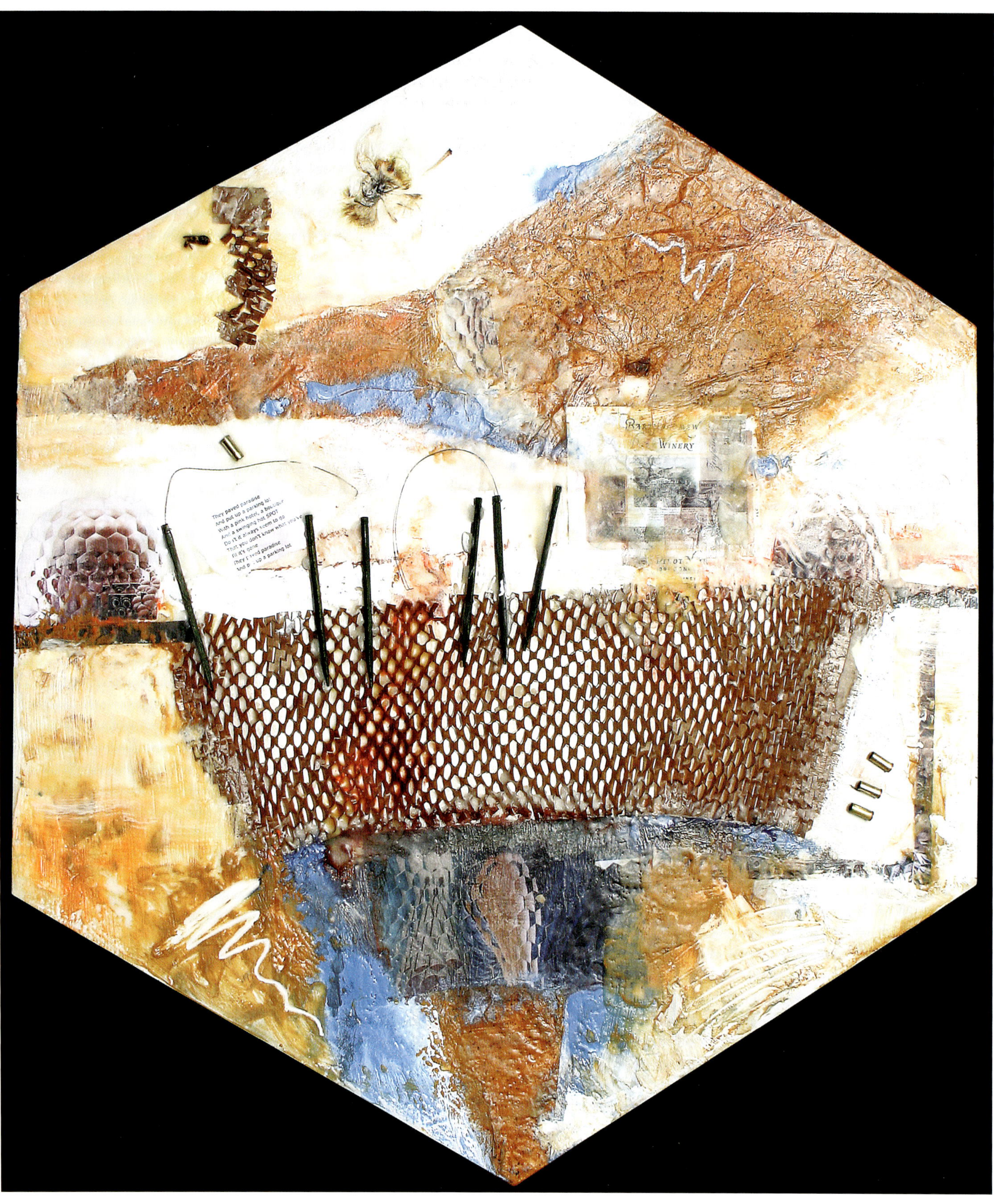
They paved paradise
And put up a parking lot
And a swinging hot SPOT
They paved paradise
WINERY

afraid that wax would not stick to whatever was already on there. I sanded and cleaned it up, then I glued down the Arches Watercolor Paper (that) I had in a roll. It was about forty four inches wide. I glued that down and weighted it overnight. The dark ground is the four inches at the bottom that I laid to cover the previous surface. I found some embossed charcoal-colored heavy paper and I glued it down. It was about the same weight as the watercolor paper, so it was fortunate, but unplanned. I put that paper on there and went from there. I meant to do some more collage work on that piece, but I never ended up doing it. What I did end up doing was what I told you before; I would start with a charcoal line and make gestural marks. I liked the way that they divided up the surface. I didn't know what I was painting, but it turned out being something that I thought of as the time between when the grasses all start drying up; between fall and wintertime. These lyrical marks that I made set the tone for me and made me think about what I was painting. I used oil pastels, I used oil sticks, and I used light-colored encaustic medium. I used a lot of medium in that painting between the oil sticks, the medium, and the fusing. The lines are the charcoal lines that I painted negatively around.

Can you tell us more about *Salute to Whistler* and the mixed media that you incorporated into it?
In *Salute to Whistler*, the reason I named it that is that I was working in a *Patina* series. I was working on some collage and I was looking through all my papers, and I found some brochures from a museum show I went to that featured Whistler's work; and I cut up bits and pieces of it and put it in with the wax with other plain papers. I work with what I find. Work is a relationship with what I find. It has been a while since I painted that one, so it is hard for me to remember exactly what I did other than that. The drawings were all black and white, but I was already using the blues and greens before I ever put those papers in. I usually don't think about my colors, but I studied a lot. Now, what I choose is fairly intuitive.

Can you tell us more about your inspiration and technique in your piece *They Paved Paradise I*?
There are two of those. The one and two I painted at the same time. We have a group called Texas Wax and we are having lots of shows. We were invited to show at the newly remodeled Art Deco building in the Fair Park District of Dallas when they reopened after the remodel. Our theme was Global Swarming. One of the members came up with the idea that we would educate people about the Colony Collapse Disorder by all of our members doing something that would refer to it. I wasn't that happy because I don't paint with a theme in mind. I kept thinking I have a year, and kept thinking "what am I going to do for that?" So finally, one day I was in the car and I heard the song the Big Yellow Taxi, a Joni Mitchell song. So, I was listening to it and I thought, "I will use that!" So then I looked it up on the internet and I printed out all of the lyrics. I fused in little bits and pieces of it. I glued in pictures of honeycomb; I made a collage out of it.

Can you tell us about what you are working on now?
I am working for a show that is coming up at the encaustic center in Dallas, it is really in Richardson, but that is a suburb of Dallas. There are two of us; it is just a two-person show. I am making plans to go to the encaustic conference. I decided to use one of the pieces for that, to enter into the show for that. I have been doing a lot of encaustic, and it is mostly with collage, of the ones that I have been doing the most of lately.

Lastly, what advice do you have for artists to make their work stand out?
I really think that you need to be true to yourself. If you work hard all the time and you do what you love to do, you will develop a style. A lot of people ask about how to have a style.

Someone else said you just can't get away from it, you will have a style. I think that is true. You just have to spend a lot of time painting. I do believe that people don't need to get carried away with being archival. But, if you ever want to sell your work, you need to make sure that you're making a painting that won't fall apart on someone. So, I highly encourage people to learn about the technicalities too. There are not that many of them once you get them set in your mind, and then you can do whatever you want to do. Just work hard, that is all I can say.

Cheryl D. McClure, *They Paved Paradise III*, 2009.
Encaustic and mixed media on wood panel, hexagon: 60.9 x 68.5 x cm.

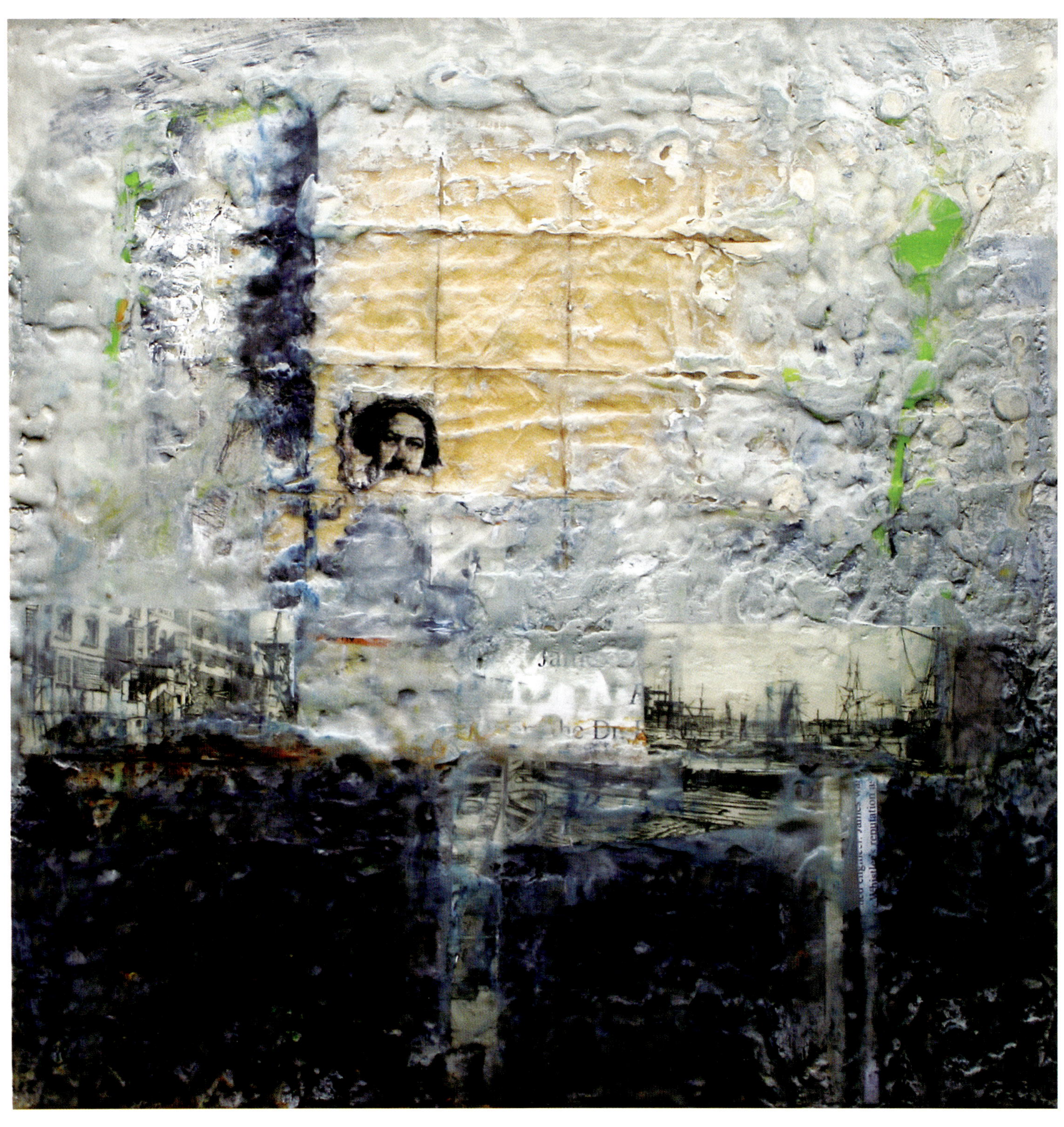

Cheryl D. McClure, *Salute to Whistler, Patina Series*, 2007.
Encaustic and found paper on wood panel, 30.5 x 30.5 x 5.1 cm.

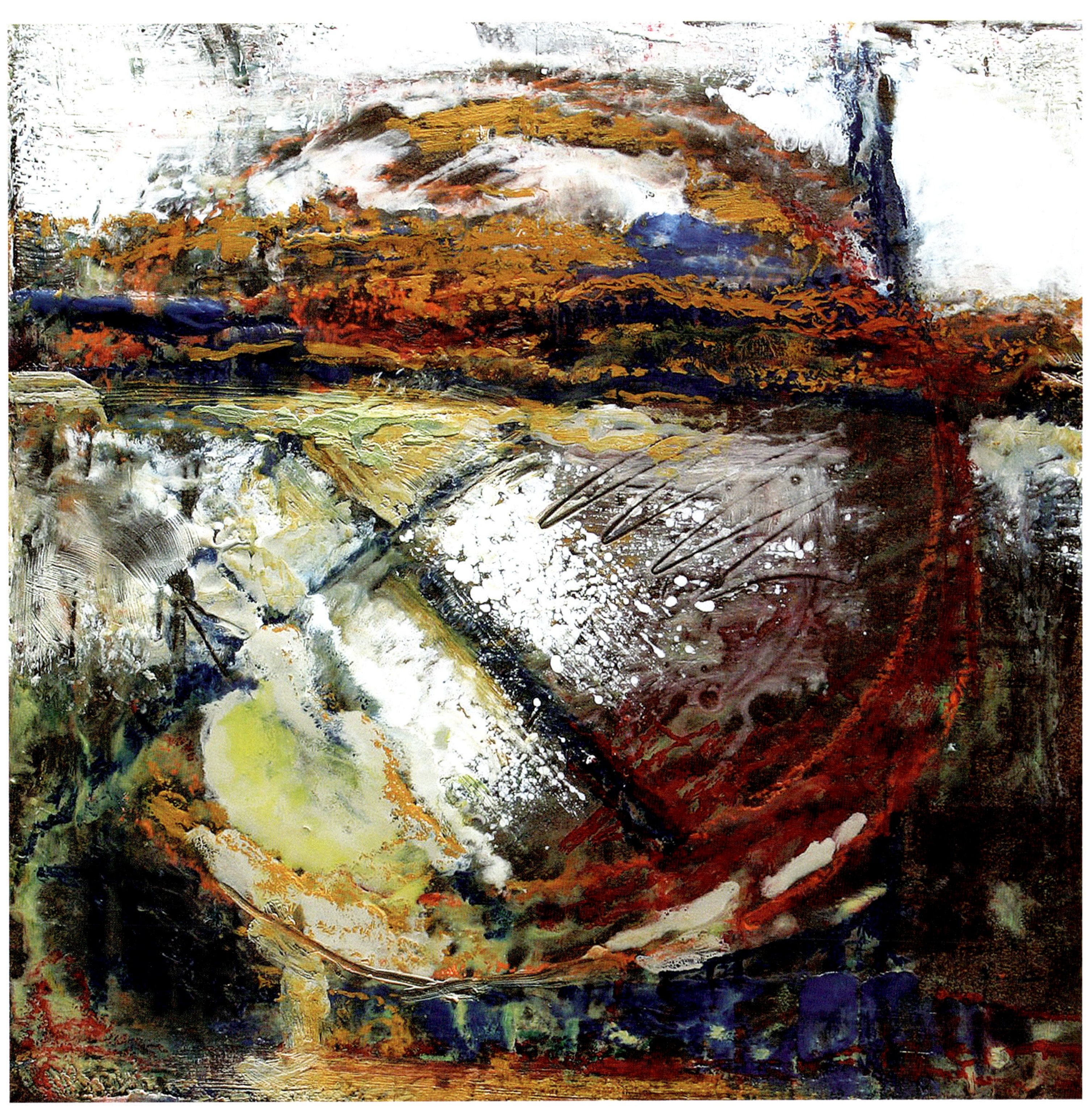

Cheryl D. McClure, *Patina 2*, 2007.
Encaustic on wood panel, 30.5 x 30.5 x 5.1 cm.

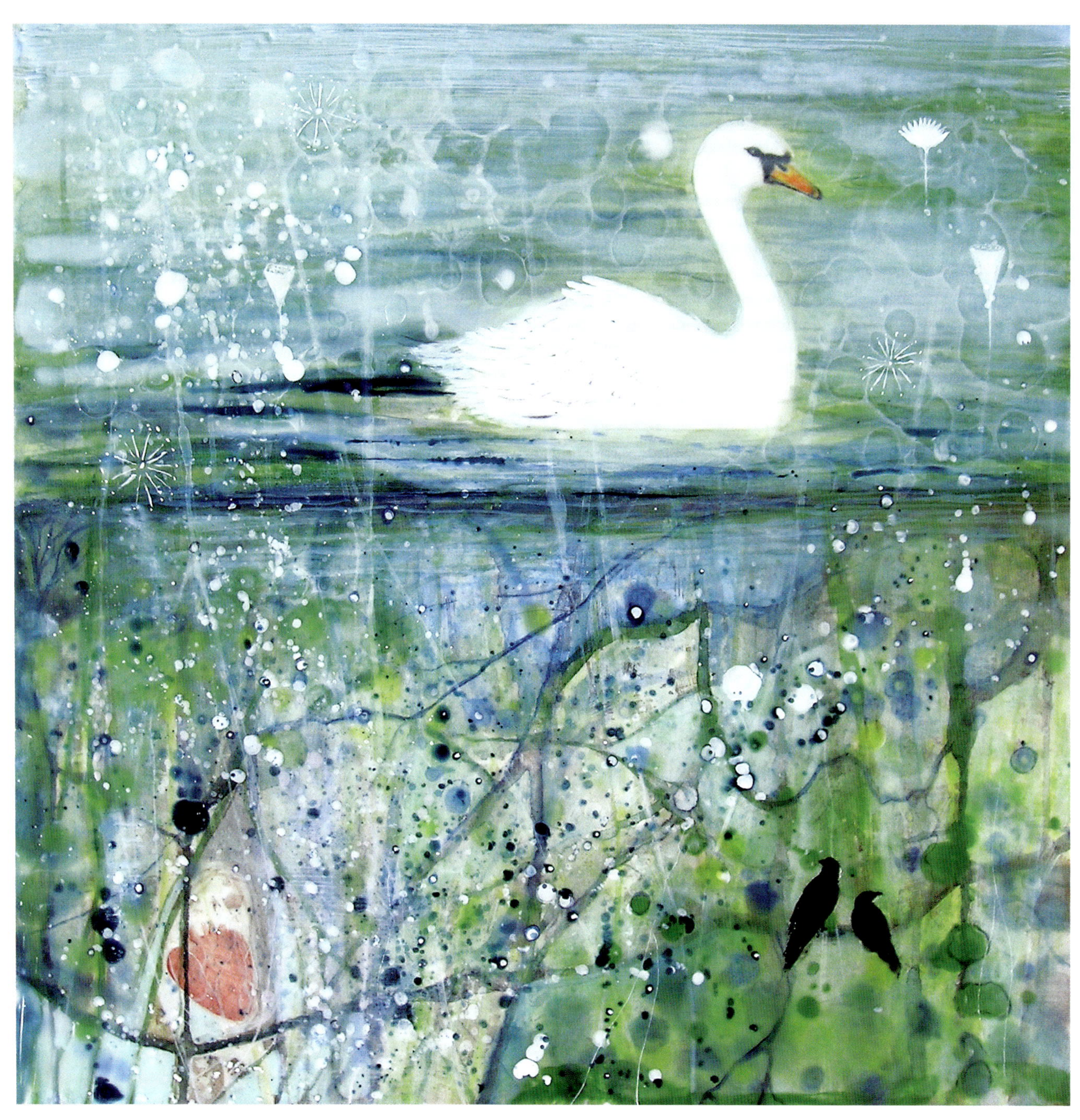

Edie Morton, *Aphrodite and the Ravens,* 2009.
Encaustic, 45.7 x 45.7 cm.

Can you tell us more about your piece *Jewels*, it has beautiful colors and seems to be very dimensional?

That piece was created also doing several pours and the sections are separated by paper. I would build a little wall out of paper, and create the taverns or spaces; and I think I did incorporate a piece of actual glass that is very jewel-like. It is in the same shape as the other organic pod shapes.

Did you build those up with a brush?

No, the little small shapes were probably done using an eye dropper.

What inspired the composition and colors in your *Landscapes* series?

I would say that in general I am inspired by Asian art and sensibilities, their poetic landscapes, Japanese calligraphy, and myths. In other words, the shapes and forms that come out of my paintings I am actually living with. There are a lot of organic objects in the materials that I bring into my studio. I collect branches that have been pruned and left on the side of the road; very tall fifteen foot branches which I bring into my studio. I bring in a lot of inspirational organic objects.

Can you tell us more about the techniques and mixed media that you used to create your piece *Lama*, which is part of that series?

The dark lines are incised into the wax using a ceramic pin tool. It is my drawing instrument and then I fill in the incised lines with oil stick. Beneath the hill in the foreground, is an ink transfer of a tiger. There are layers on top of that so it is kind of subtle. The piece was actually in honor of my cat named Jibs. He was a very Dali Lama-like cat. That piece I was working on during his last days with me. Also I used delicate petal and flower-like shapes by using a very small brush and oil.

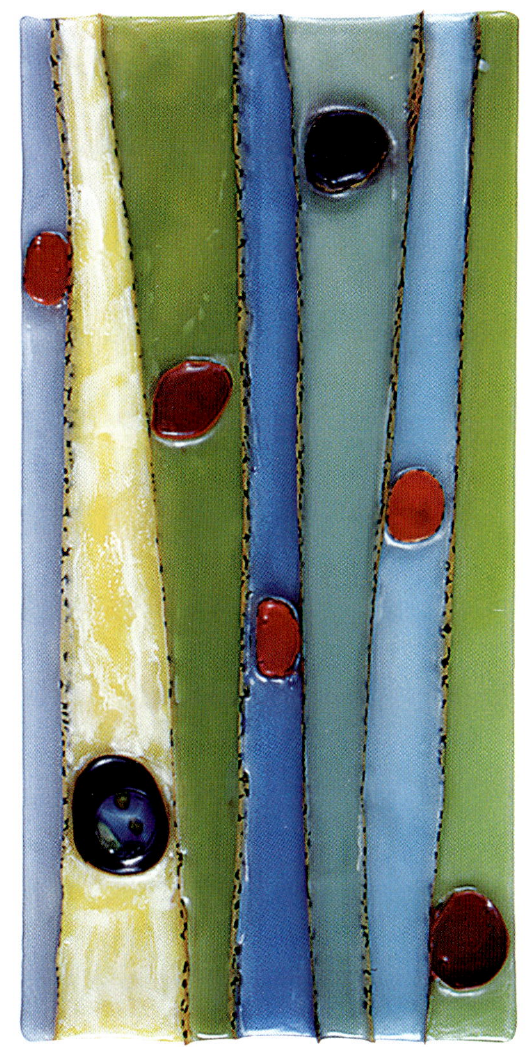

Edie Morton, *Jewels*, 2006.
Encaustic, 30.5 x 15.2 cm.

You have done some teaching as well. What have you learned through teaching workshops that would be useful to artists who are new to using encaustics?

Being present, patient, and unattached to outcome are helpful qualities to have. I find the medium quite meditative. When applying a stroke it is like a breath. Inhaling as I dip the brush in the wax and exhaling as I release the stroke to the surface. The medium lends itself to expression through painting and sculpting, enabling those possibilities.

And what advice do you have to artists to make their work stand out?

I would encourage artists to develop their own distinct language through mark making, shape, and line. Because the medium is so beautiful, it is almost as though you can do anything and you have a beautiful painting. So I encourage artists to move beyond that and work outside of their comfort zone. Explore possibilities and develop your own distinct style, mark making strokes, and shapes, etc.

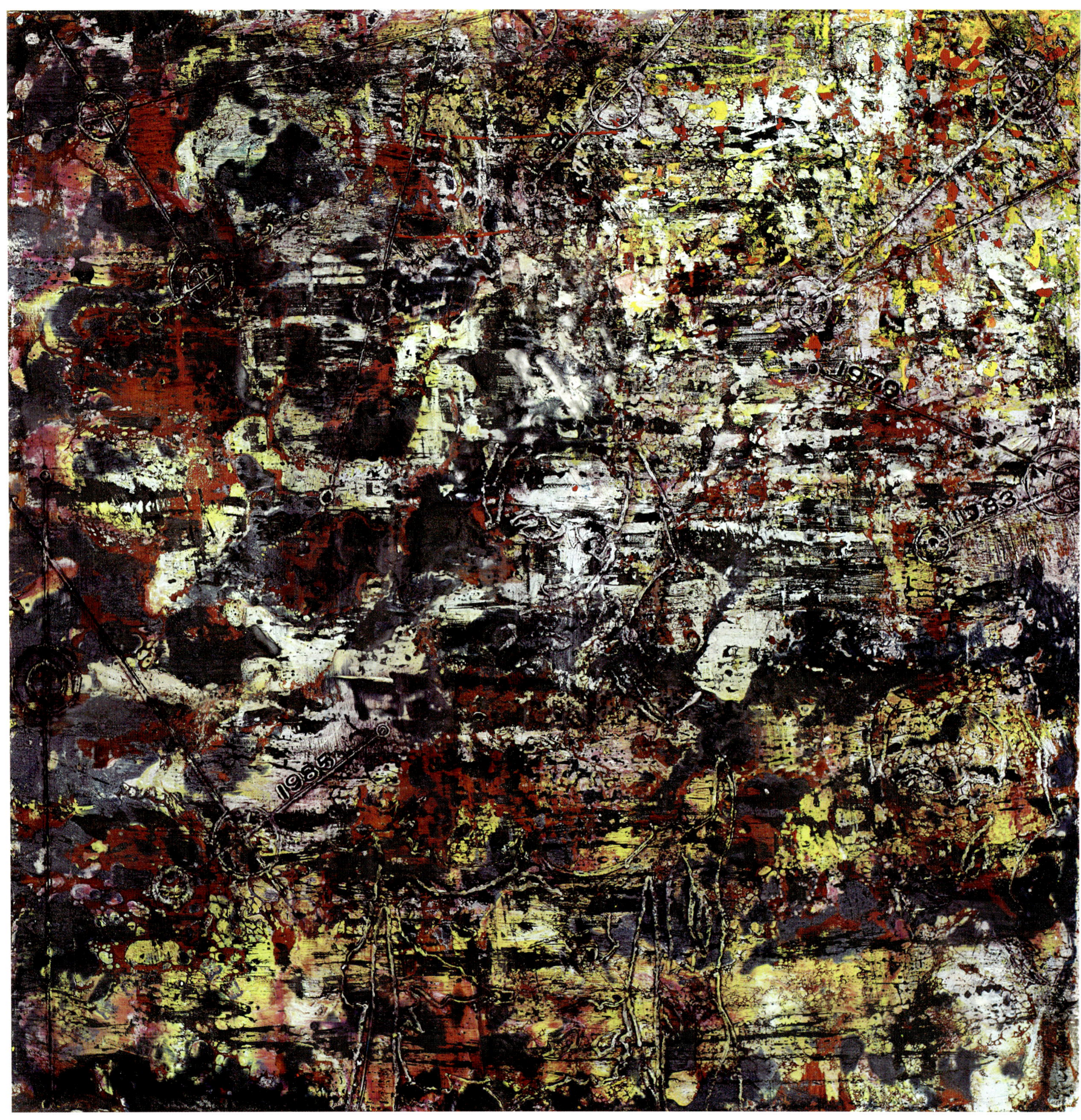

JEREMY PENN

New York City native and award-winning artist Jeremy Penn has been immersed in the world of fine arts since childhood. He enrolled in art school at age five; chose salvaged wood, lace paper, and concentrated watercolors rather than the more traditional construction papers and tempera paints.

A graduate of both the University of Maryland and the Pratt Institute in Brooklyn, N.Y. with degrees in Fine Arts, Penn's recent exhibits include the Phillips Collection, which has exhibited his work worldwide, and the Woodstock Artists Association and Museum in Woodstock, N.Y. His works are also prized by Sheikh Mohammed, the Crown Prince of Dubai.

Recently, Penn was honored with First Prize, Best Designs of 2009 by Design & Design for two of his paintings. He also received an honorable mention for recent works from the Woodstock Artists Association and Museum, juried by Doug Alderfer. Penn regularly works in encaustics, building up countless layers of encaustic paint, each color layered carefully on top of the one another, and then strategically scraped away to create a sculpture-like detailed work of art.

Currently, Penn is building an exclusive collection of paintings. In addition, he is committed to giving back to the arts by teaching the therapeutic properties in art.

Penn is a member of the International Encaustic Artists Association, Woodstock Artists Association, Woodstock Byrdcliffe Artists Guild, and the Young Home Furnishing Professionals. His work has been featured in Design & Design, Home Fashion, and Accessory Merchandising Magazines. According to Home Fashion Magazine, Penn is a "Creator of Stunning... art... known for working with unique materials while constructing color combinations intended to elicit deep emotions."

"Whether it is imbedding objects, image transfers, or highly textural paintings, encaustic is the one medium that will extend your artistic reach to places that you never thought were possible."

- Jeremy Penn

Jeremy Penn, *Timeline*, 2009.
Encaustic, 45.7 x 45.7 cm.

How long have you been working with encaustics?
I have been working with encaustics for about three years now.

What do you find challenging and rewarding about working with encaustics?
The biggest thing about working with encaustics is learning to trust your instincts. When you are using a paint that dries within seconds you need to let yourself go and just paint, which is pure process. That challenging part ends up being the most rewarding. You are working with pure process and pure instinct.

Do you normally have a clear idea what you want your piece to turn into?
I have a clear idea; but then again I let go and just work. Similarly to an improvisational band so to speak; you just go with it.

What was the inspiration behind your *Portraits* series?
I have always been fascinated by popular culture and the transition of when a person becomes an icon; and when their image becomes larger than themselves. I like to take that iconic image and either draw or paint life back into it because the soul is lost within these characters. I like to inject a new sense of life or personality back into it.

How long does it normally take you to create an encaustic painting?
It depends, sometimes I work with small canvases, and now I am going much larger. I would say it takes me about a month to complete a canvas that is about thirty-two by forty eight. That is putting a lot of time into it.

What do you prefer to use for your canvases?
The only thing that I would find actually workable for working with encaustics would have to be a hard surface like birch wood. I use Baltic birch which is a smooth, clean piece of wood that is reasonably sturdy, and I brace it in the back. For working with encaustic, it is very important for the future to not paint on a surface that will warp in any way, because that paint will potentially chip off. That is something you can prevent. So I would say (use) wood or Masonite for an inexpensive option.

What do you do on the back to brace the wood?
Depending on the size, if you are working on smaller panels, you don't need a crossbar. You can use something like a bass wood, which is light. I personally miter the corners and brace the edges. But if you are working on a bigger canvas, above eighteen by twenty-four, I would put a crossbar in to prevent any kind of warping of the wood because wood will naturally expand over time. When you are working with a more flexible material like acrylic, you know that is not such a problem. But with encaustic you need to be careful with that.

What do you do on the back so that a piece is ready to be hung and how do you frame your work?
I start off by actually signing my work. I started with a little needle, to make an incision to sign my name; and then I moved away from that and actually started to use my thumb print on the back of the panels. I found that was my little homage to a movie I had seen about Jackson Pollock. She (the character) had found a Jackson Pollock at a flea market. They did a little scientific research and they did DNA testing, and finger print matching and were actually able to identify this painting based on finger prints left on the back of the canvas. So it is my little homage to him.

For the framing, do you buy the side frame and then cut it yourself?
I actually make all of my own panels and all of my own frames. Now, one of the things I may have left out is that with encaustics, because you're working with panels, it is important, and actually looks the best, to use a floater frame: something that will float the panel within the frame. It gives it a nice look and it protects the work. You are not damaging the edges of the work by having a frame that rabbets, so to speak, right over the work.

Where do you like to get your materials that you use for encaustics?
Well, besides Home Depot, I have to say that R&F paints is the "candy land" for encaustic painters. That place is amazing. I actually have a studio up Catskill and I'm fortunate enough to have their main factory pretty close by. It is amazing there, and their paints are far superior to anything else that I've ever used. I started out getting my encaustic medium there when I was not so experienced in the process, but after a while, I just started making my own. I bought refined beeswax and Dammar Resin, and started to make it myself. It just becomes too costly. Although their encaustic medium is great, I'd rather spend the money on purchasing their paint and making my own encaustic medium.

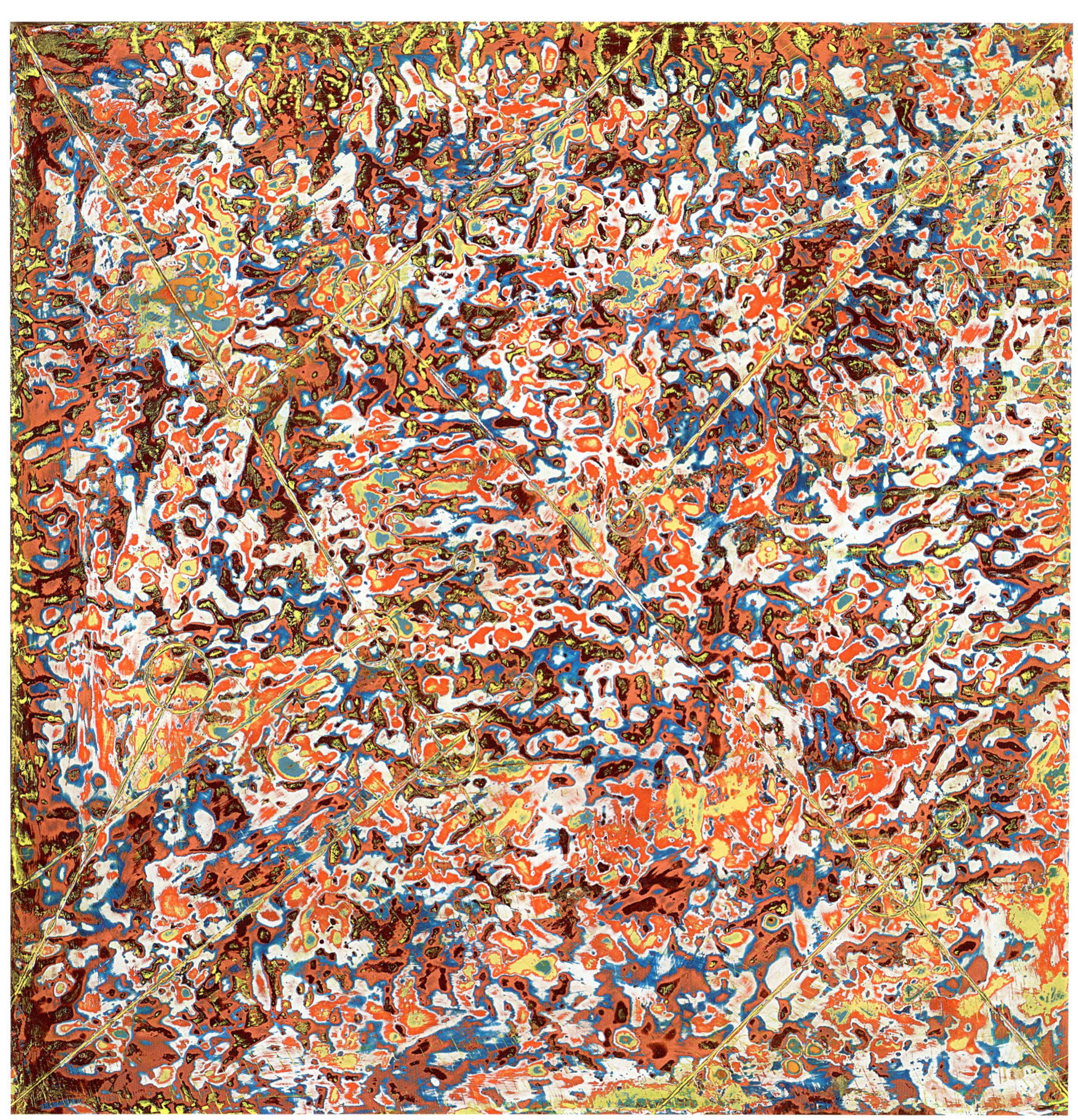

Jeremy Penn, *Thermal Erosion*, 2009. Encaustic on wood panel, 45.7 x 45.7 cm.

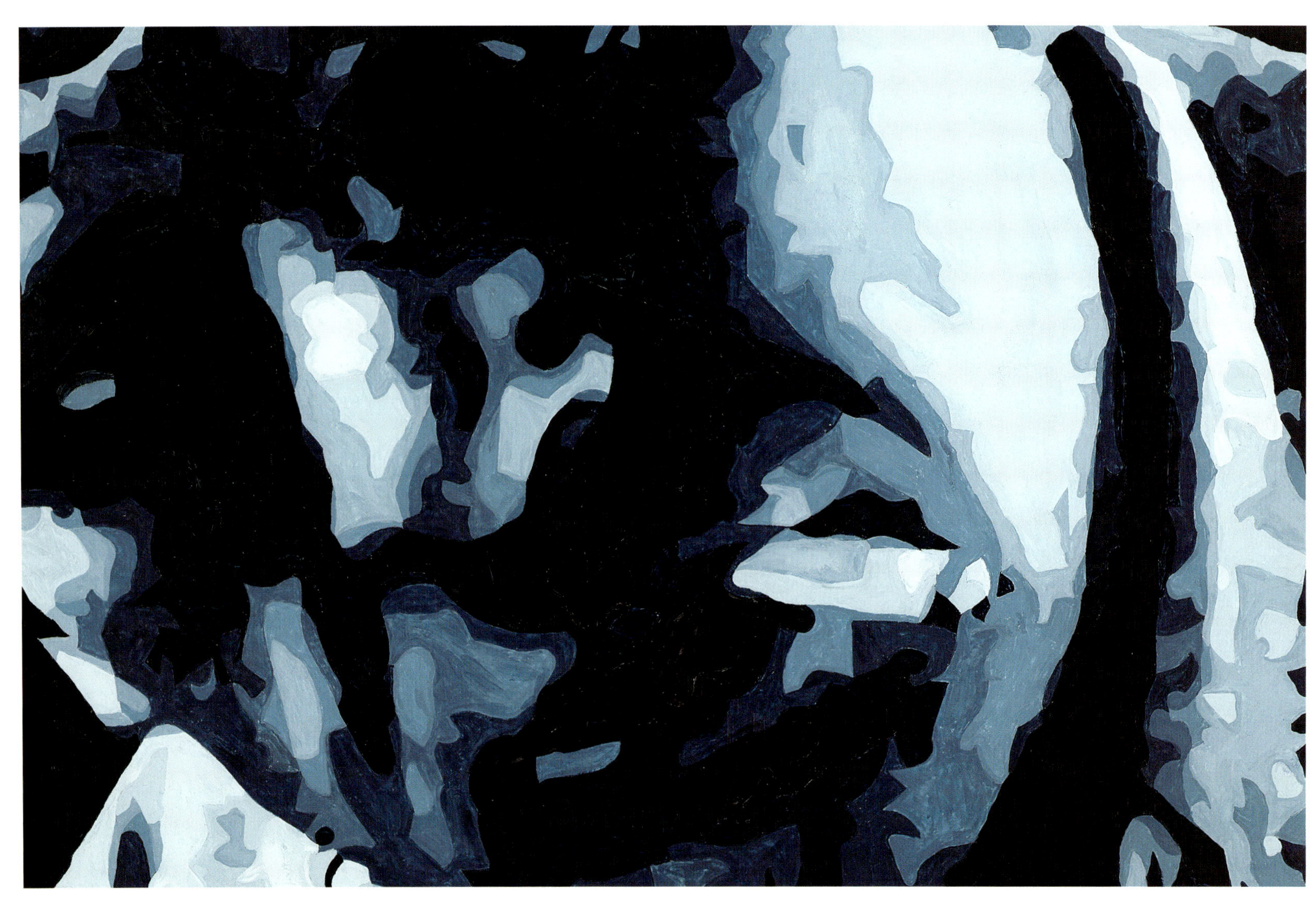

Jeremy Penn, *Jackson*, 2009. Encaustic, 76.2 x 101.6 cm.

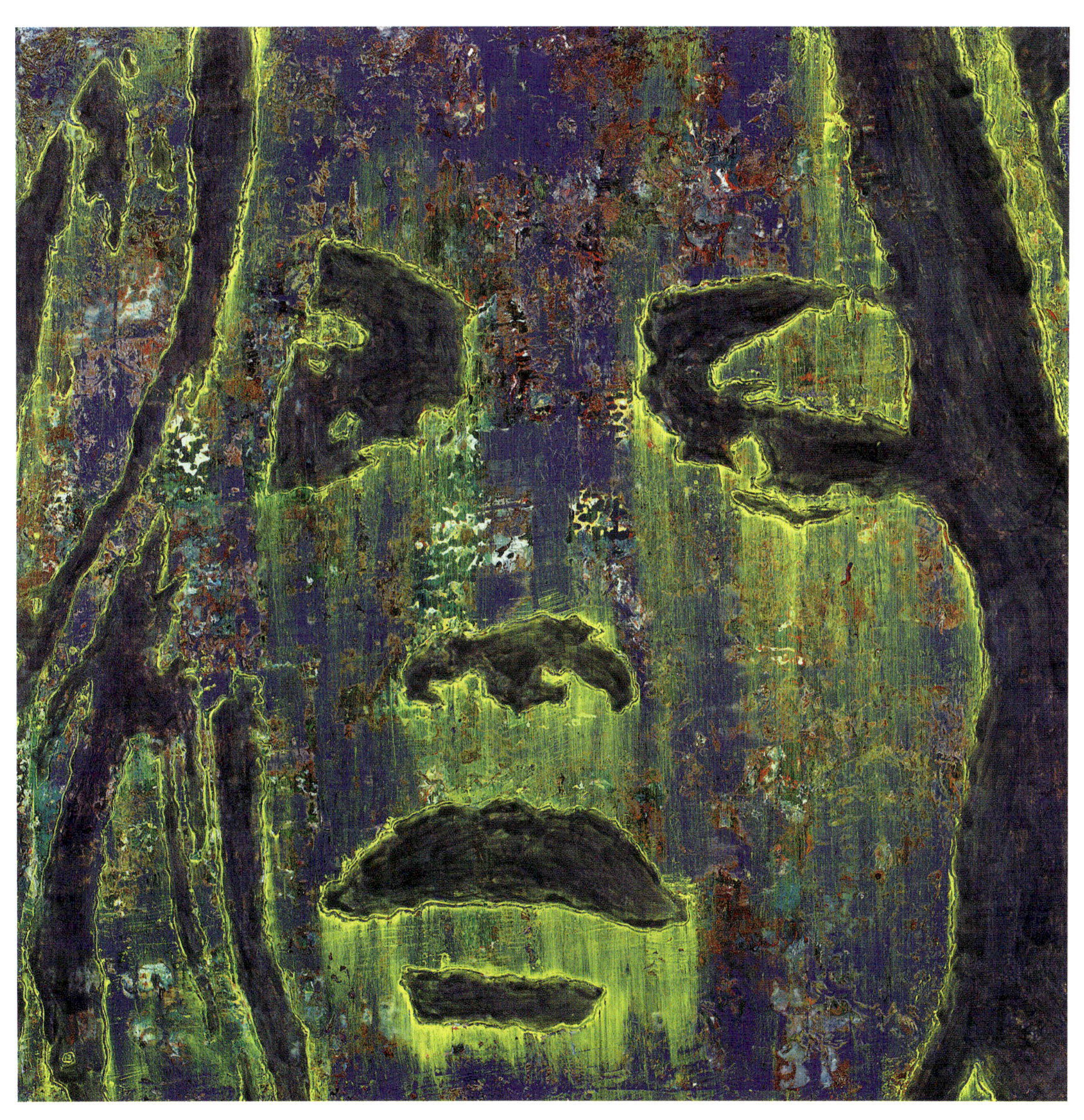

Jeremy Penn, *Moss*, 2009. Encaustic and oil paint on panel, 45.7 x 45.7 cm.

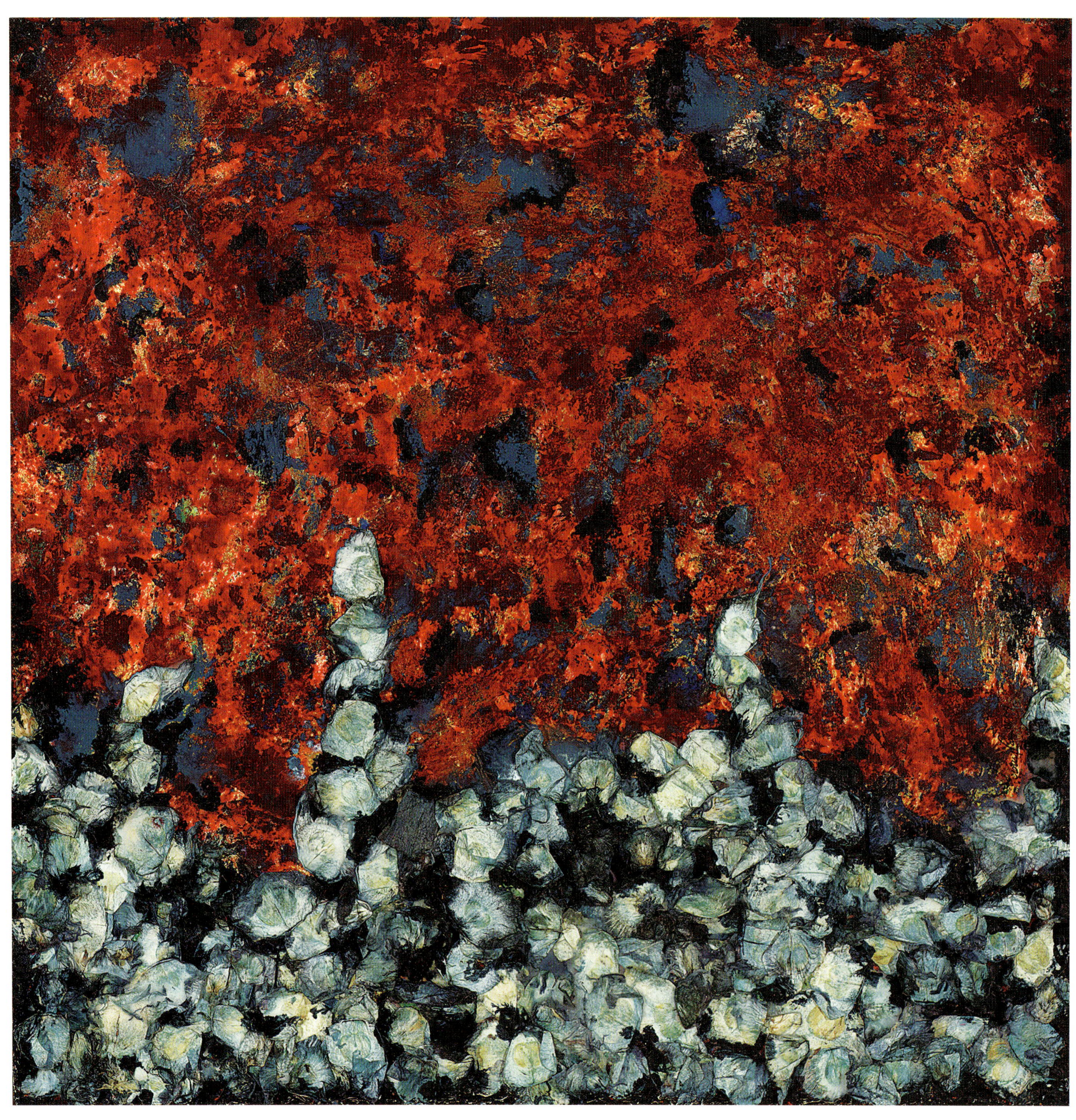

Jeremy Penn, *The Unmasking*, 2009. Encaustic, 45.7 x 45.7 cm.

When you start an encaustic, what step do you use to first get a base for your work?
Actually, R&F created an encaustic gesso, which creates the perfect rigid surface. I always start off with that. I put (down) about two coats of encaustic gesso; it is slightly more rigid than any acrylic gesso that I have used. This is just a personal preference, but I always coat the gesso with a clear layer of encaustic medium to get the wax on there. It is just my way of working.

With your *Portrait* series, what techniques did you use to create such clear lines and detail?
Well, I started buying dental tools and pottery tools to create incisions in the work. I think the term that is used is Intaglio. I bought dog dental tools, for a veterinarian actually. They are very thin with a nice handle. They are similar to what you would see at a dentist's and with that you can make very precise incisions. Then, after I make these incisions, I use an oil stick. I know R&F makes it and there are a few other companies that make them. The oil and the encaustic actually work pretty well together. After I make my incision into the wax I will coat the entire painting with an oil stick, and then I will wipe away the surface.

What is left is the oil that remains inside those incisions. Then I use a blow torch to gently heat the incision lines. It creates a nearly three-dimensional surface where the incision was, so it really pops out. For whatever reason it pops out, it just does; and it creates a really nice line. It is something that I have experimented with and it worked out very well.

You have a piece called *Moss*, which is a portrait of a face. What technique did you use to make the green line? It has a smeared down effect.
That was the same technique, but I controlled that smear. I wiped it down first. I thought it was a very interesting effect, but it wasn't intentional. I was intending to wipe everything off except what was in the incision lines, but for me, it is not thinking about what to start with, it is knowing when to stop. That is a perfect example of forcing yourself to stop working and leave it the way it is, and it had a nice result. You see that there are multiple layers of paint, and I started off with gold leaf. Gold leaf is just another material, like any material, that you can use with encaustic paint. One of the things about working with encaustics is that the possibilities are limitless. You could work with anything and it is pretty amazing. What I did with that, is I that I layered it down and then set it on fire, which is not for the faint-hearted. I don't recommend anyone doing this. I do it in a controlled environment, but it burns through all the layers of gold. What you see are different layers, you see hints of gold and hints of dark. It makes for a very nice look.

I love the color gradients in the pixilated piece *Jackson*. Can you tell us more about this piece?
This piece was my transition between portraits and abstract work. I was working on portraits, then I was working on strictly abstract work and this was something I wanted to work on within both of those. It is a very, very tight color scale that I used to create that. The funny thing about that painting is that people to this day don't see what the painting is. They see it as an abstract painting. It was just featured on the Discovery Channel for a show that is coming out and the set designer took the piece and turned it sideways because she thought it looked so good vertically.

She didn't see, and she didn't realize, that it was actually an abstract portrait. And once you see it, you see it forever. Sometimes it takes people a while to see the image that is in there, so I guess it was a success in that way. It is an abstract, yet it is still a portrait. That piece was a tedious process. I used very thin brushes too create the shapes, and it took me a while. I approached it like I do my oil paintings when I was growing up and being trained. I think that encaustic lends itself to many different techniques. One of the things that is most beautiful about working with encaustics is working freely and openly. With this I was a little too precise, so it took me a long time to complete.

In your abstract pieces, what techniques did you use for paintings like *Thermal Erosion*?
I was actually a color theory major back in college. I wanted to explore with encaustic. With encaustic, when I started working with it, I started realizing "wow, I could really do anything with this." So, I created a color scale, like a color palette, and what I started doing was layering colors on top of one another.

What you see there is probably about seventeen or eighteen layers of color all fused together, and then scraped back. I started scraping back with a razor blade. I thought that might be a good way to scrape back because it is controlled, it is nothing too big.

However, I found that I started cutting back the edges and it wasn't as controlled as I would like. I reached out to another encaustic artist in the city called Richard Purdy. He is a master at scraping and he was kind enough to share his technique with me. What he uses is a cabinet scraper, which doesn't have those really sharp edges, so you have a lot more control. For me, it took everything to another level. You know when to stop, you have a little bit more control over everything, everything is less unpredictable, and that is definitely the tool to use when it comes to scraping as far as I'm concerned.

What is the inspiration behind the colors you choose for your abstract paintings?

I wanted to create a color palette of really vibrant colors. I was looking at some colors from R&F and I found that they sell a color called Warm Pink. I found myself attracted to that color as a top coat. So I used that to start a palette, with colors like Naples Yellow, Indian Yellow, etc. That is how the color palette of just vibrant colors came through. That was my inspiration behind it, that color palette; and I used that through a couple of different paintings.

What advice do you have for an artist who wants to take their work to the next level?

I have got to say to just experiment. One of the things about encaustic, is that you are able to create art in multiple dimensions. You know, whether it is imbedding objects, image transfers, or highly textural paintings, encaustic is the one medium that will extend your artistic reach to places that you never thought were possible. I am a traditional oil painter. That is what I was trained in.

Once I started with encaustic, that was it, it was a game changer. I looked at it like I was having a dream. Things were possible yet impossible. Things were so far out of reach, and yet within reach. Encaustic lets you live within that world of limitless impossibilities. I would say, get started in it, and you might have some frustrating experiences at first, but they will be learning experiences.

You can do anything within this medium, besides some scientific blending with acrylic paint with encaustic. Taking these rules into account, you can really do anything with this medium. It is the medium, I think, that really lends itself to an artist who really wants to try anything and be all about process. Just keep going with it.

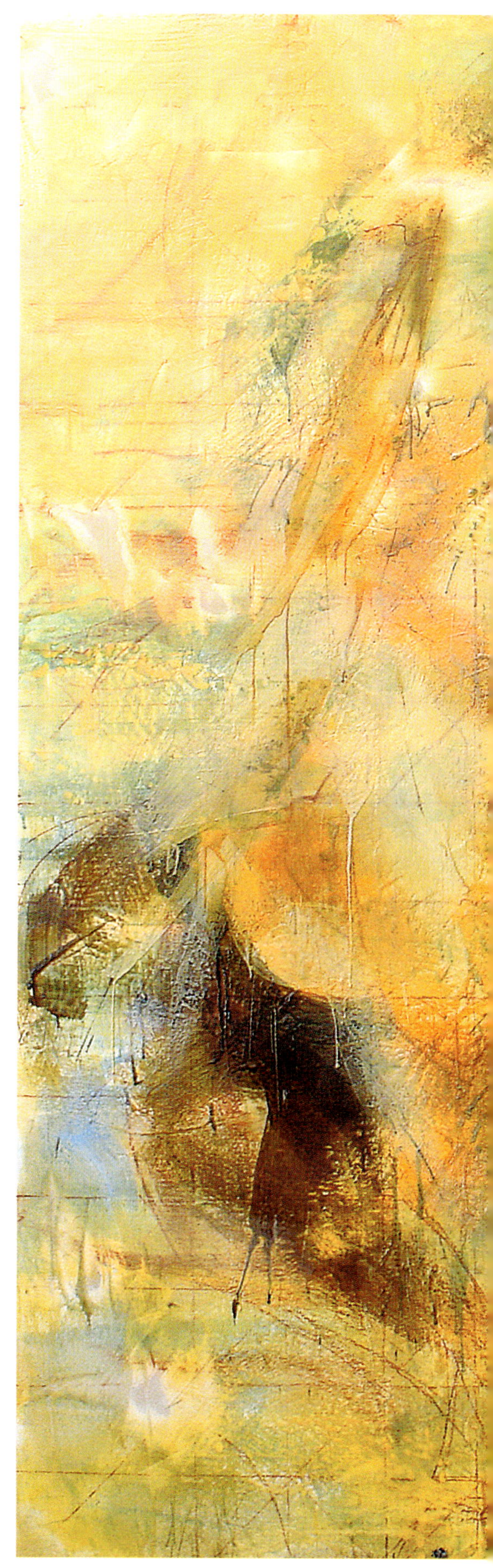

Tony Scherman, *Penelope* (detail), 2008-2010.
Encaustic on canvas, 213.3 x 243.8 cm.

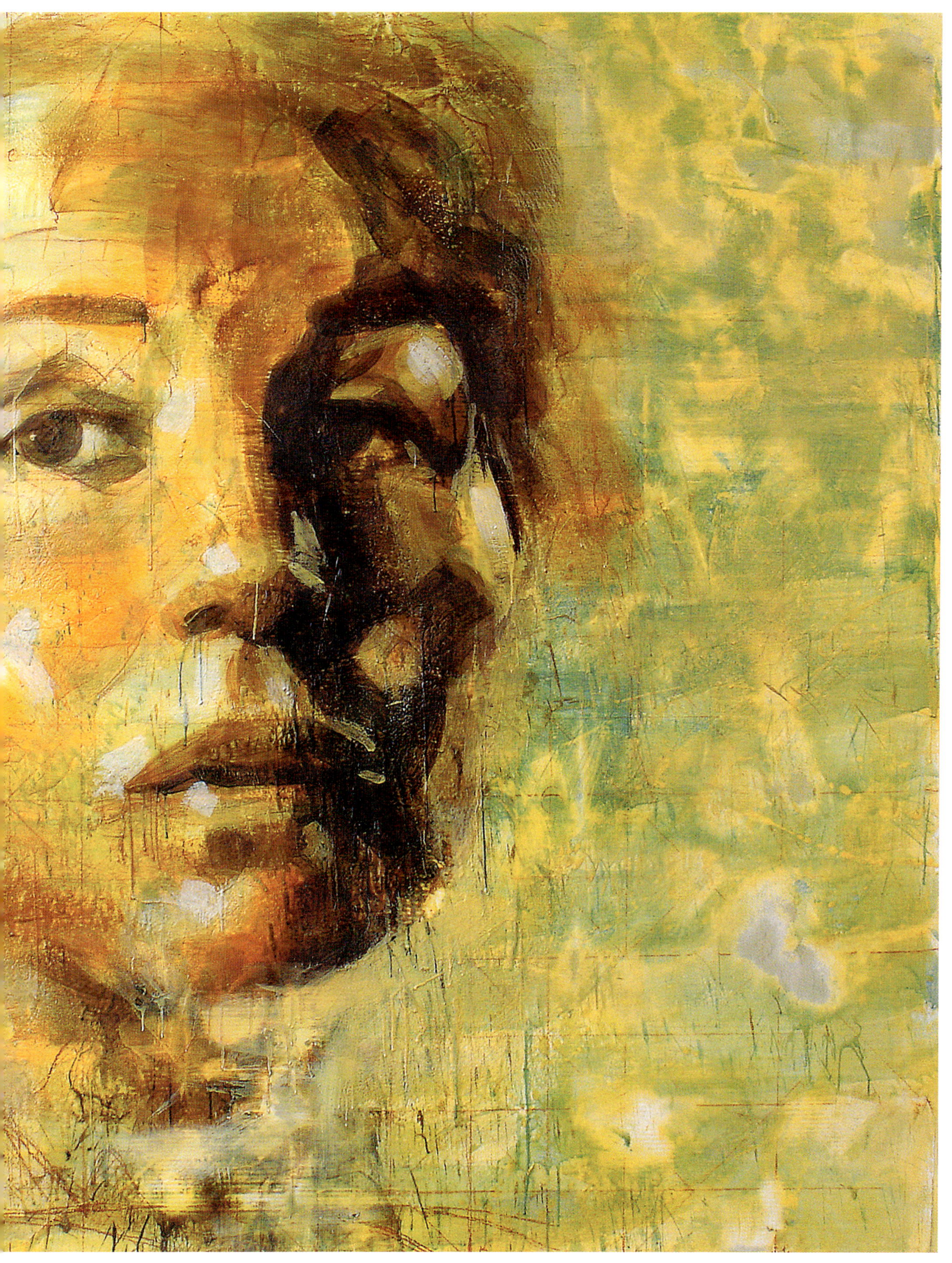

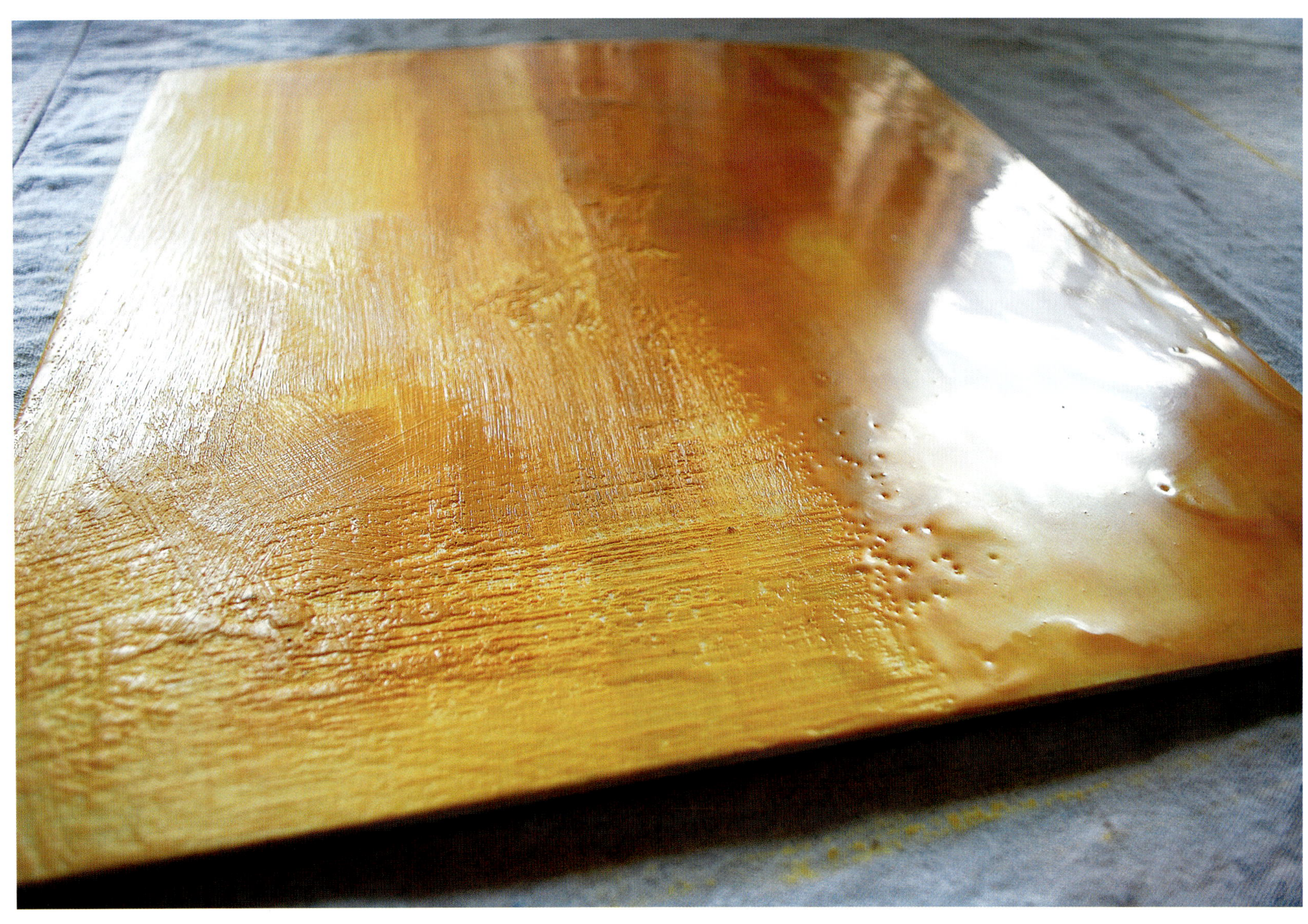

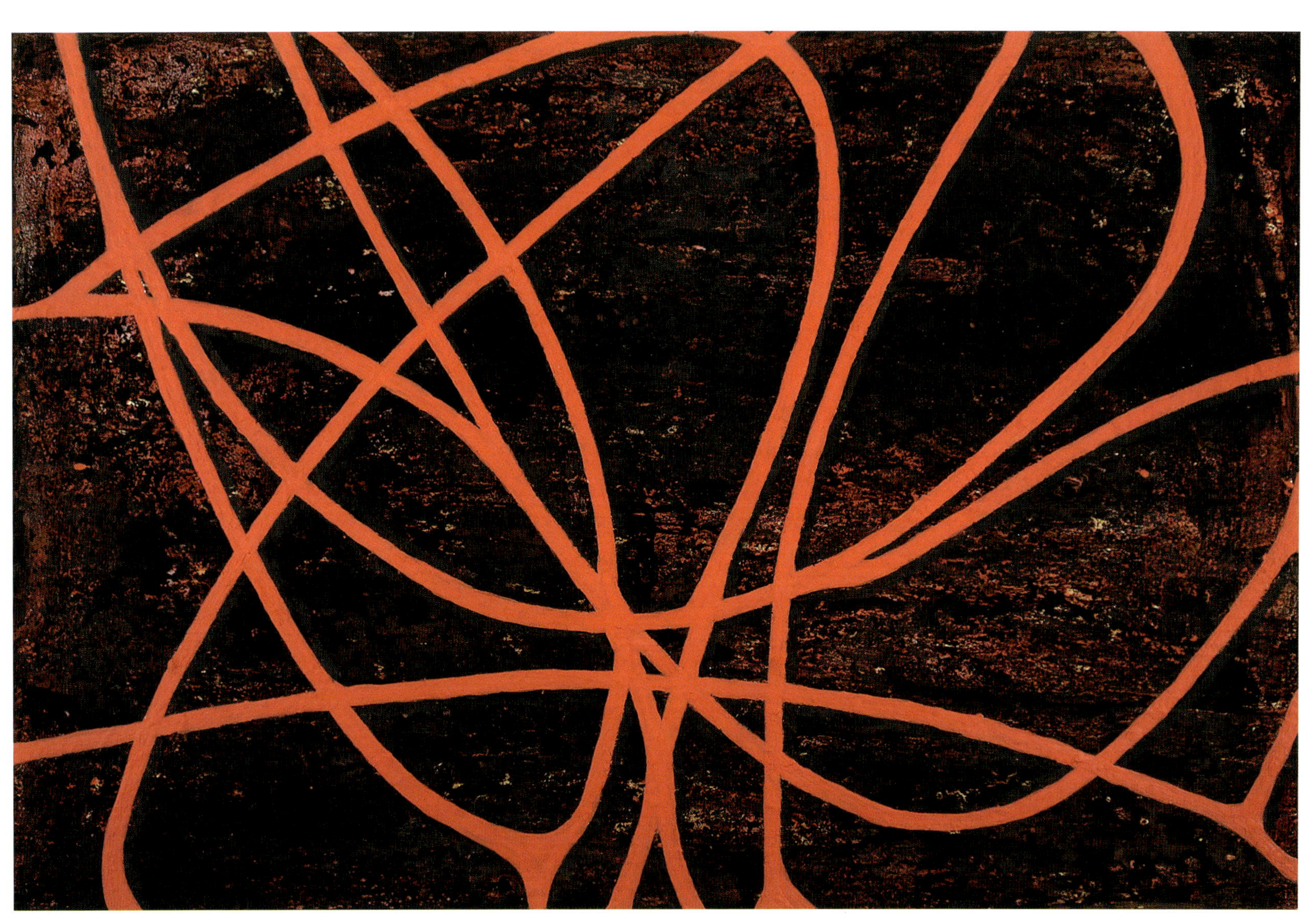

Jeremy Penn, *Industrial Glam*, 2010. Encaustic, 81.2 x 121.9 cm.

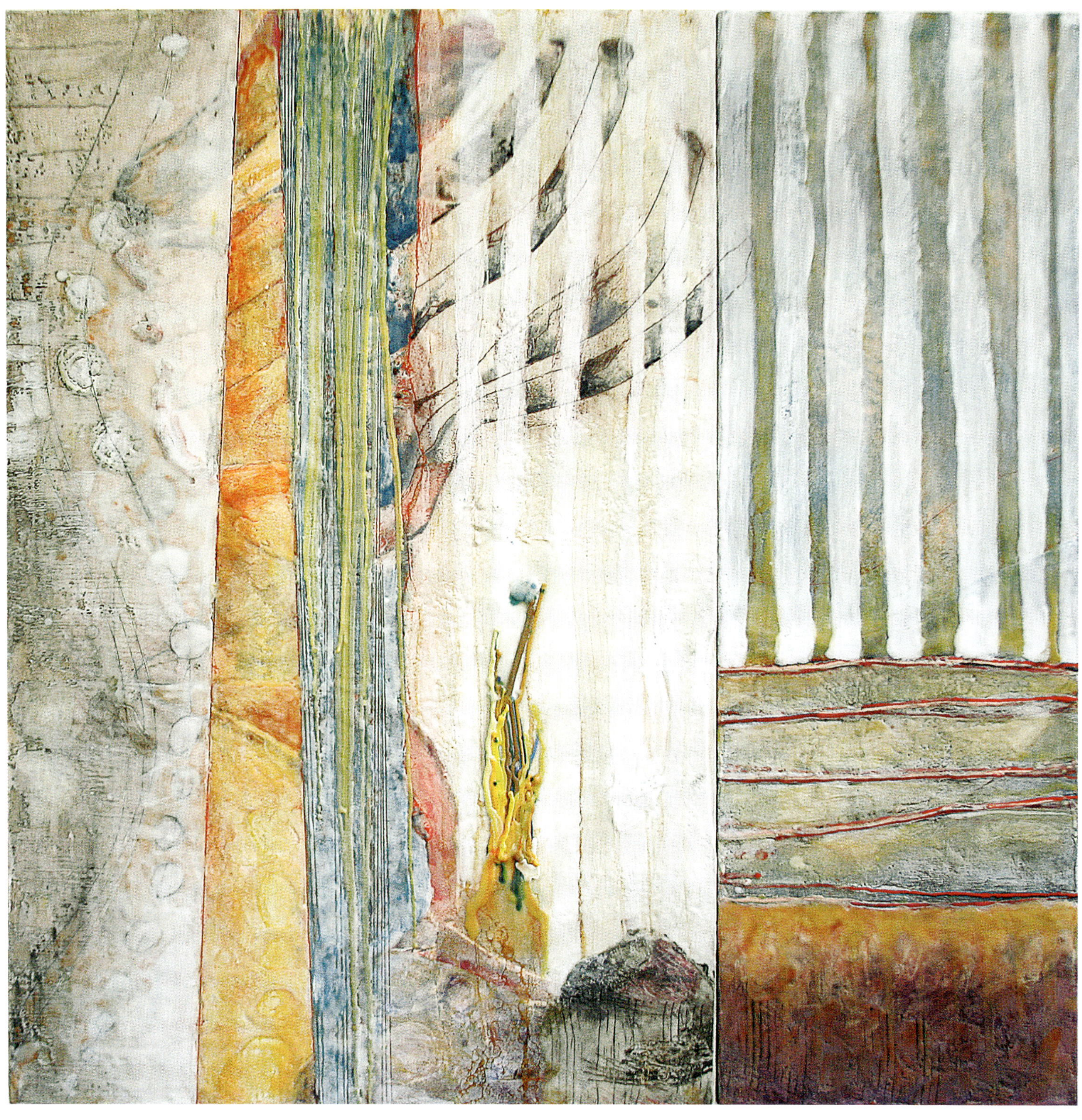

Amy Royce, *Envy*, 2008. Encaustic with mixed media on panel, 91.4 x 91.4 cm.

Amy Royce

Bend, Oregon painter Amy Royce explores communication, body language, and non-verbal expression, engaging the senses and emotions through paint. Royce received her BA in Art with a painting emphasis from Humboldt State University in Arcata, California. She received a scholarship to Anderson Ranch Arts Center in 2006 to study with Harmony Hammond. More recently, her work was selected by Judy Chicago and awarded the Artistic Merit Prize for the 20th Anniversary Women's Works Exhibit in Illinois. An avid 1940s era swing dancer, she enjoys the translation of sound, rhythm, lead, and follow into a conversation without words.

"It is a real give and take when I paint. I do a lot of additive and then subtractive. That is when it reveals that luminosity and variation of tone in the paint."

- Amy Royce

How long have you been working with encaustics?

I started experimenting with encaustic in college and that was about twenty years ago. I stuck with it, but more sporadically. It was about eight years ago that I got a dedicated studio space for myself and that was when I really started painting more seriously with encaustic.

What are the inspirations behind your paintings?

My paintings always go back to the human figure. You don't always necessarily see figures in my work because I abstract them. There is always an attempt to express the physicality of the figure and it happens to come from more of an internal space. They have become more biomorphic forms and shapes, but are still very rooted in the human figure.

What unconventional materials do you like to use?

One thing I love about encaustic is that the medium itself is a bit unconventional because you need heat to manipulate it. I don't think there is any other medium, in painting at least, which needs heat to be manipulated. That in itself is experimental.

Probably the most unconventional technique I use is using Shellac in my art. When you paint amber-colored Shellac over the wax and then fuse it in, it creates these really interesting textures and shapes that change as you heat it. However, I think a lot of encaustic artists do use that. I am also starting to play with encaustic print making. So you build a plate of sorts, kind of like a collagraph plate, but you build it with wax over Plexiglas. That has been exciting in that it forms my encaustic paintings as well, because sometimes I will use those prints as collage elements in my work.

Can you tell us more about the technique for doing encaustic printmaking?

Encaustic printmaking is basically taking the encaustic paint, (and) you are definitely going to need color because you are going to be inking it later. You paint some encaustic medium onto a piece of Plexiglas or metal, in the shape that you want. Just like in encaustic painting, you can scrape back or incise lines. You could even engrave into the plate as well, and then just like any form of printmaking, you would then ink it and run it through a press with paper; and when you lift the paper off you get a print. You can do additions or you can then draw on them like I sometimes do. I will tear them apart and incorporate them into encaustic again. It is basically another layer of what the medium can do.

What steps do you take when you start a painting?

Even though I don't do a lot of drawing in preparation for a piece, I try to remember that every color, shape, or material has a built-in meaning to our society. So the viewer of that work is going to automatically have a meaning, whether you want that meaning to be taken that way or not. So, I try to take all that into account when I begin.

I like to have kind of a no-holds barred approach for the under painting. I just begin, and trust my intuition to put down shapes and colors. I know later I can change, scrape them out, cover them up, or turn them into something else. But it opens me up to the creativity so that I can stay out of my own way, and sometimes I get happy accidents that can make the work really special. The more I practice that, the freer I am, and the work builds itself for a while.

So, the beginning of a painting is very spontaneous, and then as I get closer to finishing, I just want to slow down and ponder more. Take areas more deliberately, and ideally, I still retain that first spontaneity, yet get something that is well developed. For actual technique, when I start, I tend to paint on raw wood panels and so for the initial sealing of that wood, because the wax can really soak in. I will also put a layer of clear medium on first and fuse that in; and then I can begin with color, or sometimes a light wax layer to get a nice light ground on there first.

Other times, I actually will glue down collage elements first and then start putting wax down on top of that. Other times, I will wrap the panel in canvas, or I'll lay down a sheet of paper, like plain white paper, if I want a nice white or creamy substrate on first. The texture of a nice rice paper is nice to paint on.

A lot of your pieces are in multiple panels, how do you deal with attaching the panels together?

Sometimes I bolt them together, but often I still keep them separate. I find that just having them have a little space from each other is nice. If I want them to truly be unified together, then I will drill holes in the sides of the panels and bolt them together.

Can you tell us about why you often choose to use long vertical panels for your pieces?

Even though my imagery is abstract, like I said, I go back to that humanistic era. I have been influenced by Alberto Giacometti, and his long tall narrow figures that move through space. I always think of those when I paint these

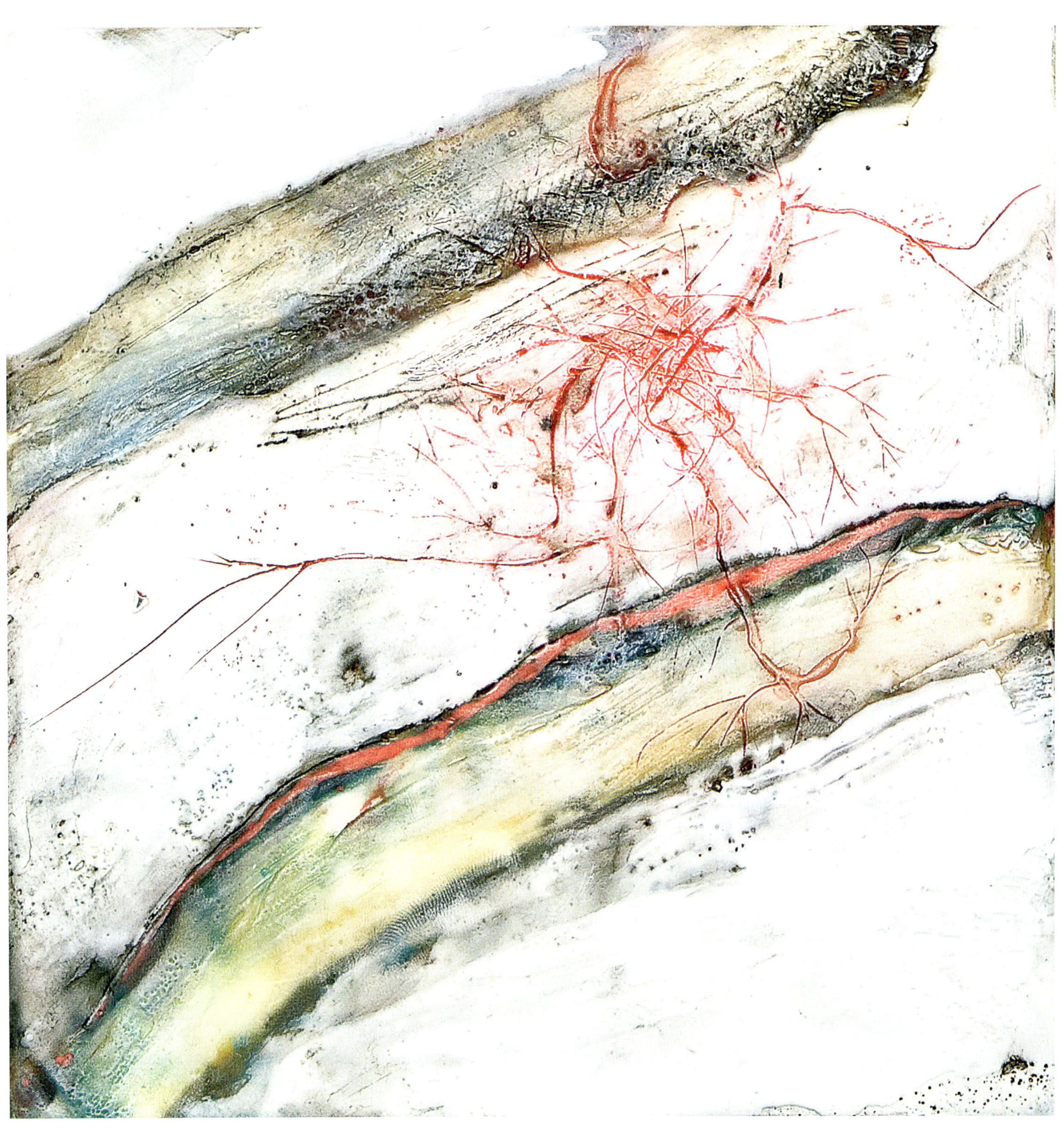

Amy Royce, *Breathe a Word*, 2008.
Encaustic mixed media on panel, 15.2 x 15.2 cm.

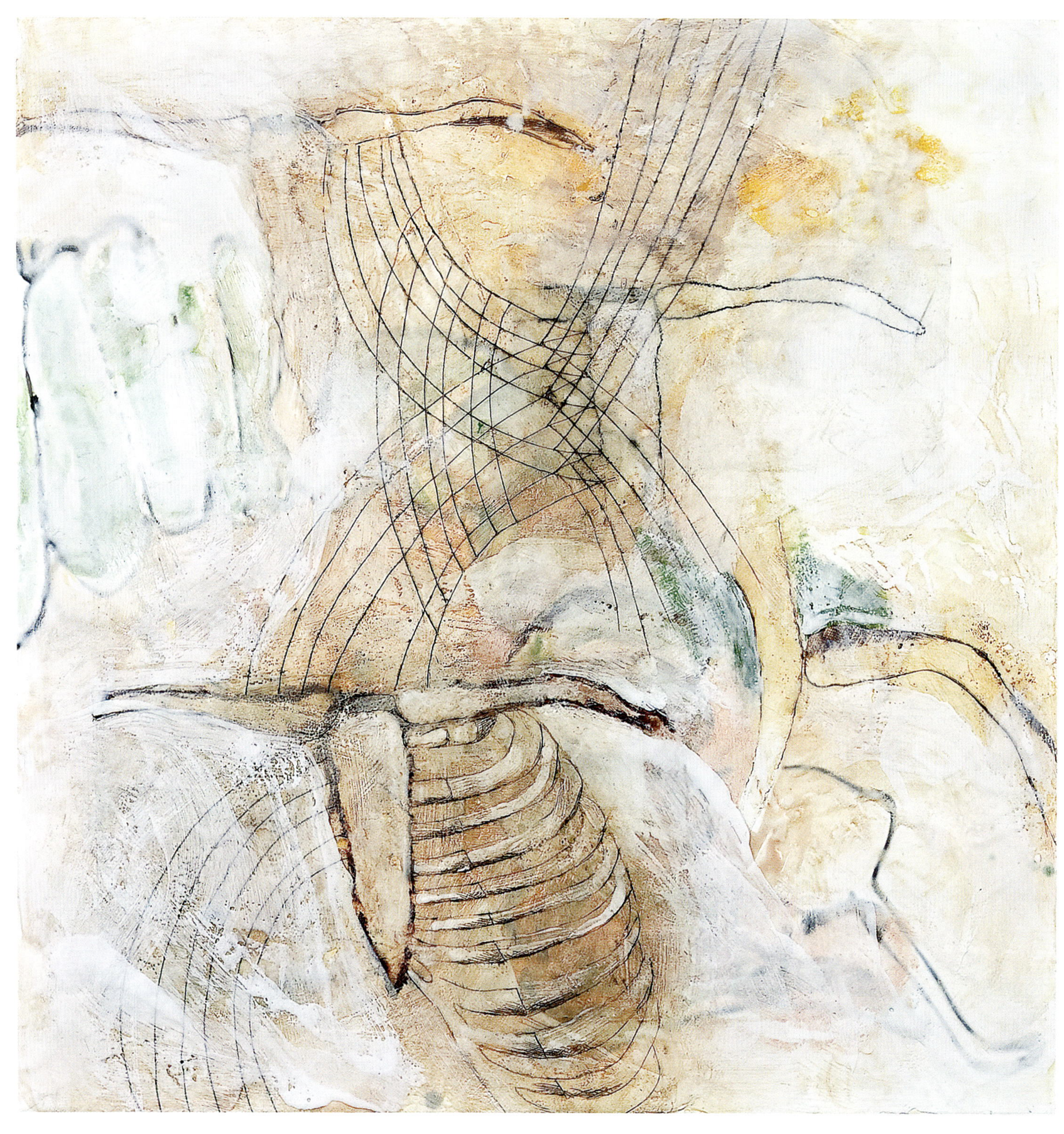

Amy Royce, *Source of Support*, 2007.
Encaustic with mixed media on panel, 60.9 x 60.9 cm.

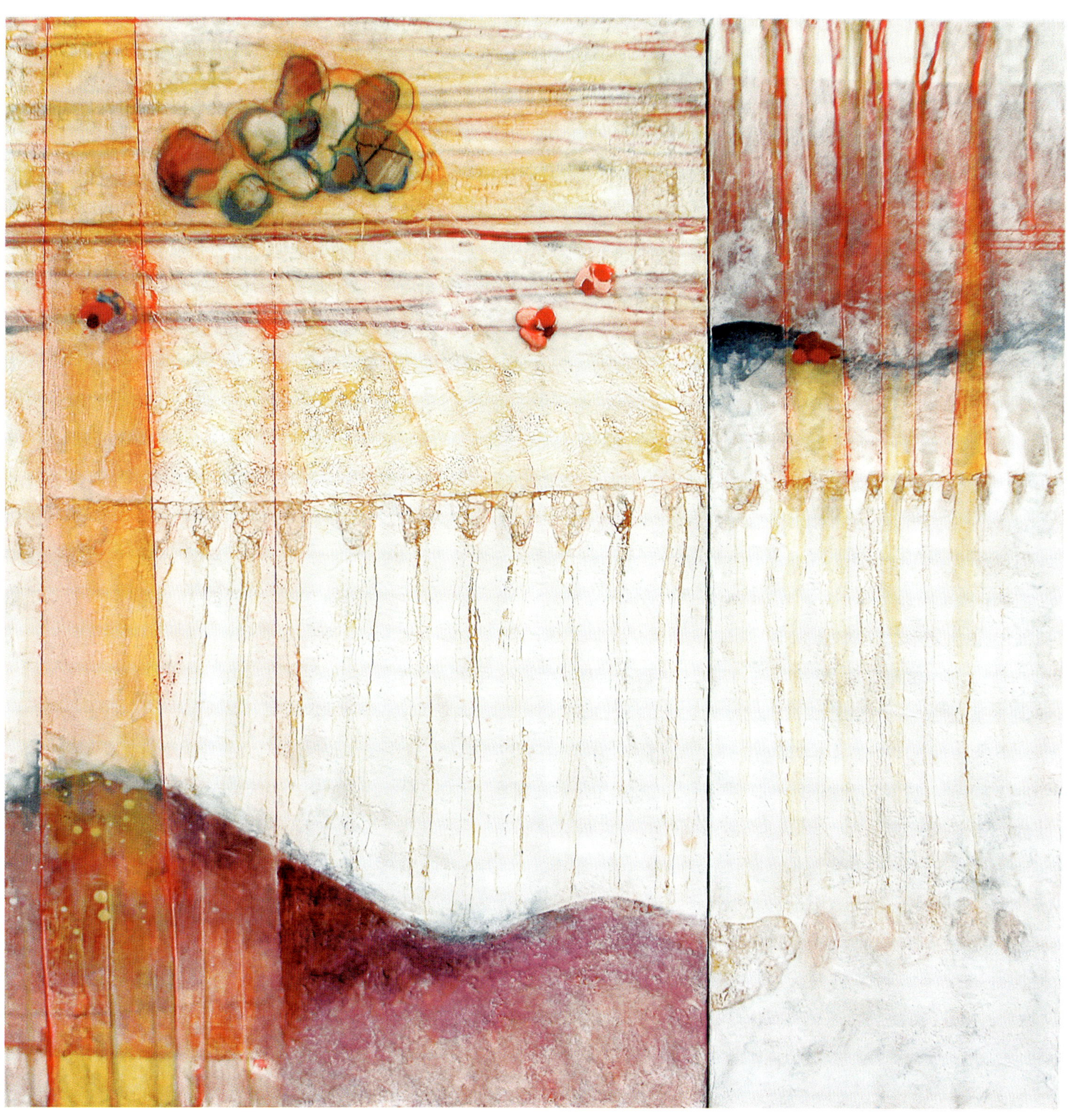

Amy Royce, *Aire Libre.*
Encaustic with mixed media on panel, 91.4 x 91.4 cm.

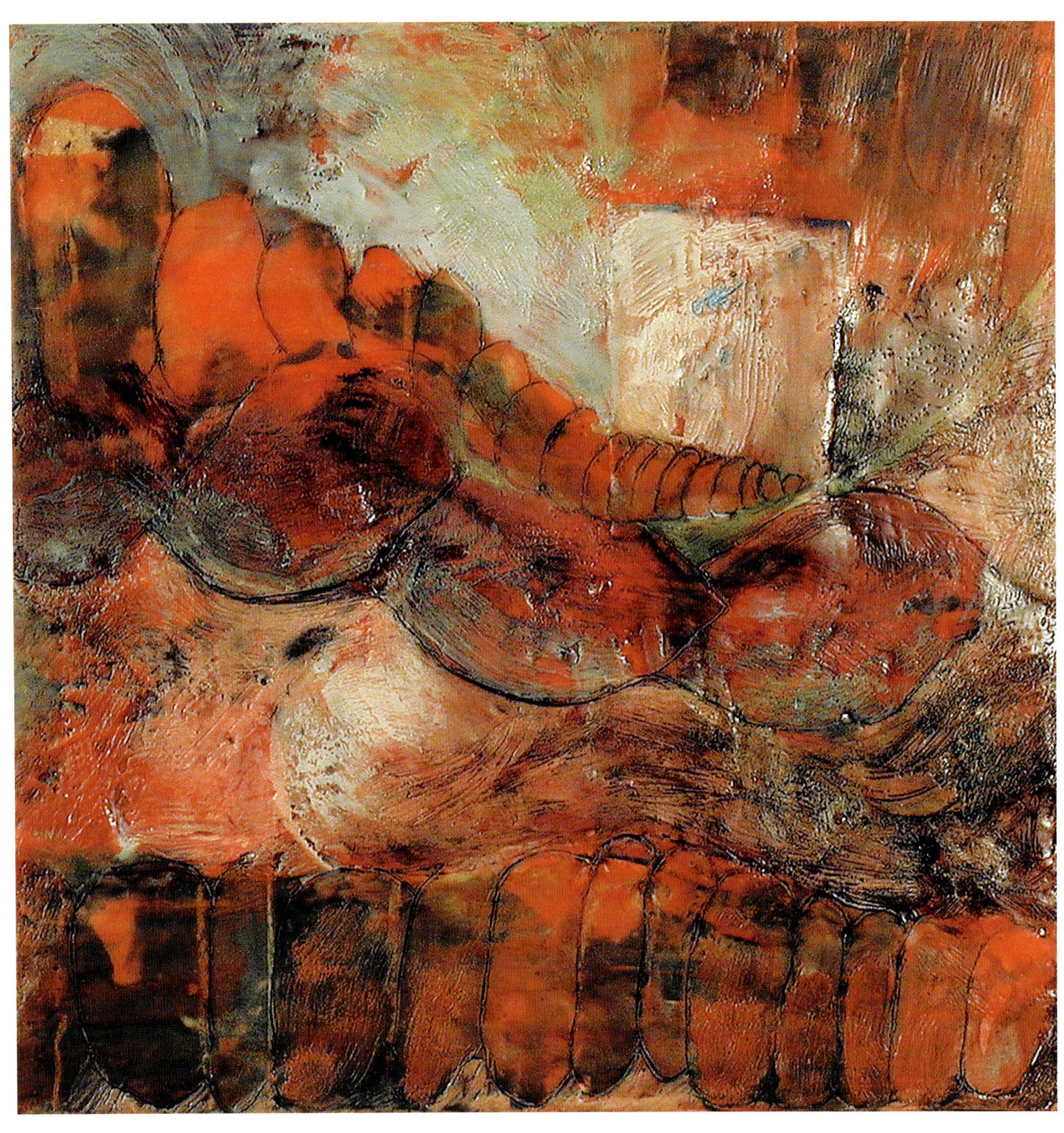

Amy Royce, *Vertebrate II*, 2007.
Encaustic with mixed media on panel, 30.5 x 30.5 cm.

long vertical panels. Somehow, because they are box panels, they are about three inches deep as well; they feel figurative to me. And obviously they are still rectangles, but there is still a figurative feel to me that they are upright, reaching. (They have) kind of an upright movement, so to speak. That format appeals to the sculptor in me. There is a symbolic height and grace that I want to give the pieces and that format feels good to me.

Also, the constraint of that narrow space challenges me to fit a composition into that space and then if I do want to add more panels to it, there is an expansion. So, I like the contrast between the constraint and this expansion. I also love the square format. I am starting to incorporate some tall narrow pieces and then creating a square with another panel.

Can you tell us about the inspiration for your piece *Pirouette*, which is in that same vertical format that we were just talking about?

That is a multiple panel piece and I wanted to incorporate that upward expansion as well. Both with the color of the varying shades of yellow, and with the shape of the foreground, it is a spiraling figure.

I really love dancing. I am a swing dancer, specifically Lindy Hop, which is a 1940s swing dance. I also love watching all kinds of dance, and I like to incorporate the feel of the way dancers carry themselves, and the way the human body in itself can do all these amazing graceful movements. That just fascinates me. There is that physicality that I am trying to express. The uplifting of the yellow colors and the sort of spiraling twisting shapes of the foreground made me think of a pirouette.

Can you tell us about the techniques you used in this piece and how you created the depth in the vertical stripes in the background?

The vertical stripes are fun for me because you can really play with the color and create almost like a vibrating effect. I do that by taking a cake of wax color and a hot iron. I will hold the cake against the bottom of the iron so that it drips down the vertical face of the panel. Then I carefully fuse it with a torch and continue to build each line. Then when I am satisfied with that I will paint a layer or two of clear medium to build up the surrounding areas.

It does not have to be clear medium, it can be a color and then scrape back so that those drip lines are revealed again. That also creates a stronger fuse. The longer the panel is, the faster you need the drips to go, because it can cool quickly. So, I like to build up around it as well with more wax so that it does not get knocked off. The foreground shapes were torn up encaustic prints. We were talking about encaustic prints earlier, and I wanted the spiraling shape, so I was able to arrange them to create that. I will dip them in the clear wax to get them soaked in wax, and then apply them to the panel and fuse them in; and as appropriate, I will make sure there are no air bubbles under there and just make sure it is fully fused so that it won't release itself from the panel. Then I continue to paint on top of that to create the shapes that I want.

Can you tell us about the technique and mixed media you used to create *Breathe a Word*?

I love the technique of being able to etch fine lines into the wax with a pencil or some other sharp tool. In this case, it was towards the end of the painting.

I like printmaking, so sometimes I will use them as collage elements as under painting. So, I had glued down a piece of a print and used that to get started. I then built up the painting and then when I was ready to etch the fine lines in there, I used a pin tool which has a very small diameter to make the lines.

Sometimes I use oil bars, but sometimes I use oil paint. In this case it was oil paint. So I took a paint brush and brushed the paint into those fine lines. Then I took a rag so that I could gently wipe off the excess and that reveals the lines and the other color. In this case, it was the red color. The other red line I carved more deeply with a woodcut tool, and then I filled in with a red magenta encaustic paint. Then I scraped back, because it is sort of a messy thing. You just fill that groove that you made with the woodcut tool and when you scrape back you reveal the hard edge of that groove, only it has been leveled out and made into a different color. It gives you a greater sense of control that I find necessary in my work. I want a balance between the looseness between some of the painted encaustic paint and the definition of some of that line work.

What was your inspiration and painting process for your piece *Source of Support*?

Back to the figure, I love all things to do with the body. I love the shapes of bones; in this case, the ribs, clavicle, and sternum. I like to play with symbolic meanings associated with them.

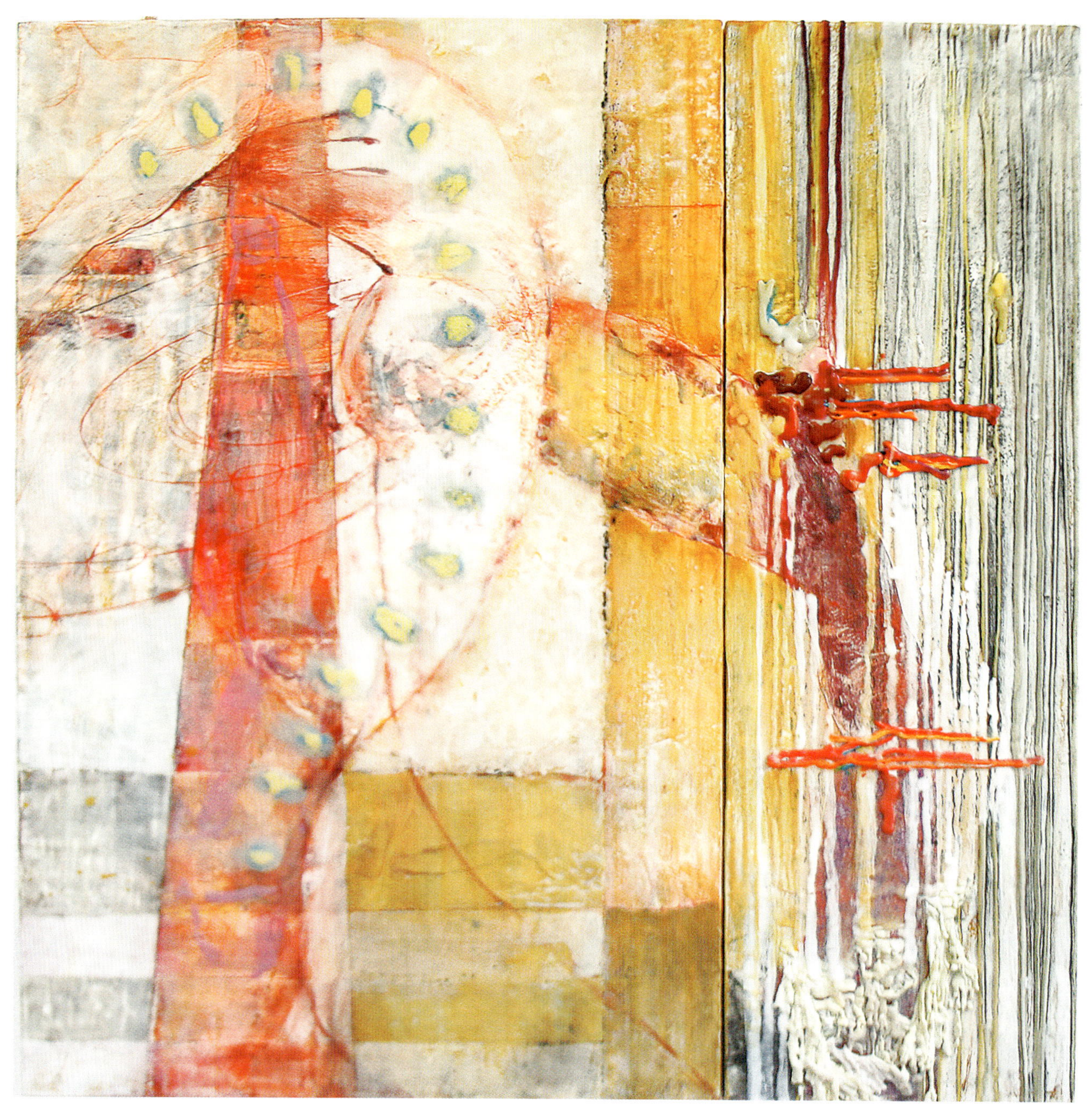

Amy Royce, *Extension.*
Encaustic with mixed media on panel, 91.4 x 91.4 cm.

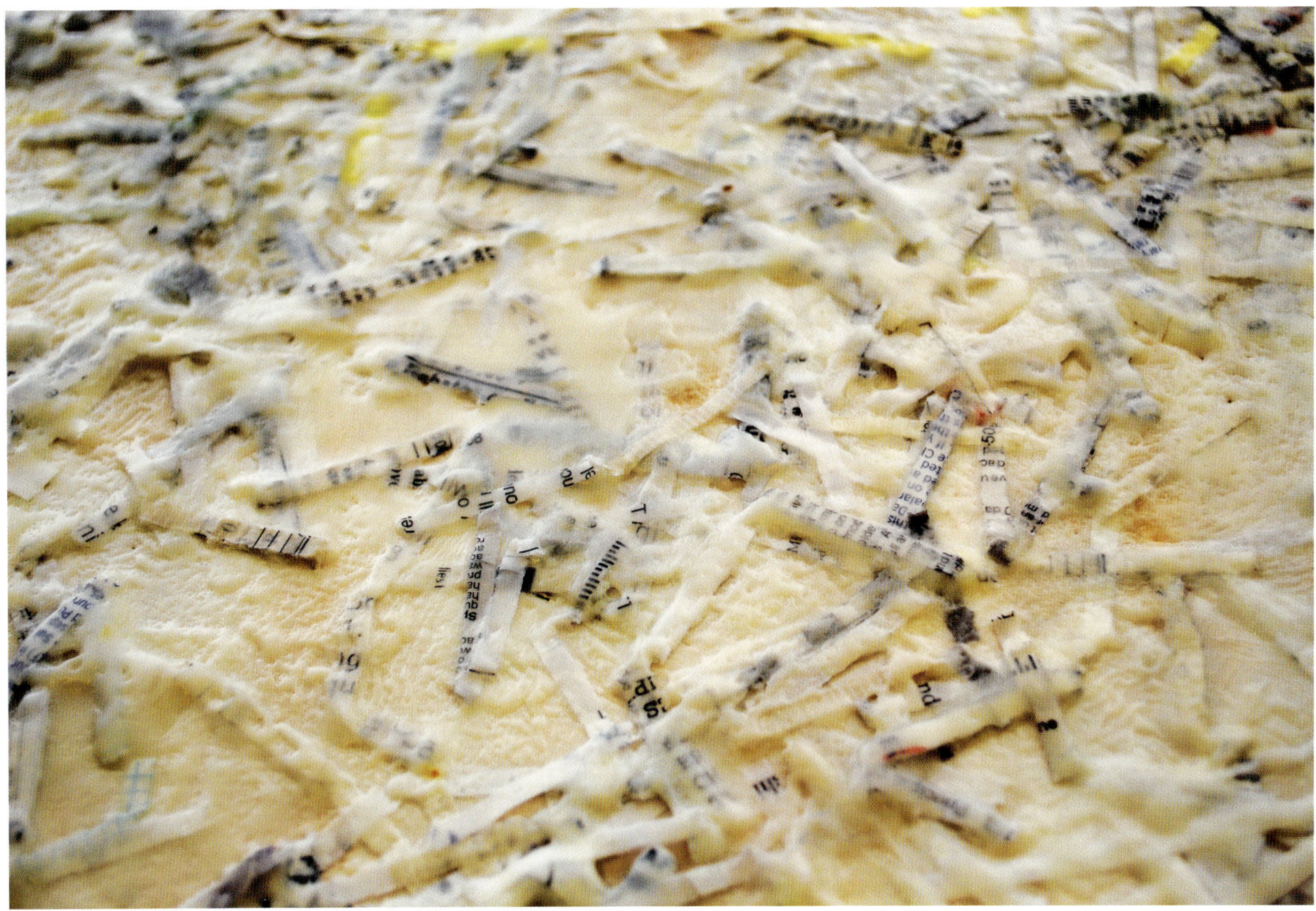

Jasper Johns is the root influential artist for me. But often, my artistic idols are sculptors, or at least they divide their time between second and third. Like Kiki Smith, Manuel Neri, Nathan Oliveira, and Richard Diebenkorn. They are the West Coast artists that I really adore. Sculptors like (Alberto) Giacometti, and Louise Nevelson have been a great influence on me. Robert Mallory and Eva Hesse are both sculptors. Also, painters such as Helen Frankenthaler and Joan Snyder, there are so many. I love to look at art and try to incorporate certain elements that really inspire me.

What advice do you have for artists to make their work stand out?

I would say experiment a lot. Let go, make mistakes, and take risks. Don't be afraid to mess up something; don't get focused and protective of the work, because that is when you get those happy accidents and surprises in the medium. It is so variable, and there are so many ways to get what you want.

One thing I also like to do is take a class in another media, and try to figure out how you can incorporate, or at least influence your encaustic painting. It keeps you fresh and you get new ideas. And just have fun.

You have a quote that says "My art is not smiling, pretty, passive, or silent. My art is moody, earthy, and corporeal". Can you tell us more about what you mean by that?

Yes, it expresses me as a human being. That it is not always pretty. There is certainly something to be said for beauty that makes you feel good, but I like to see beauty in the reality of all the different emotions. And maybe it is a reaction to the "Sunday painter" artists that I see, who have their place absolutely. I want to see beautiful art as well that makes you feel good.

But my art, for me it needs be a little bit challenging as well, including to myself as I am painting; it challenges who I am, and that is not always beautiful or pretty. It is physical. It pushes you and it challenges you and sometimes it is not pretty. But it is important. So that is how I want to express myself.

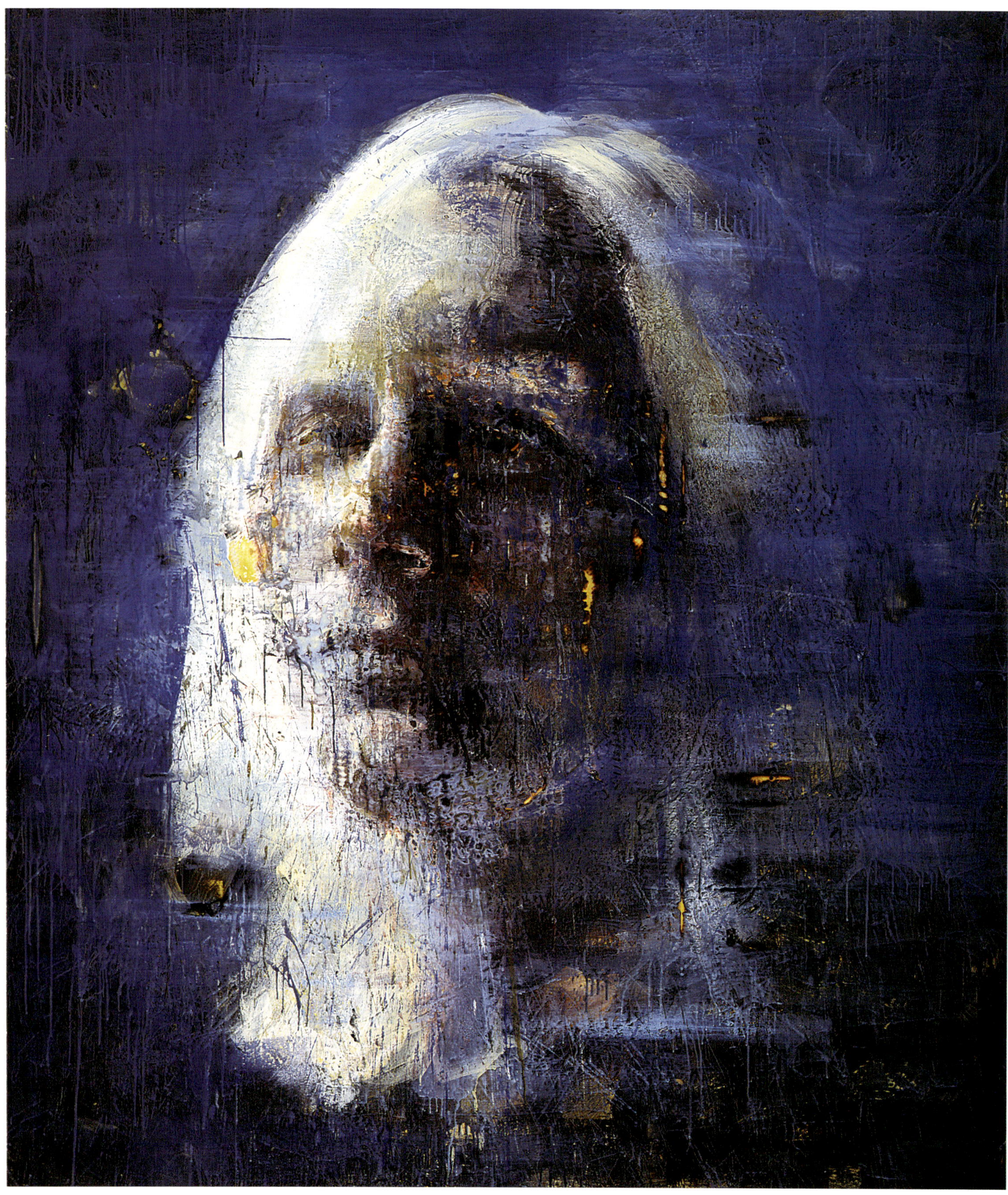

Tony Scherman

Canadian artist Tony Scherman, born in Toronto in 1950, received an M.A. from the Royal College of Art in London, England, in 1974. Since then he has exhibited his works in solo and group exhibitions in North America and Europe. He has also been a visiting critic and lecturer at universities, art colleges, and art galleries in North America and Europe.

"When you are looking at one of my portraits, you are constantly in a battle between the physicality of the encaustic and the fact that you have an illusion of the picture frame. I wanted that contradiction to be heightened."

- Tony Scherman

Tony Scherman, *Johnny Winter*, 2001.
Encaustic on canvas, 243.8 x 213.3 cm.

Can you tell us about how you got started with encaustics? I was at the Royal College of Art from 1971 to 1974 getting an M.A. in painting and I got painter's block, I just couldn't paint. I was drawing for about a year and I was doing drawings with wax crayons.

My tutor Tom Golden basically said to me "you have got to paint, it is a painting degree," and then he said "why don't you try encaustics"? And I knew a little bit just by portraits and I knew Jasper Johns' work, but his use of encaustics had not interested me per se. So, I kept trying to do it and nobody knew (how).

A guy in my studio said to get some wax and some pigment, melt the wax and put it on the brush. So I went to get some wax and I remember I had a little burner in my studio. I took a pencil and drew out a still life on some paper; it is unusual in encaustics to use paper. I remember putting some crimson in the frying pan and it looked like a dye. Then I put it on, and the moment it hit the paper and dried I knew exactly what I was going to do with it.

Nobody was working in it. Basically, encaustic painting had died. There was cold wax by Rembrandt with beeswax and turpentine which is goo that you mix with oil paint and you get a body that dries and has several types of properties. But hot wax really fell by the wayside. Victor Brauner and a few people used them, but not too many.

What influence has your work been on encaustic painting? Probably huge, I am saying that because my agenda was very different than to Jasper's. I remember when I was in college and I had already done a couple of encaustic paintings. And there is an artist called Keith Milow, he is from New York, a British artist. And he was a good friend of Jasper's at the time.

I remember him saying to me "You can't paint encaustics, only Jasper paints encaustics", and I remember looking at him and saying "watch me". I had a completely different agenda. I wanted to take encaustic up to the level of oil painting. I wanted to bring it into the body of painting and I wanted to use it with 18th and 17th century technology for painting.

So basically I reinvented the medium completely. I was showing internationally, at various art fairs, slowly but surely. There was a major change to the medium because I went to a microcrystalline wax. I wanted to paint with oil paint, and encaustics, and I was working with beeswax. The whole history of art conservation is to battle with oxidation. It is a battle to retard the oxidation of the paint because as the oil dries it cracks. It is a figment of thermodynamics that is at work here. The beeswax paint was fine as long as I didn't use pigments that had a lot of oil per volume in them. But the whites had a tremendous volume of oil in them. If you mix titanium white it is a pigment, and the amount of oil you have to put in is a lot more than with an earth-colored paint.

So what was happening was that the oil content in the encaustic paint was very high. That would not have been a problem, except for the fact that beeswax oxidizes as well. Any time you heat beeswax above its melting point and then bring it back down, it is tempered like steel or glass and it becomes more and more brittle. What that means is that beeswax is very vulnerable to cracking.

Problem B is that I like to paint on a canvas. It bounces and I came from oil painting and I started in a particular kind of a way and I wanted the give. I have never liked painting on board. For me, I needed to deal with the fact that because of the amount of oil left on, my grays and my whites started to crack. They did not crack on their own, but they were very vulnerable. If you shipped a painting overseas the hold could be -15° on the Atlantic. Any turbulence would crack paintings, it could happen.

I needed to find a way of painting in encaustic and put something in it that would prevent the oxidation. Heating the wax less was not possible because it wouldn't flow. All the techniques I had ever read by Max Doerner and other people about encaustics were only good for painting encaustic on wood. So it is not going to be as likely to be cracking, although that it is definitely heightened by the varnish is no question. It is probably not going to just happen, but with the bouncing canvas it could.

I set to work and talked to chemists. I went to Ohio where there was a big conservation at a paint gallery, so I talked to those guys. It was about a year until I figured out a chemically stable medium. So I basically reinvented the medium by using microcrystalline wax, which is a long chain molecule.

What happens with beeswax is that it is also a long chain molecule, but every time you heat it the chains get shorter and shorter, which is why it becomes more brittle. With microcrystalline wax on the other hand, you can heat it to its flash point, and then bring it right back down again and the molecules don't change.

Microcrystalline was invented in the 1930s and is a petroleum by-product. Before I even used it, I remember going to an antique market in London and buying some lipstick from the 1940s and melting it, because it was made with microcrystalline wax. Lipstick comes in all different

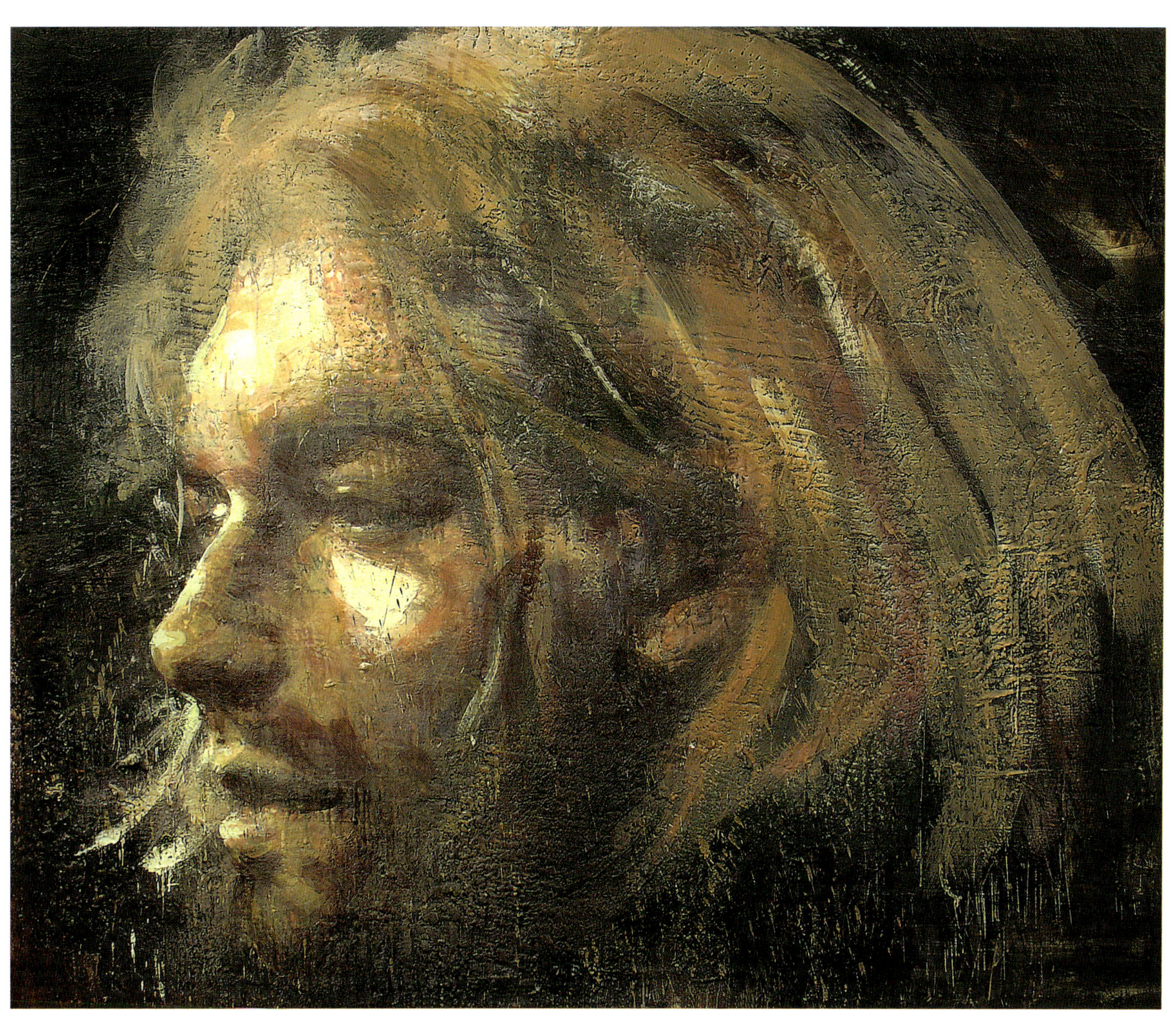

Tony Scherman, *Kurt C*, 2007-2008. Encaustic on canvas, 152.4 x 182.8 cm.

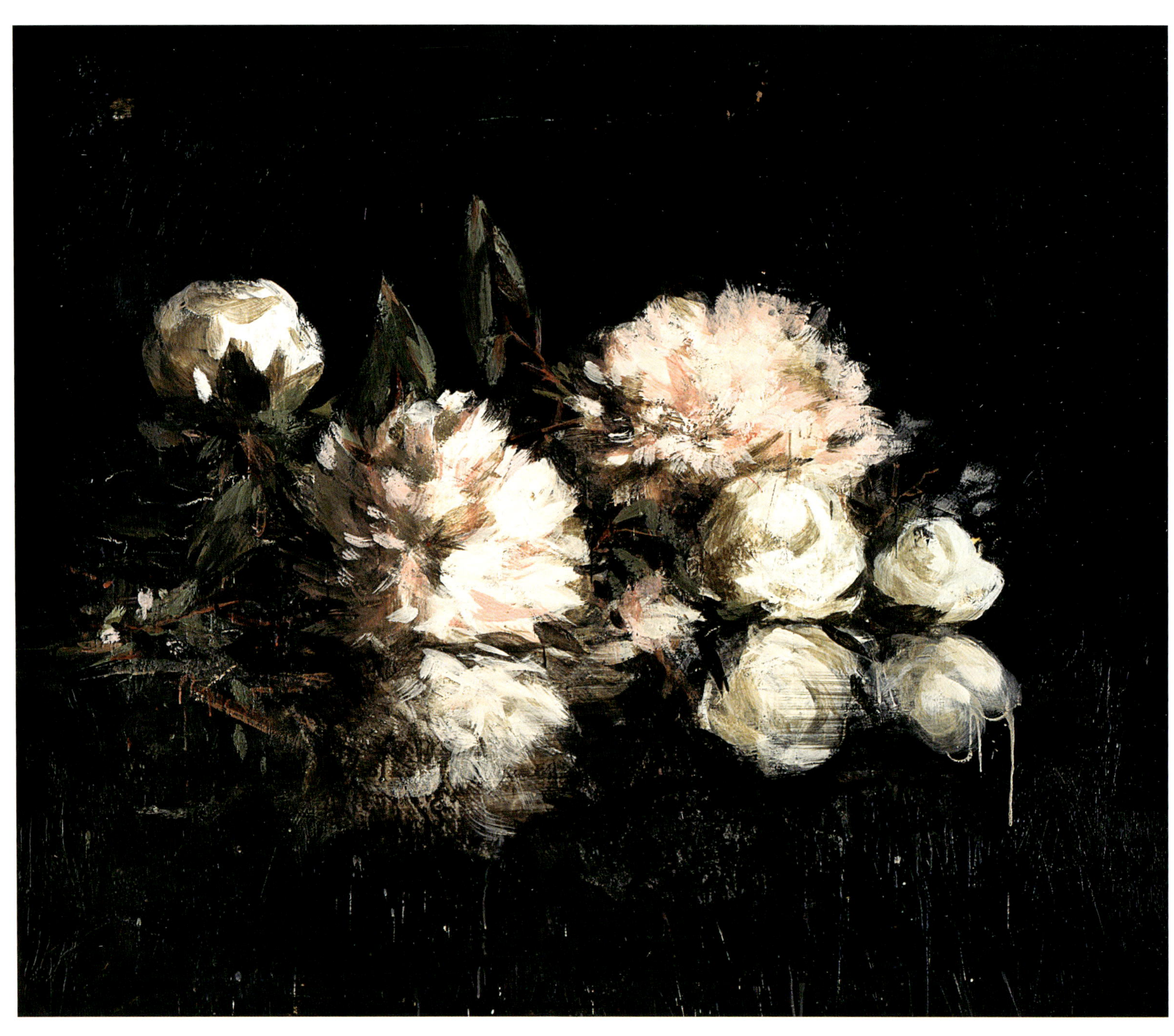

Tony Scherman, *Conversations with the Devil*, 2000-2002.
Encaustic on canvas, 152.4 x 182.8 cm.

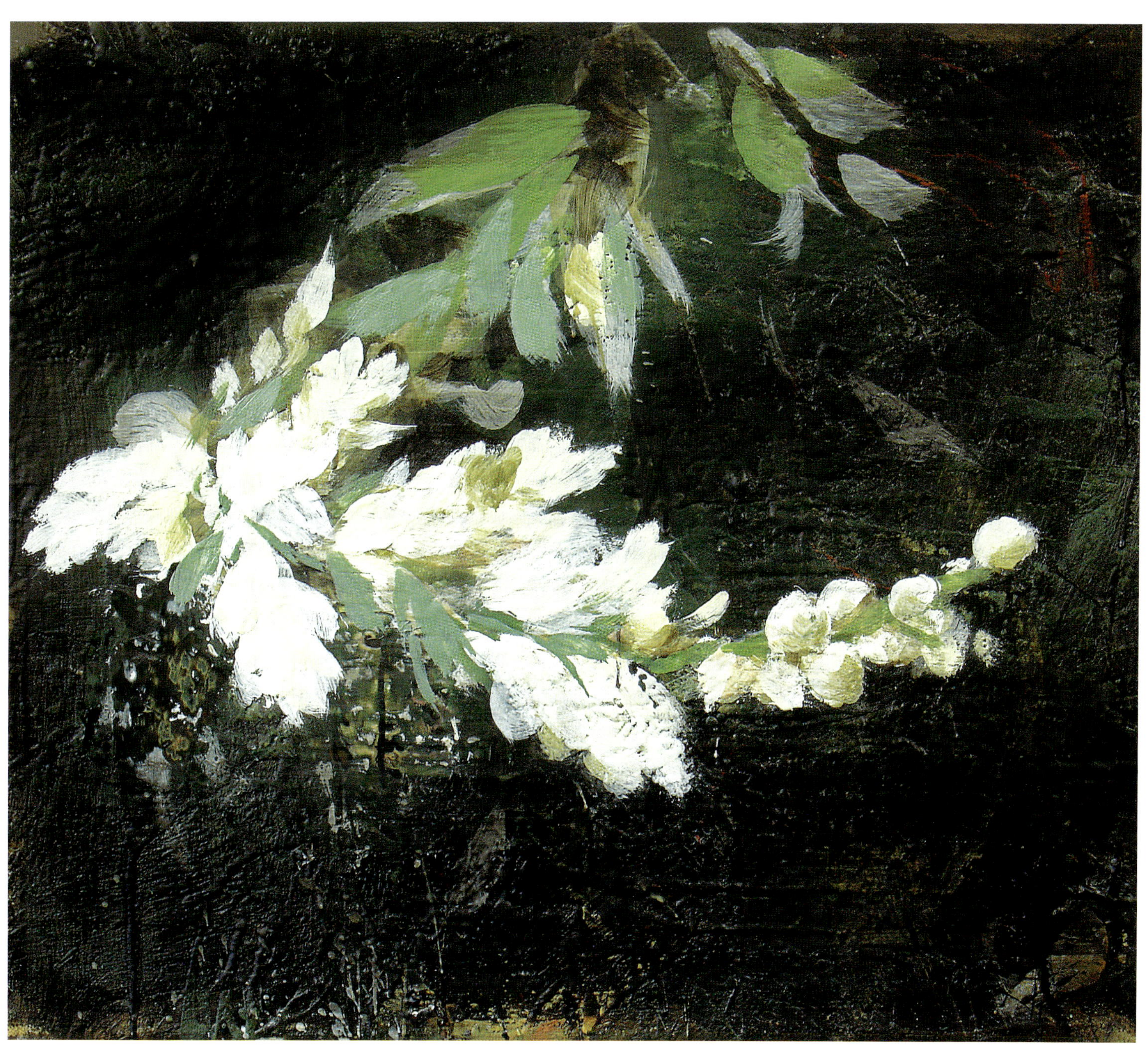

Tony Scherman, *Conversations with the Devil*, 2006-2008.
Encaustic on canvas, 60.9 x 71.1 cm.

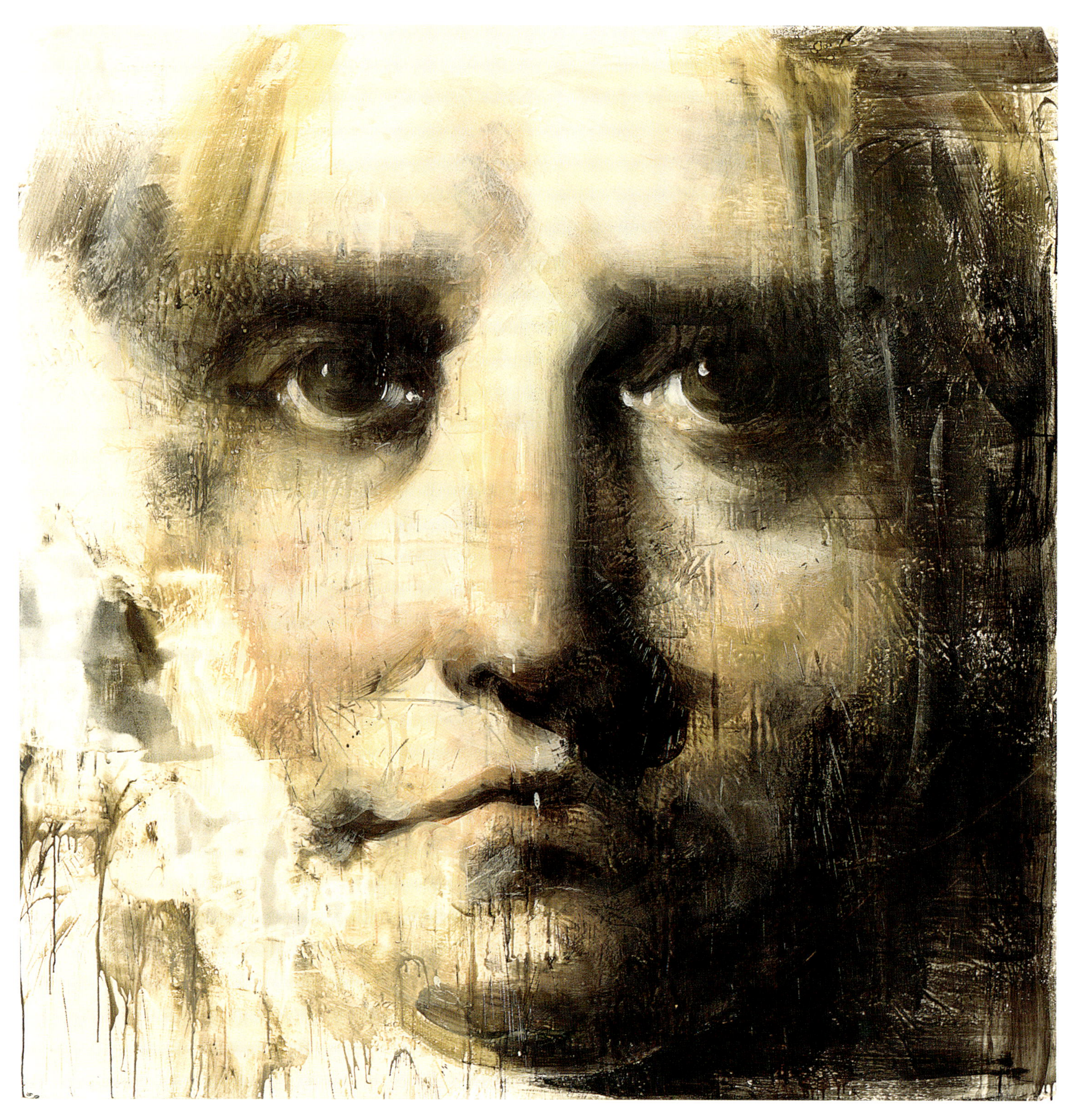

Tony Scherman, *Bonaparte: Italy*, 1998. Encaustic on canvas, 182.8 x 182.8 cm.

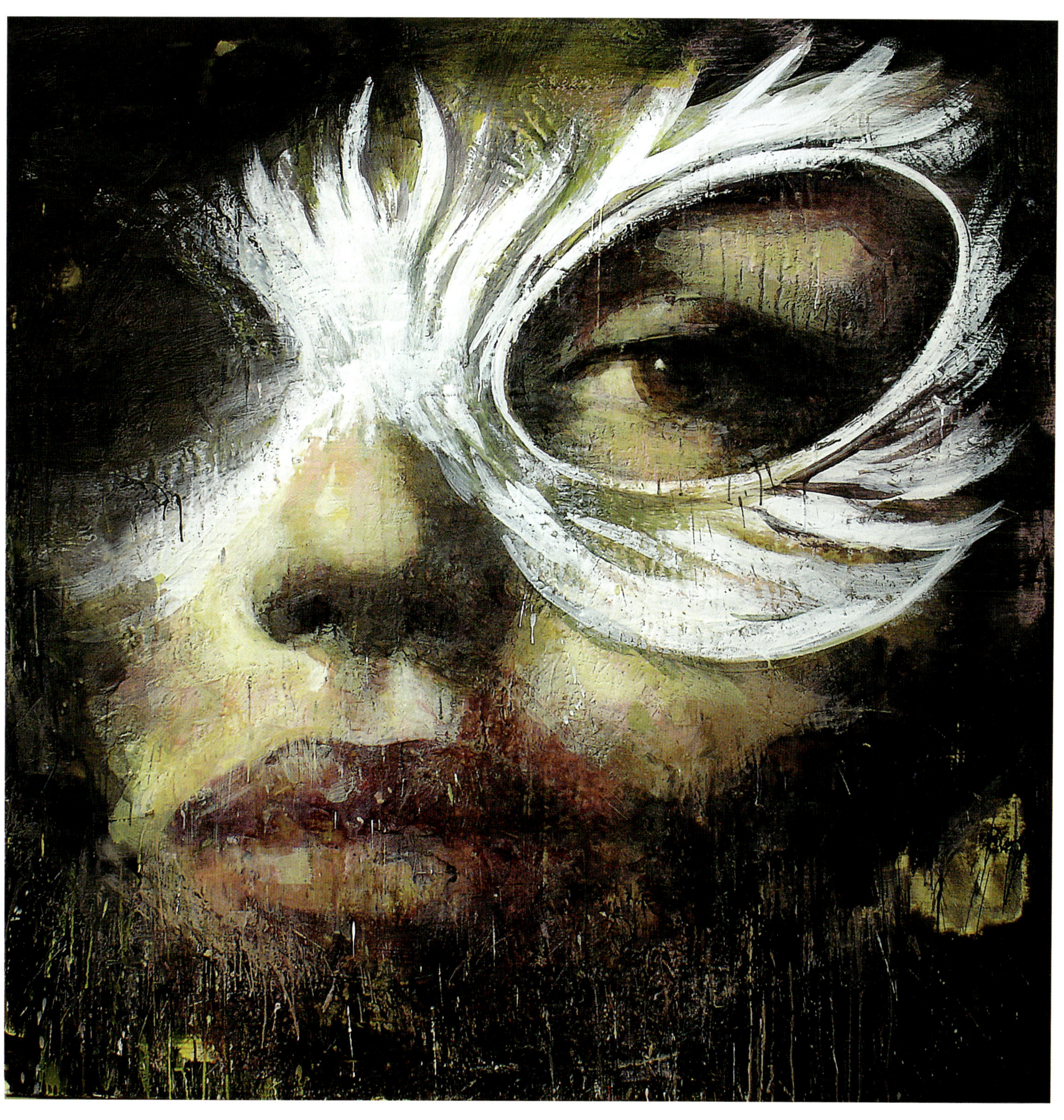

Tony Scherman, *Circe*, 2008-2010. Encaustic on canvas, 152.4 x 152.4 cm.

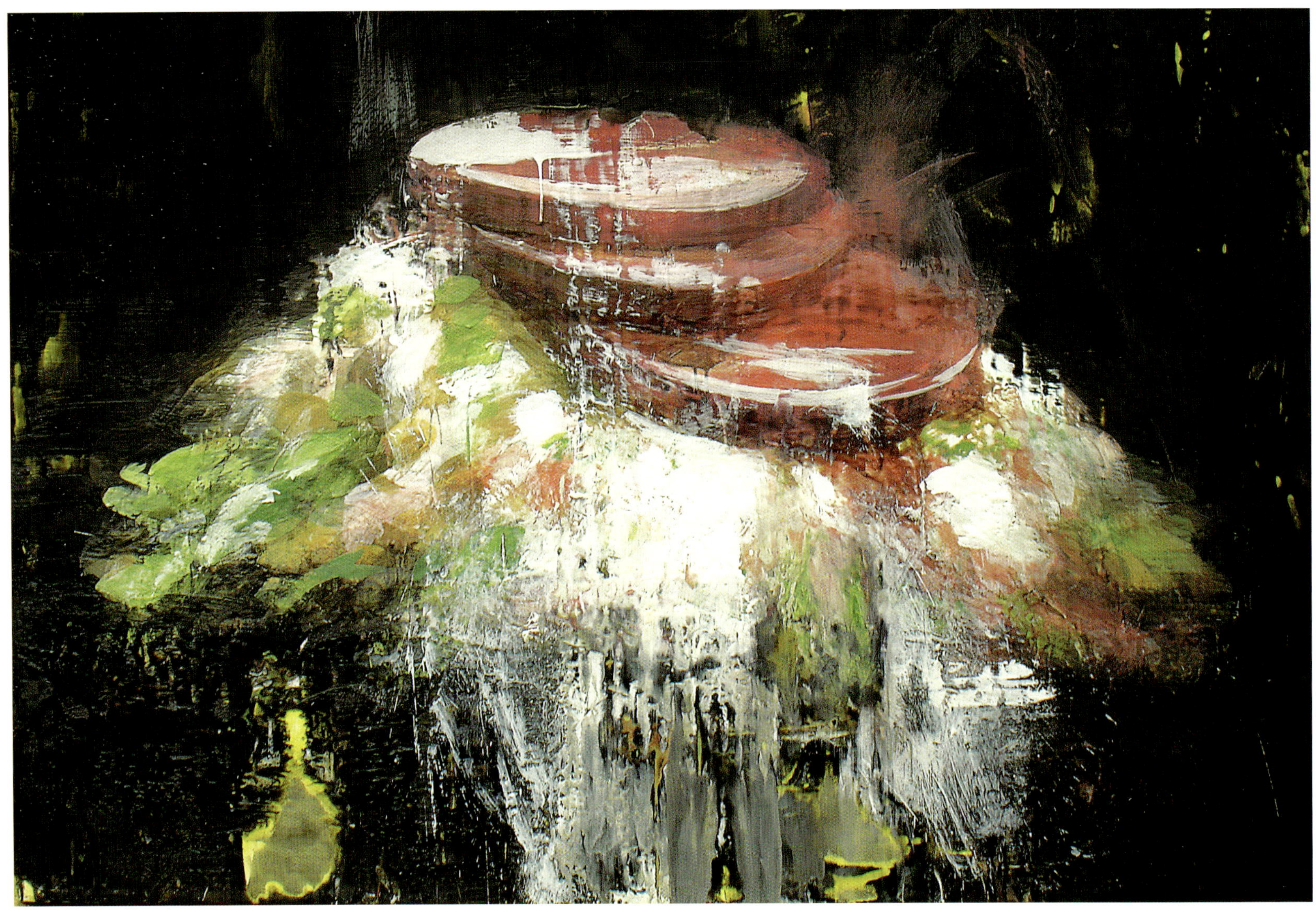

Tony Scherman, *Untitled Still Life*, 2007-2009.
Encaustic on canvas, 137.1 x 152.4 cm.

really huge and it is a great medium. Encaustic did not appear again besides being used by just a few artists here and there, and I am talking about hot encaustic not cold.

Jasper kind of revived it, but he pretty much used it like paint and now a lot of it is cracking. So it is not a good medium. I use it, but I have a very specific purpose in mind and I curse it every single day. I love it and I hate it. I think you really need to have a reason to paint in it if you want to sustain a career in it.

I feel like right now is a very exciting time for encaustic painting because a lot of people are trying very revolutionary techniques. How do you feel about that?
I think it is great. My biggest caution and biggest advice is do not mix. The more elements you put in, the more unstable it is. The simpler the better, I talked to a lot of chemists and they all told me the same thing, keep it really simple. If you add varnishes, you better expect some cracking somewhere down the line.

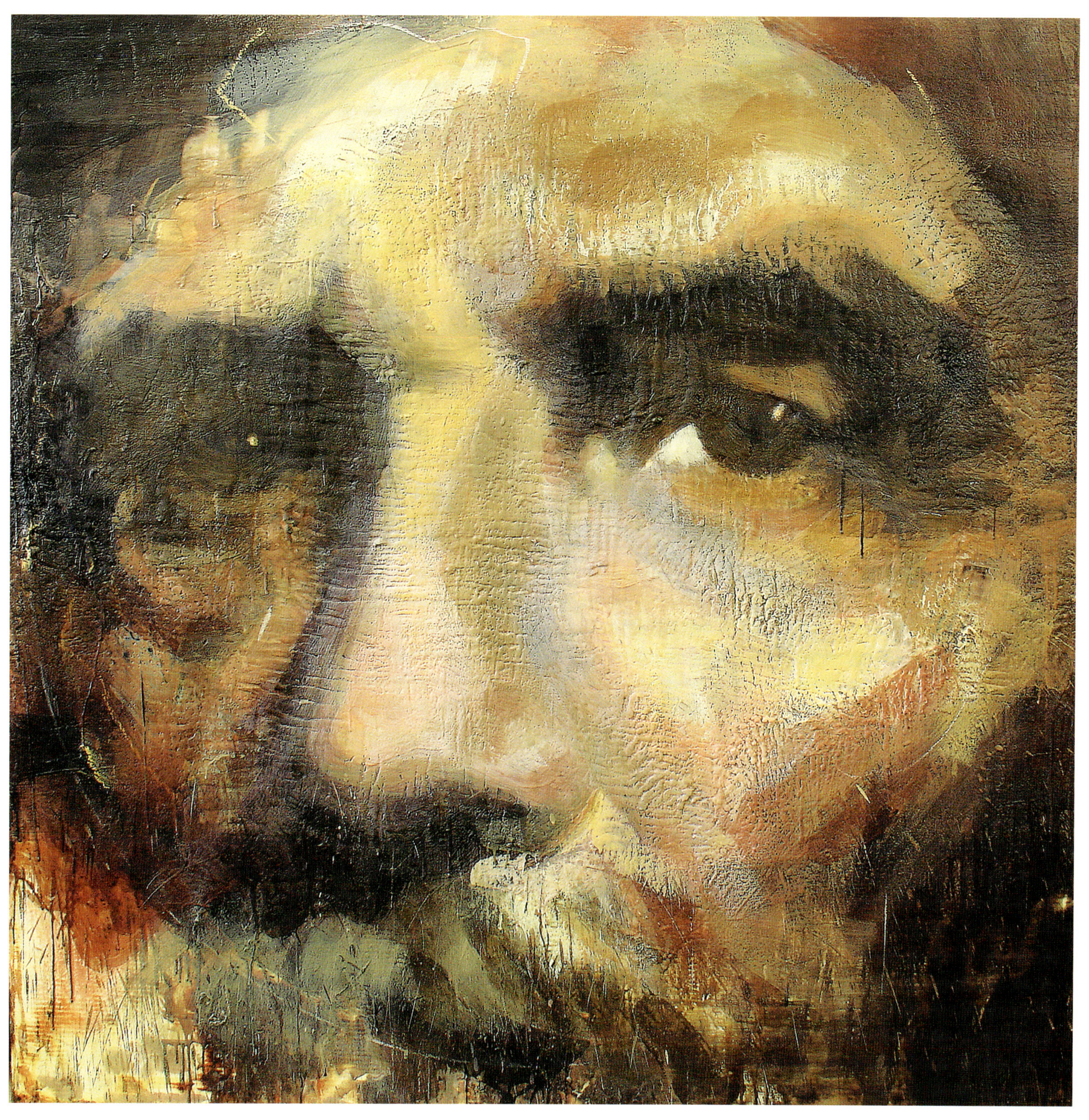

Tony Scherman, *General Bob at Cold Harbor*, 2004-2006. Encaustic on canvas, 152.4 x 152.4 cm.

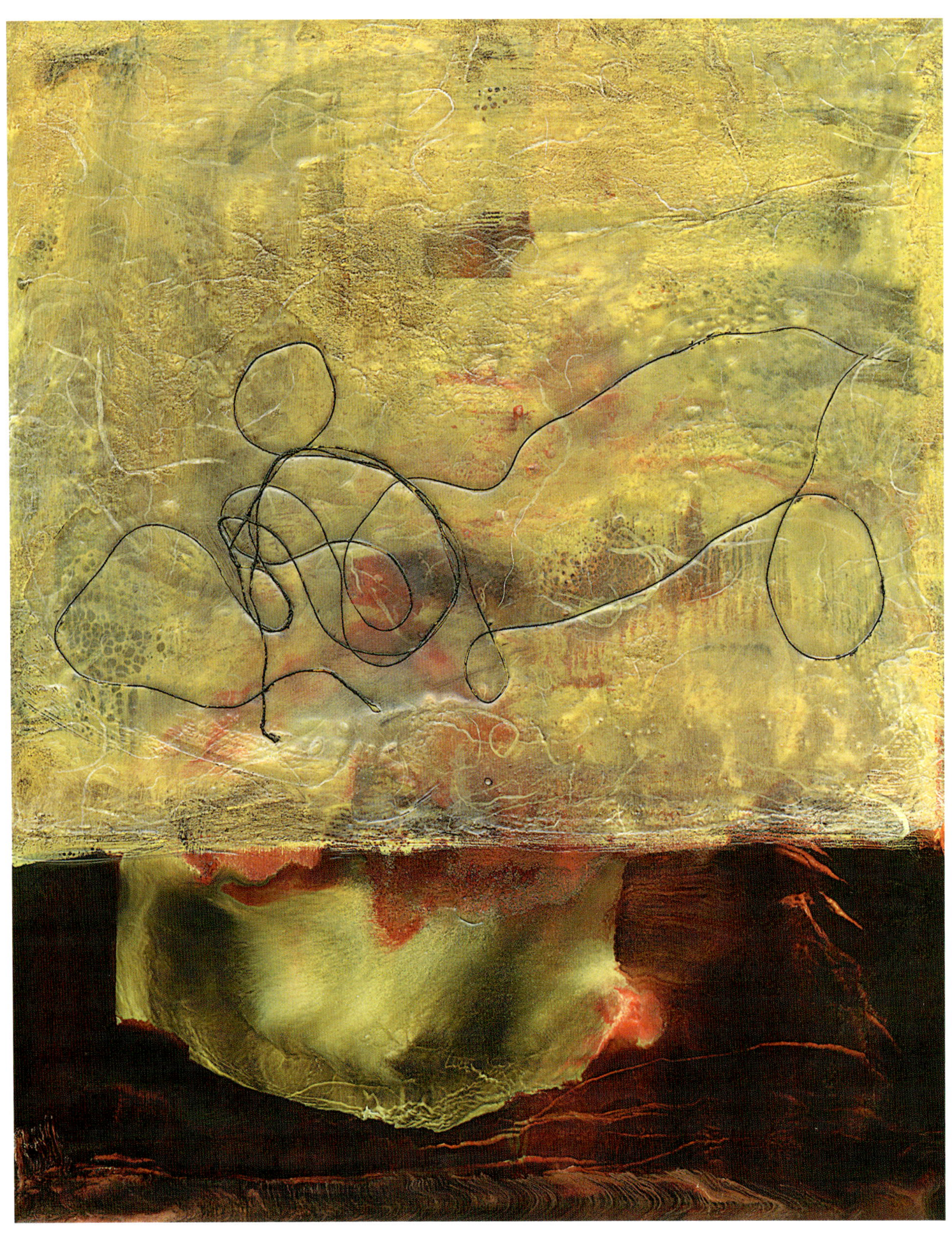

Steven DaLuz, *Expectant*, 2008. Encaustic, 30.5 x 22.8 cm.

Encaustic Image Gallery

Selection of Featured Artwork Collection by Contemporary Encaustic Artists

Steven DaLuz

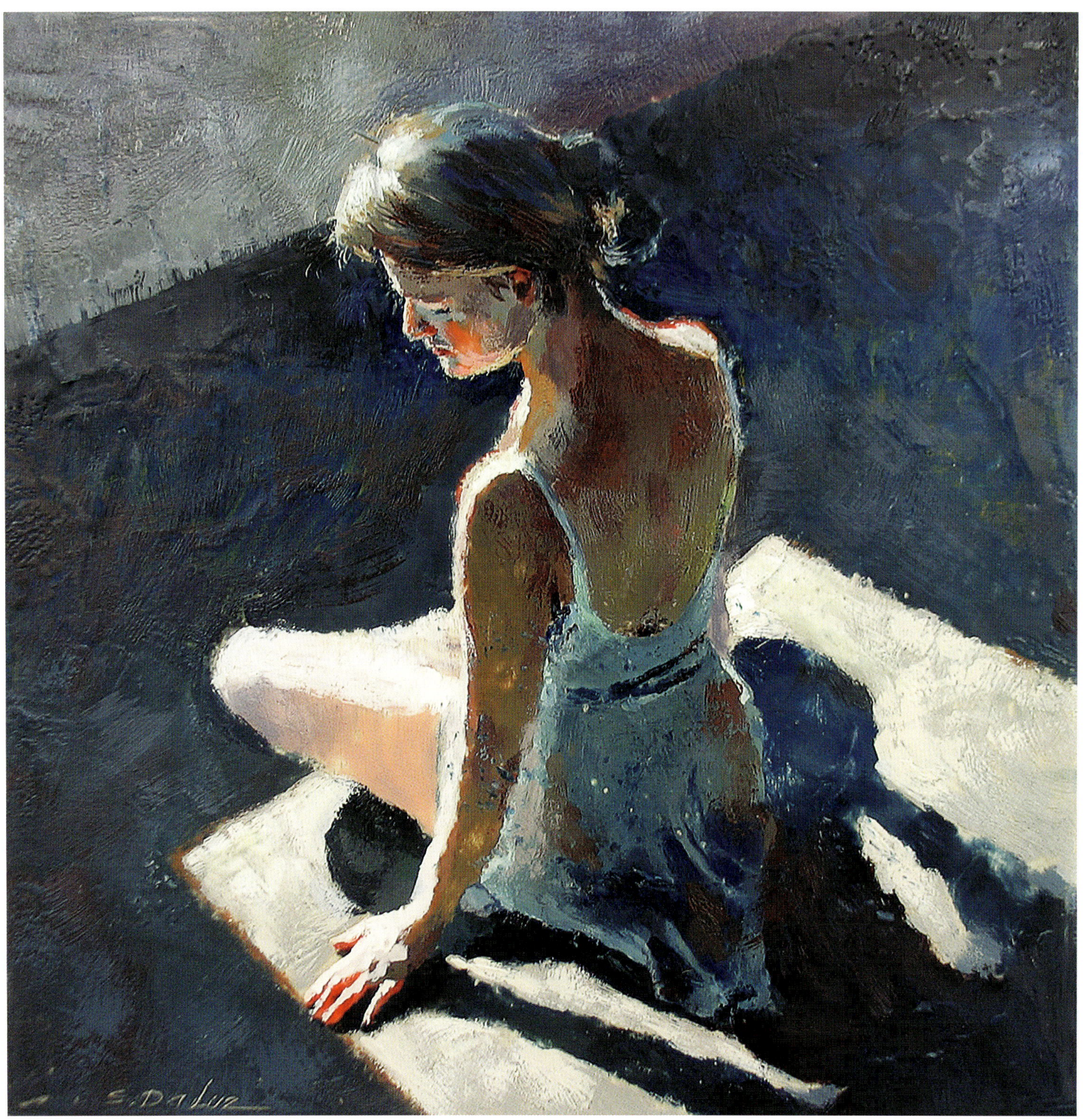

Steven DaLuz, *Contemplation*, 2008. Encaustic, 30.5 x 30.5 cm.

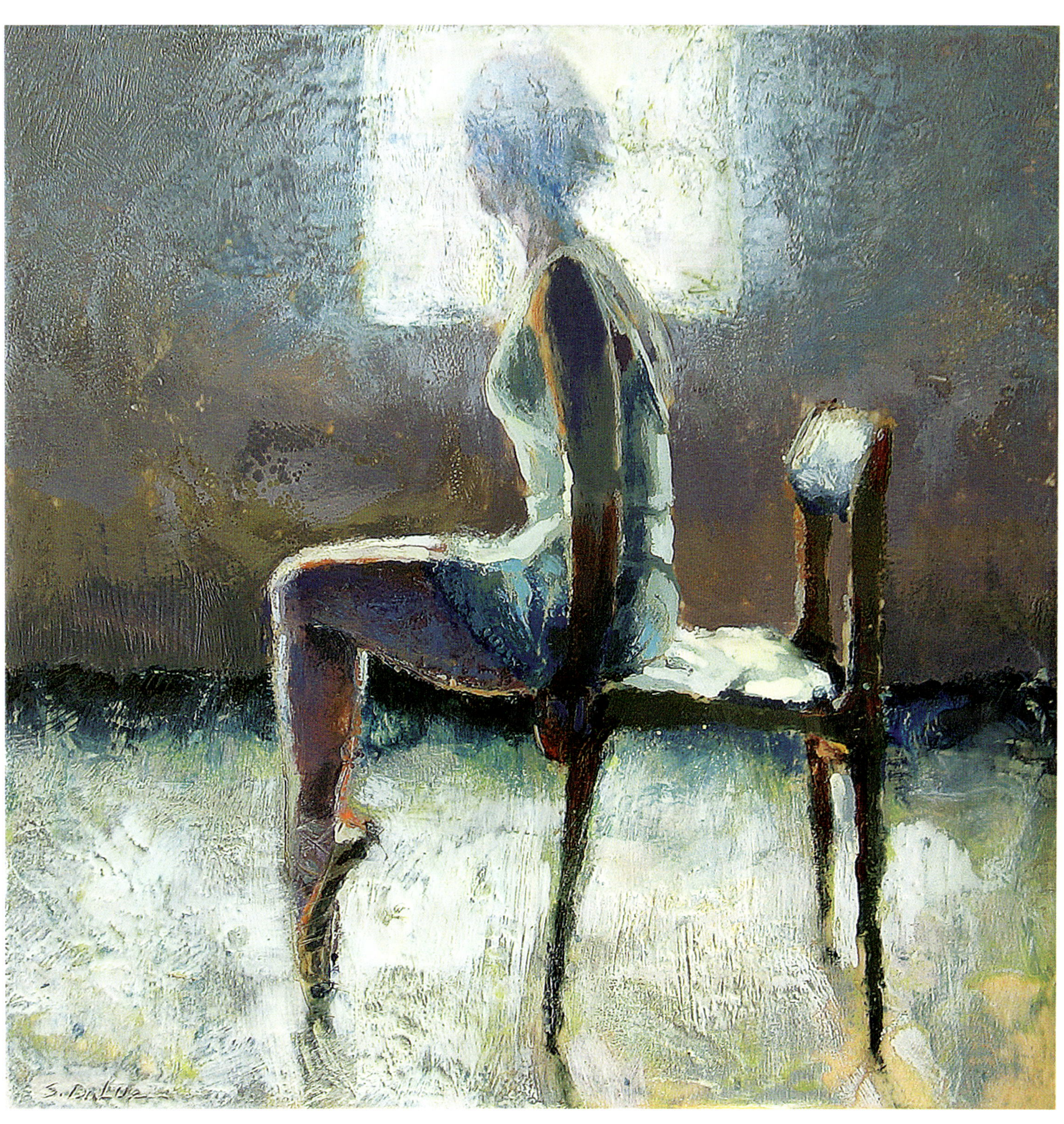

Steven DaLuz, *Dancer in a Chair*, 2008. Encaustic, 30.5 x 30.5 cm.

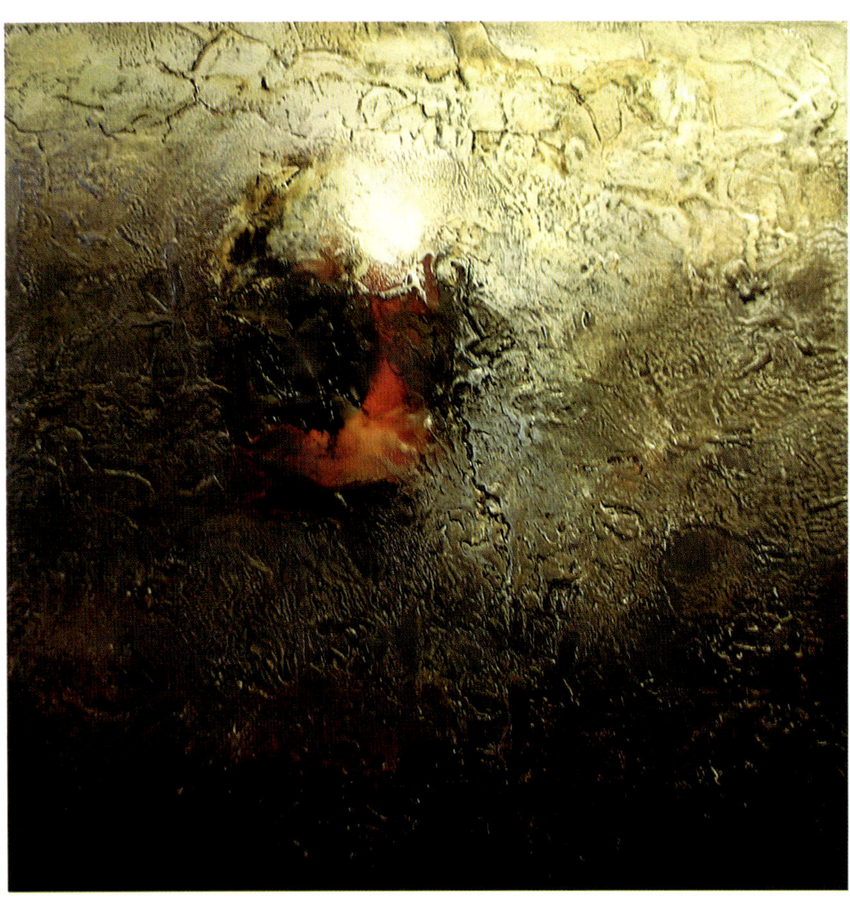

Steven DaLuz, *Birthstone*, 2008.
Encaustics on wood, 24 x 24 cm.

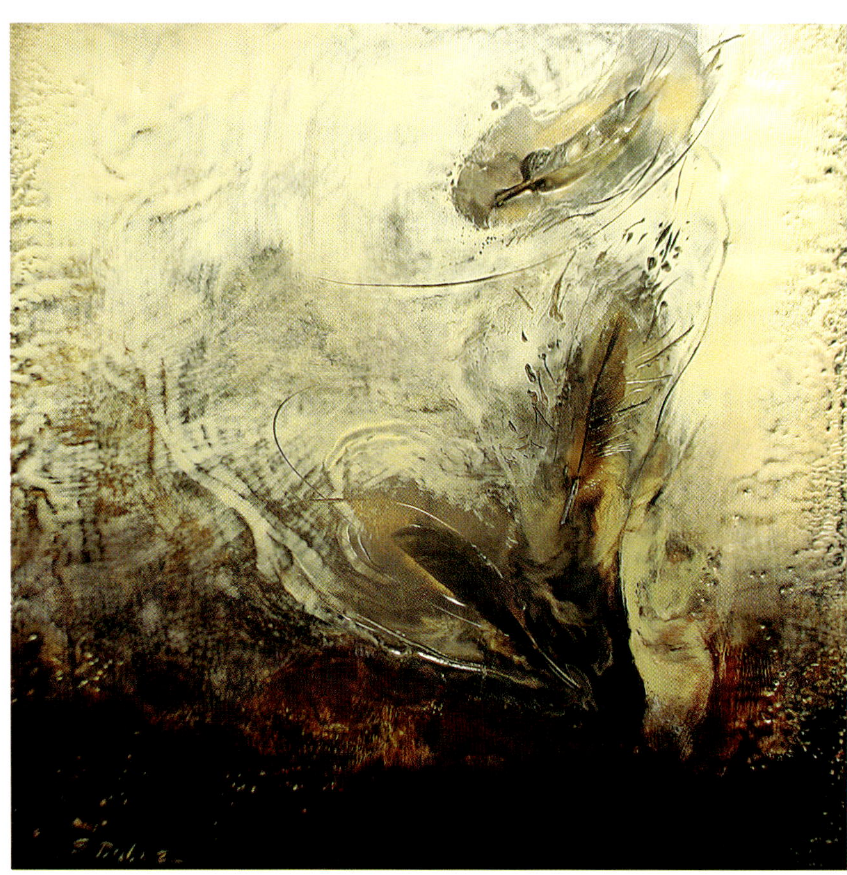

Steven DaLuz, *Icarus*, 2010.
Encaustic and bird feathers, 30.5 x 30.5 cm.

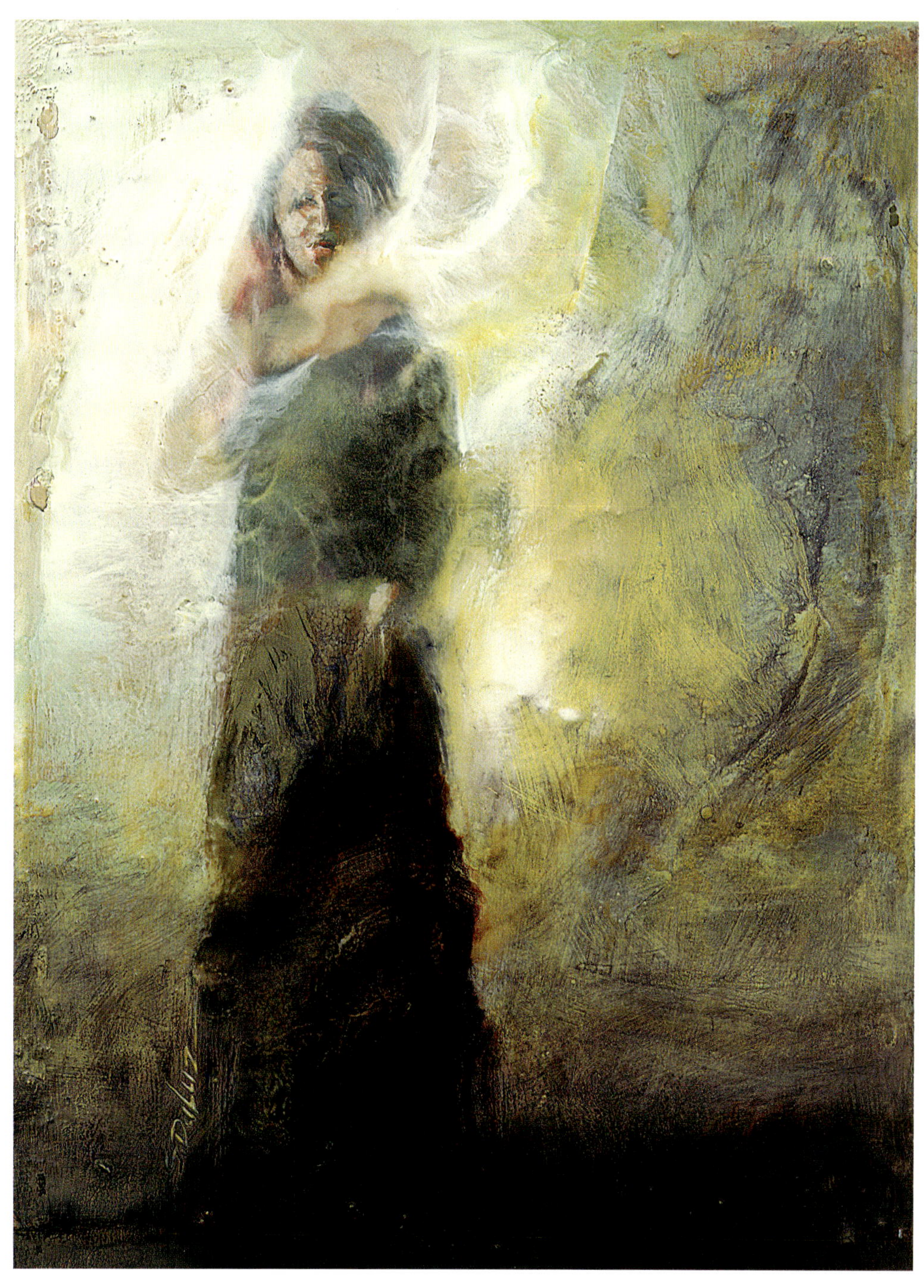

Steven DaLuz, *La Llorona* (detail), 2009. Encaustic, 30.5 x 22.8 cm.

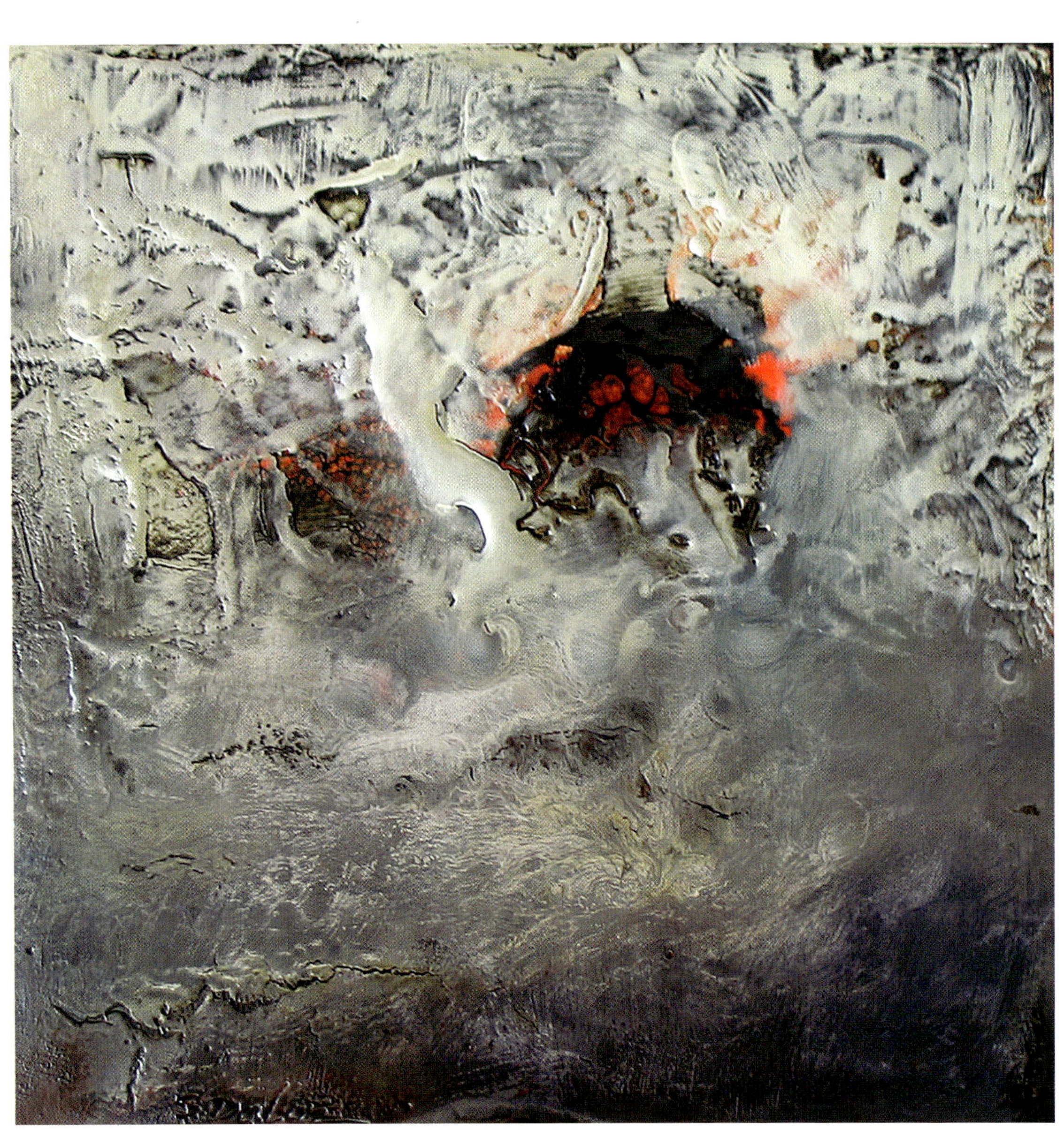

Steven DaLuz, *Composition in Gray #722*, 2008. Encaustic, 30.5 x 30.5 cm.

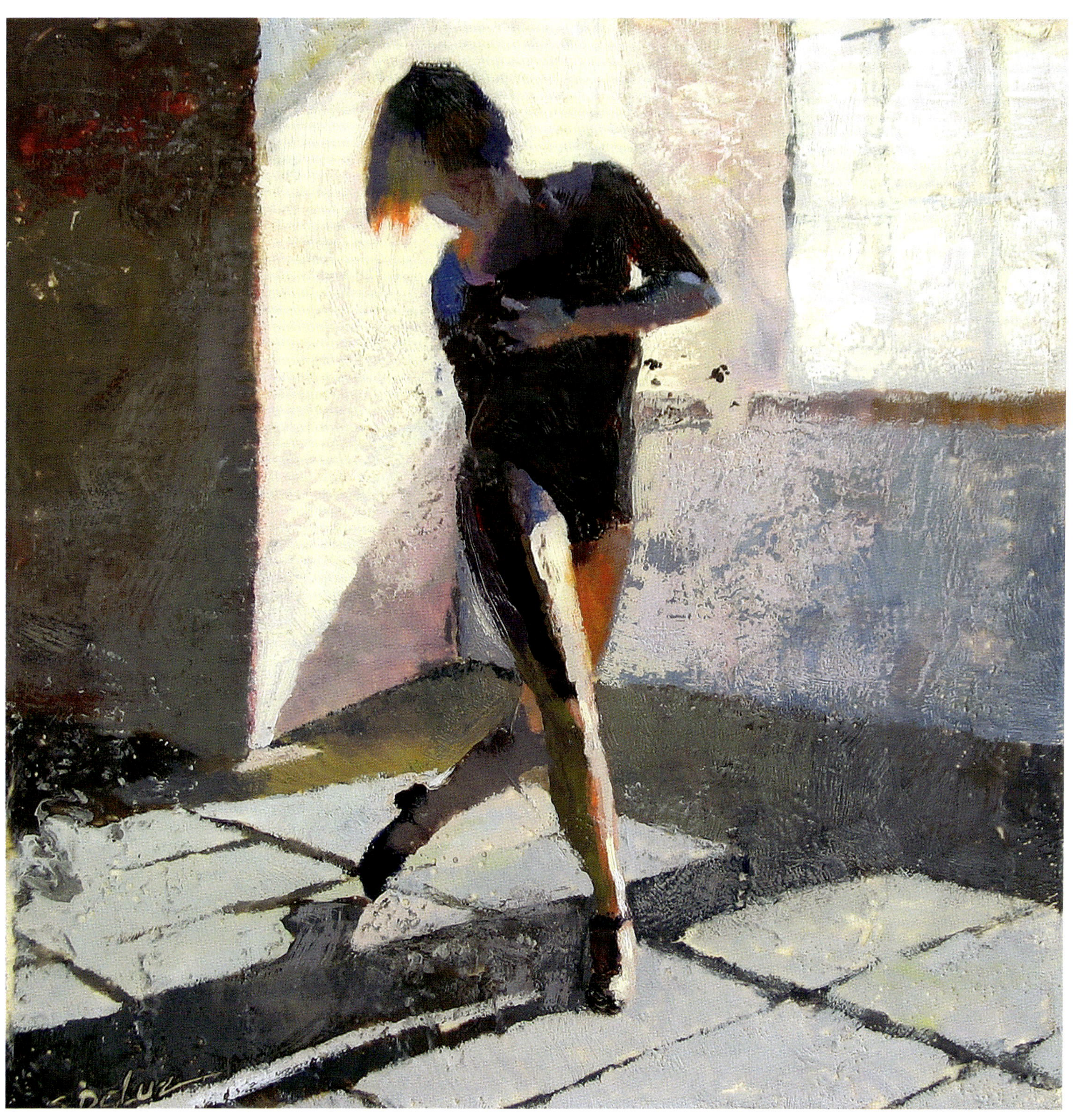

Steven DaLuz, *Jazz Solo 2*, 2008. Encaustic, 40.6 x 40.6 cm.

Stephanie Hargrave

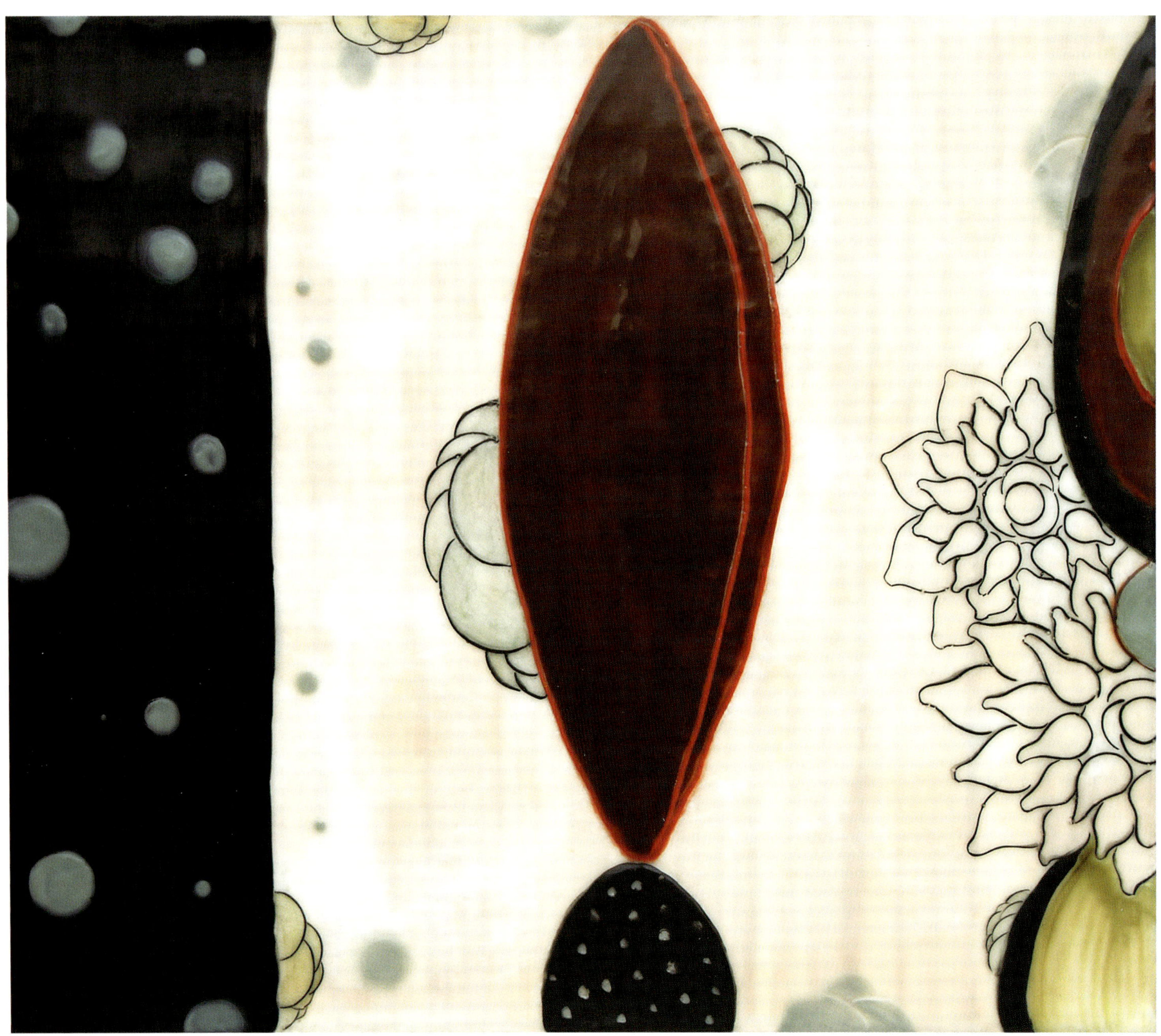

Stephanie Hargrave, *Pods and Pollinia 2*, 2010. Encaustic, 62.2 x 71.1 cm.

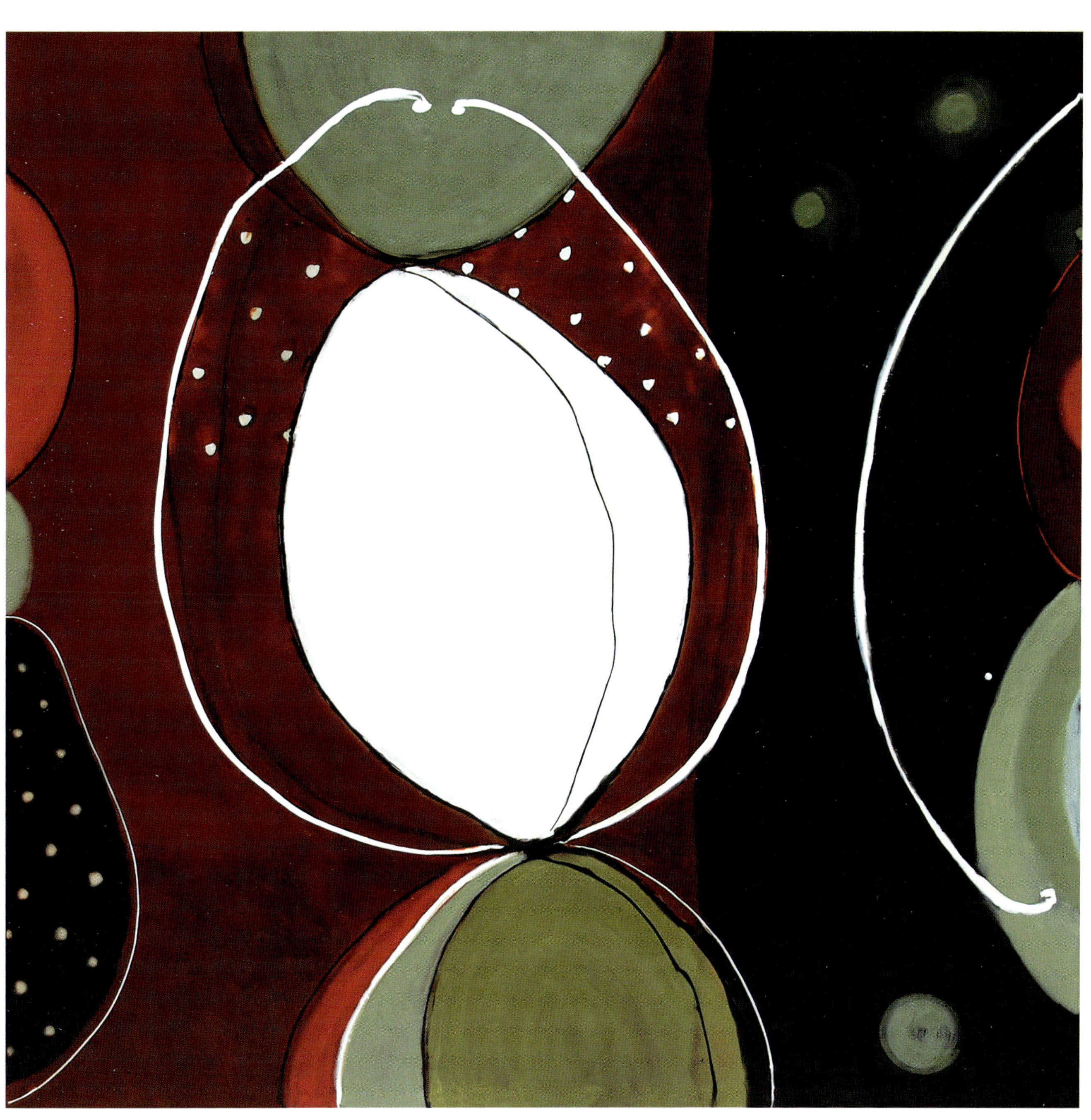

Stephanie Hargrave, *White Pod 4*, 2010. Encaustic, 91.4 x 91.4 cm.

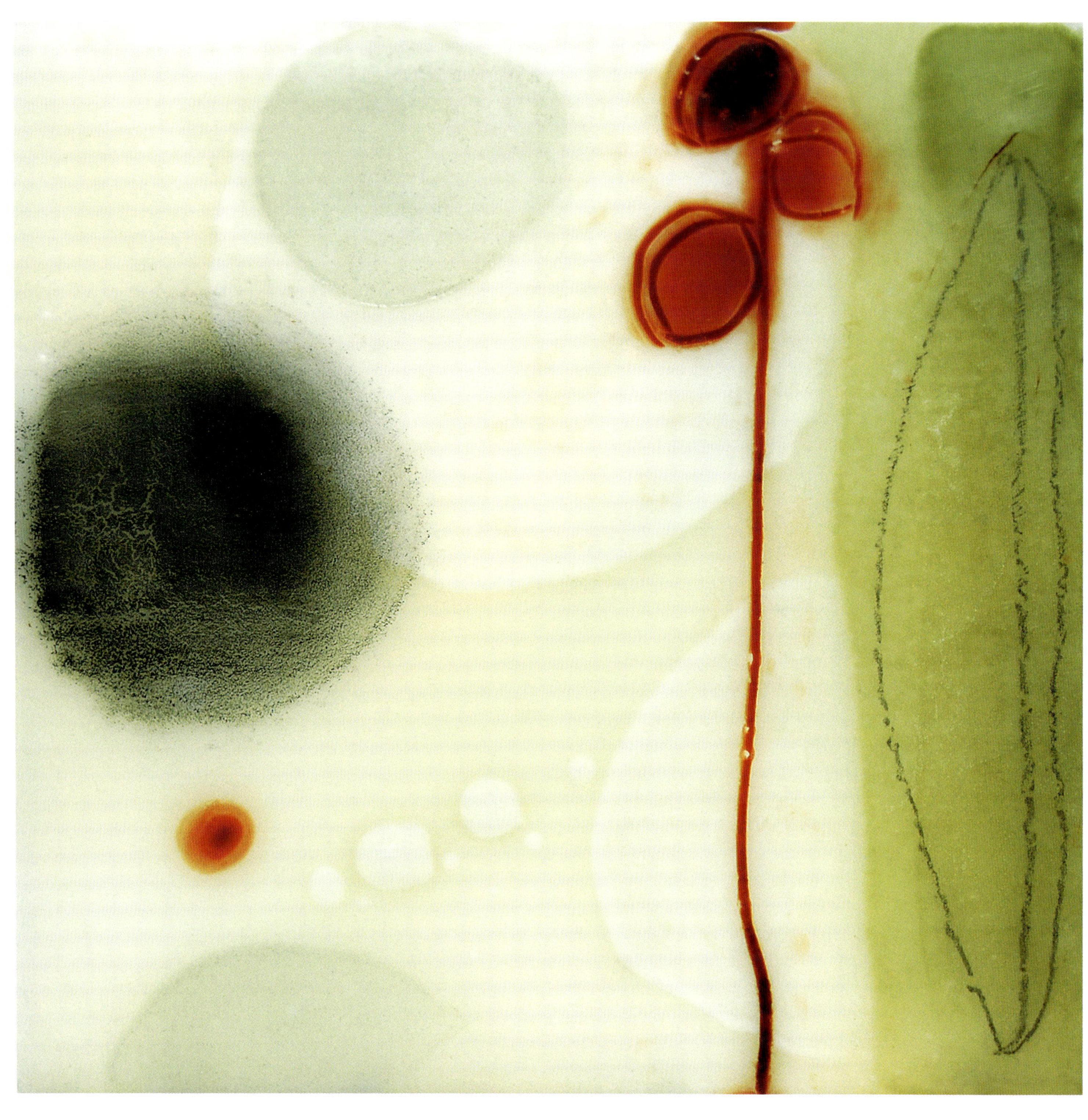

Stephanie Hargrave, *Cross Section 4*, 2007.
Encaustic, 60.9 x 60.9 cm.

Stephanie Hargrave, *Red Flower 2.2*, 2009.
Encaustic, 10.1 x 10.1 cm.

Stephanie Hargrave, *Seed Pod 5*, 2007.
Encaustic, 45.7 x 60.9 cm.

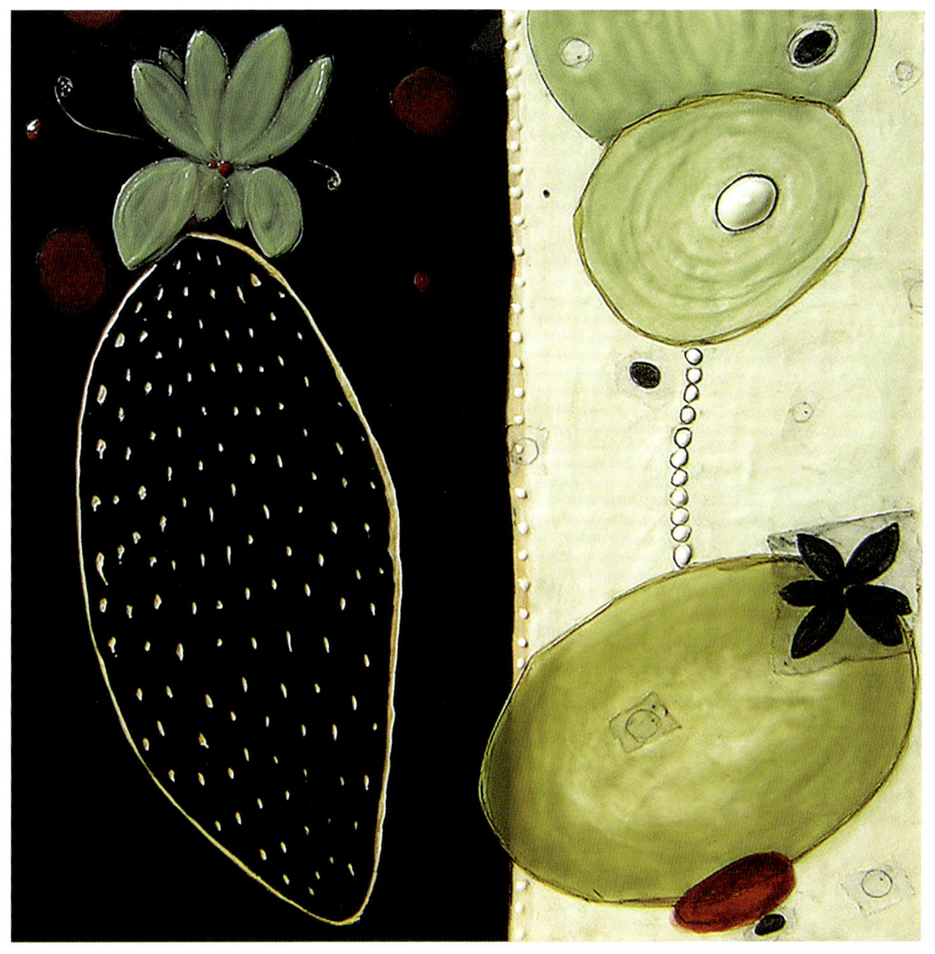

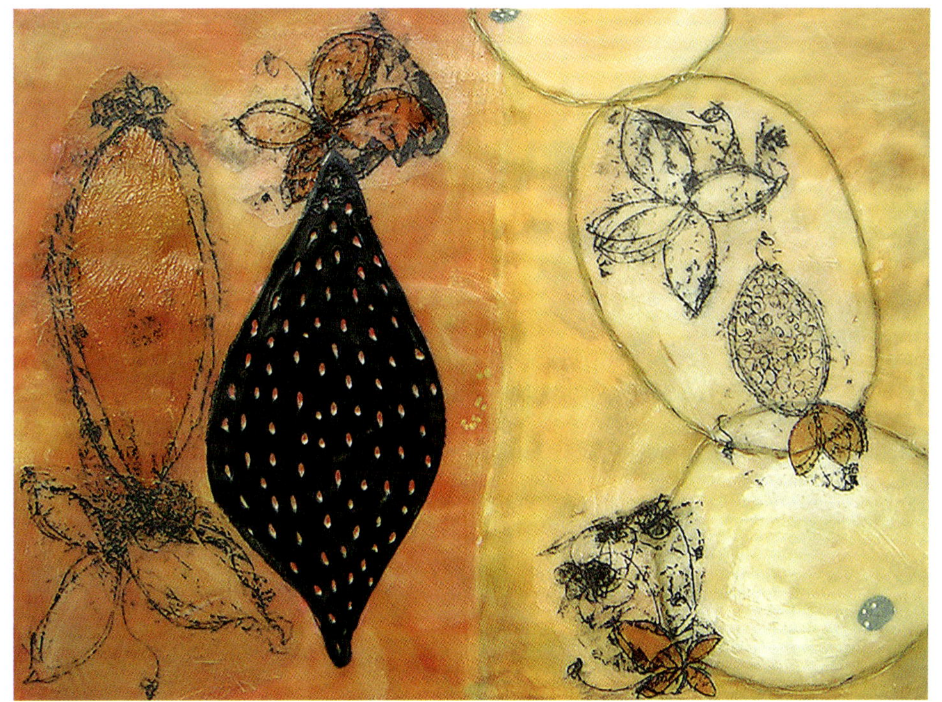

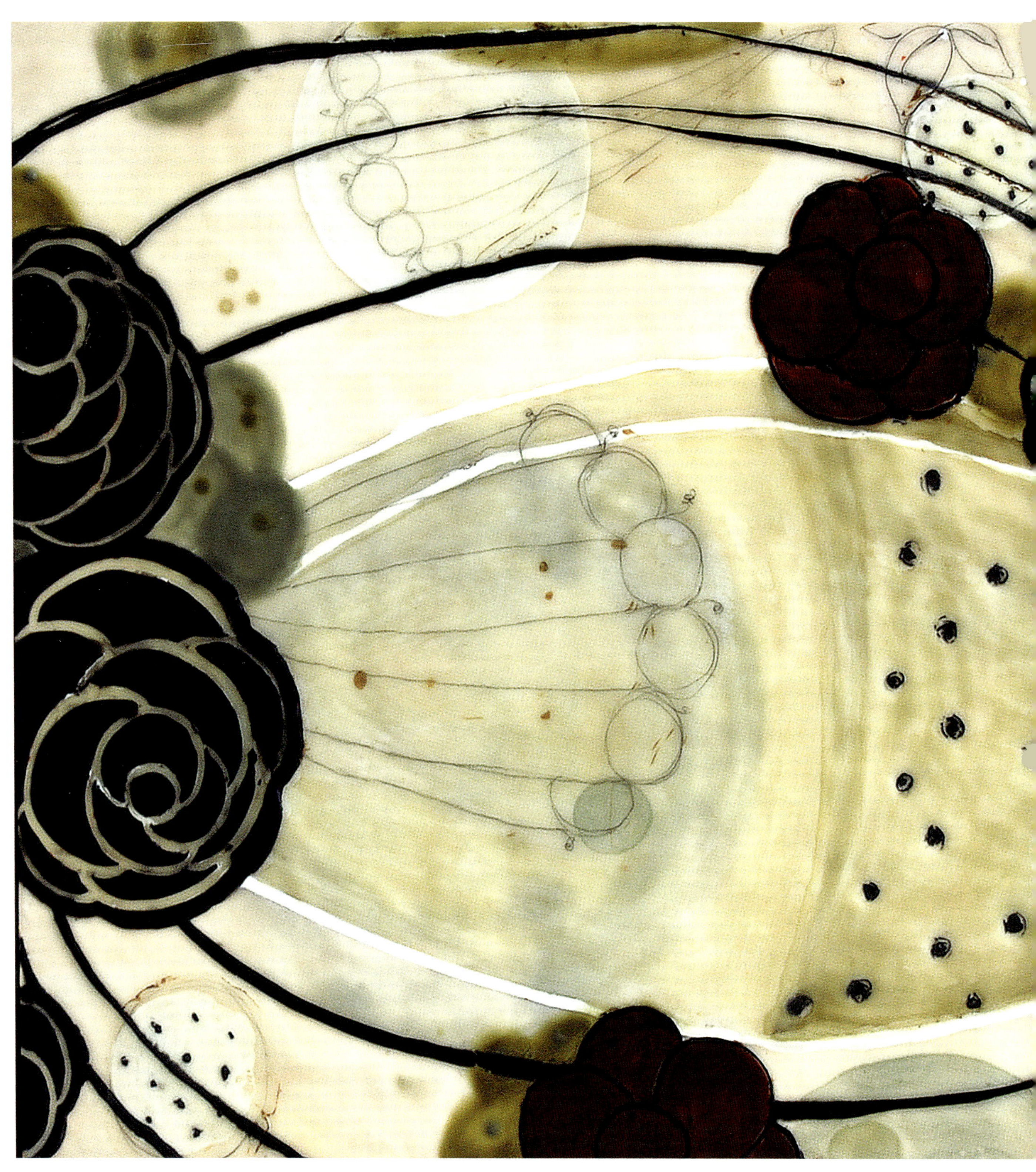

Stephanie Hargrave, *Balance 26*, 2009. Encaustic, 60.9 x 121.9 cm.

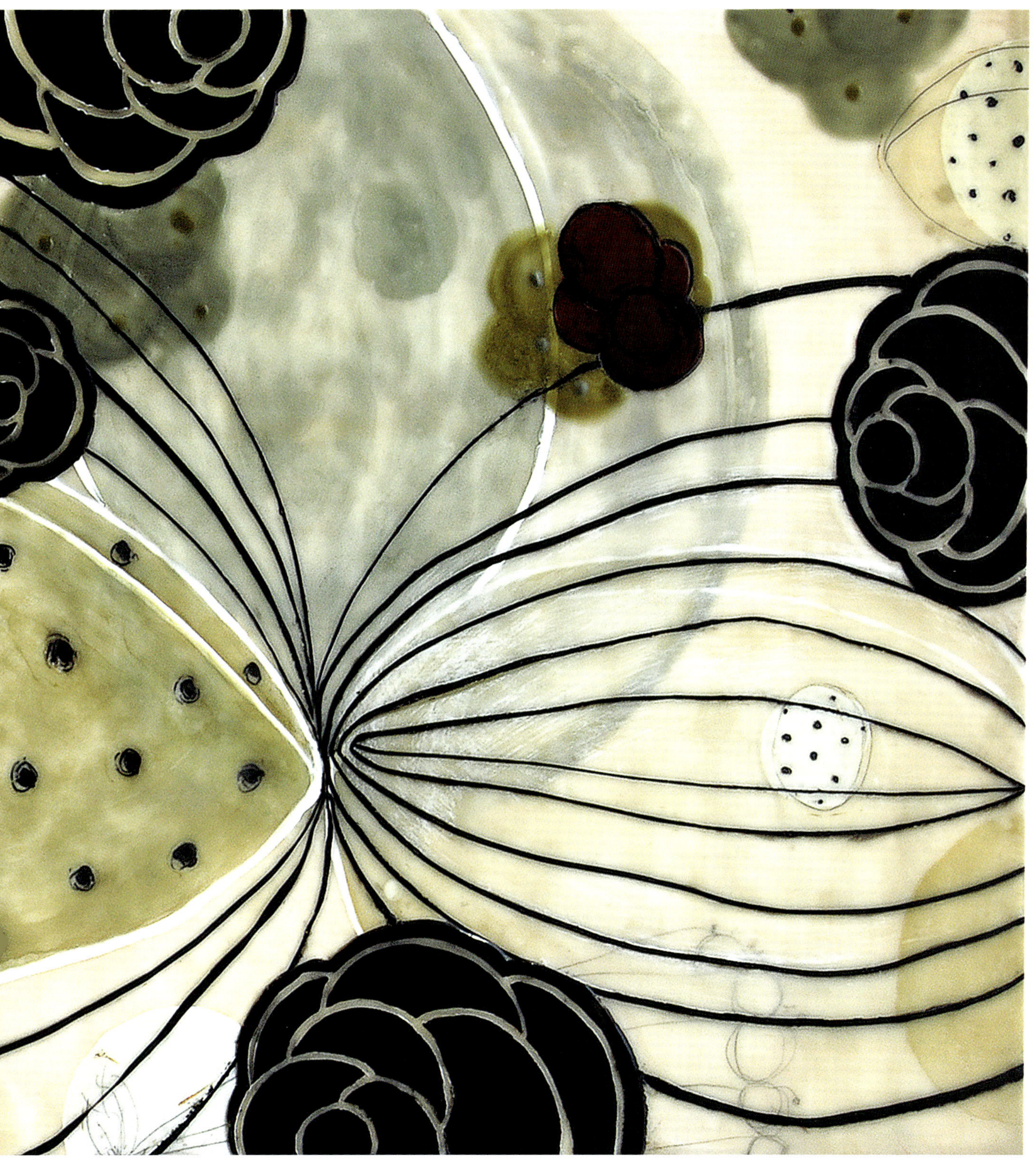

Lorraine Glessner

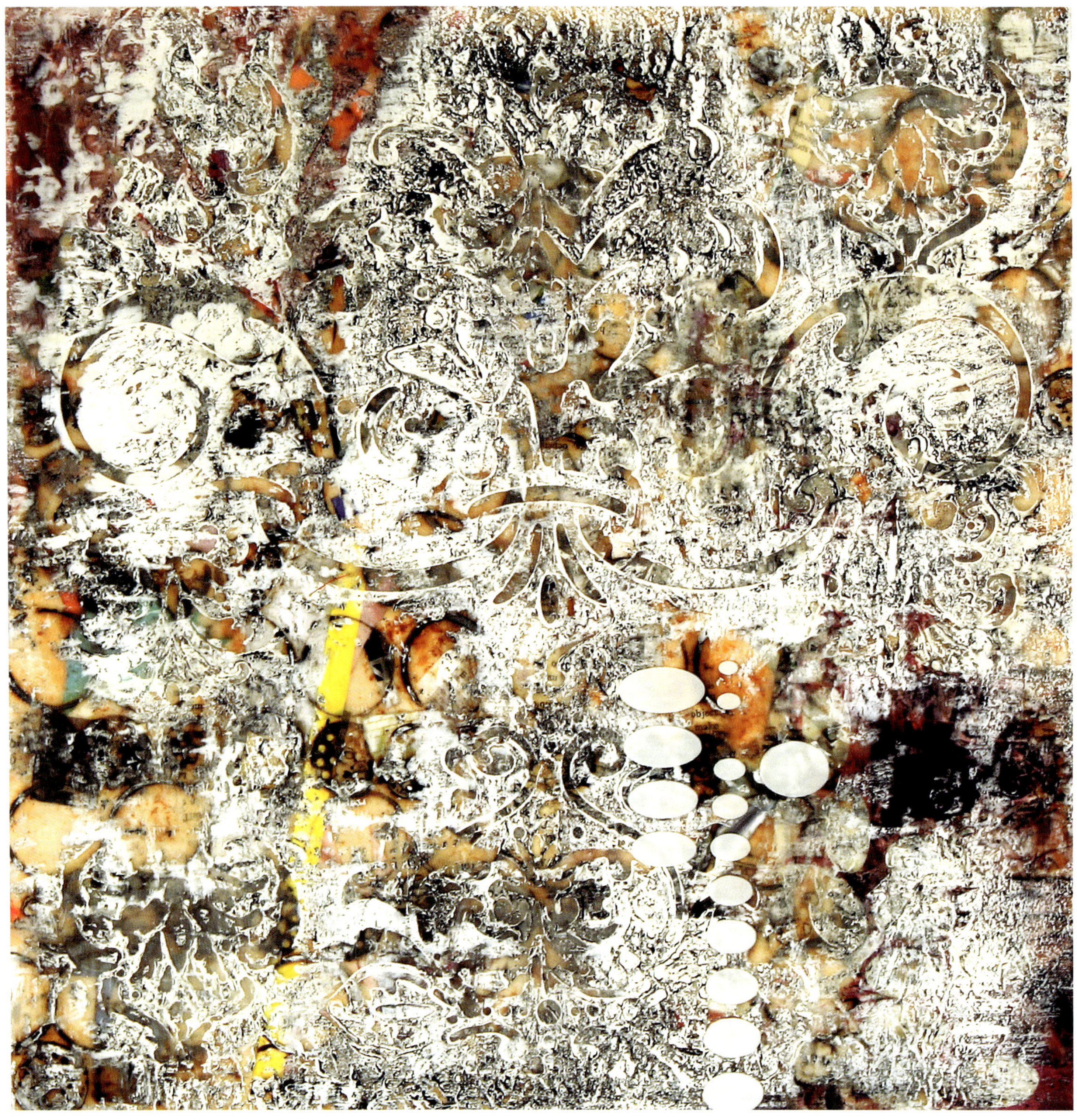

Lorraine Glessner, *Rows: Bank*, 2010.
Encaustic, horse and human hair, collage, mixed media on rusted and branded silk on wood, 40.6 x 40.6 x 2.5 cm.

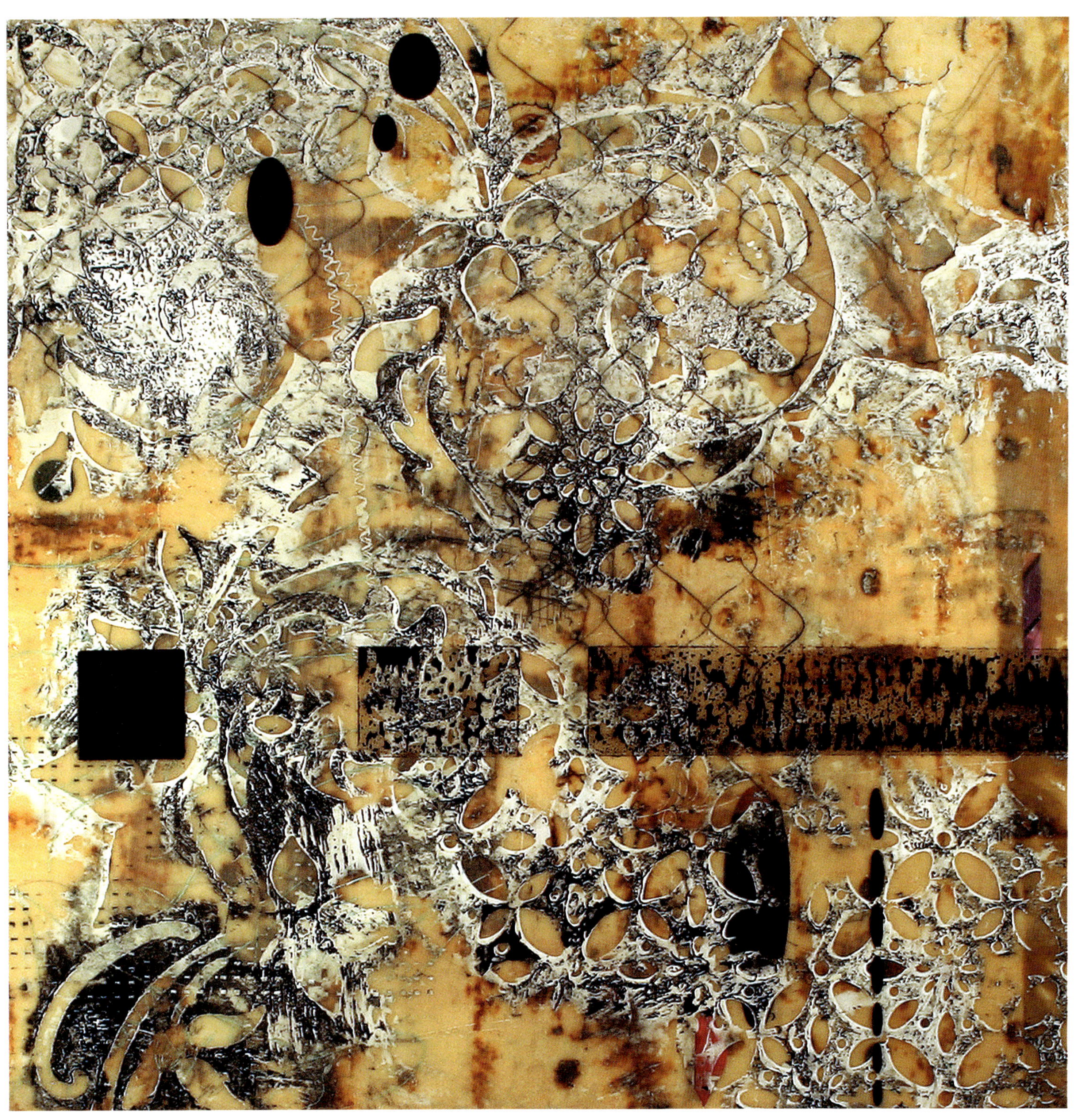

Lorraine Glessner, *Rows: Painted Lady 2*, 2010.
Encaustic, horse and human hair, collage, mixed media on rusted and branded rayon on wood, 40.6 x 40.6 x 2.5 cm.

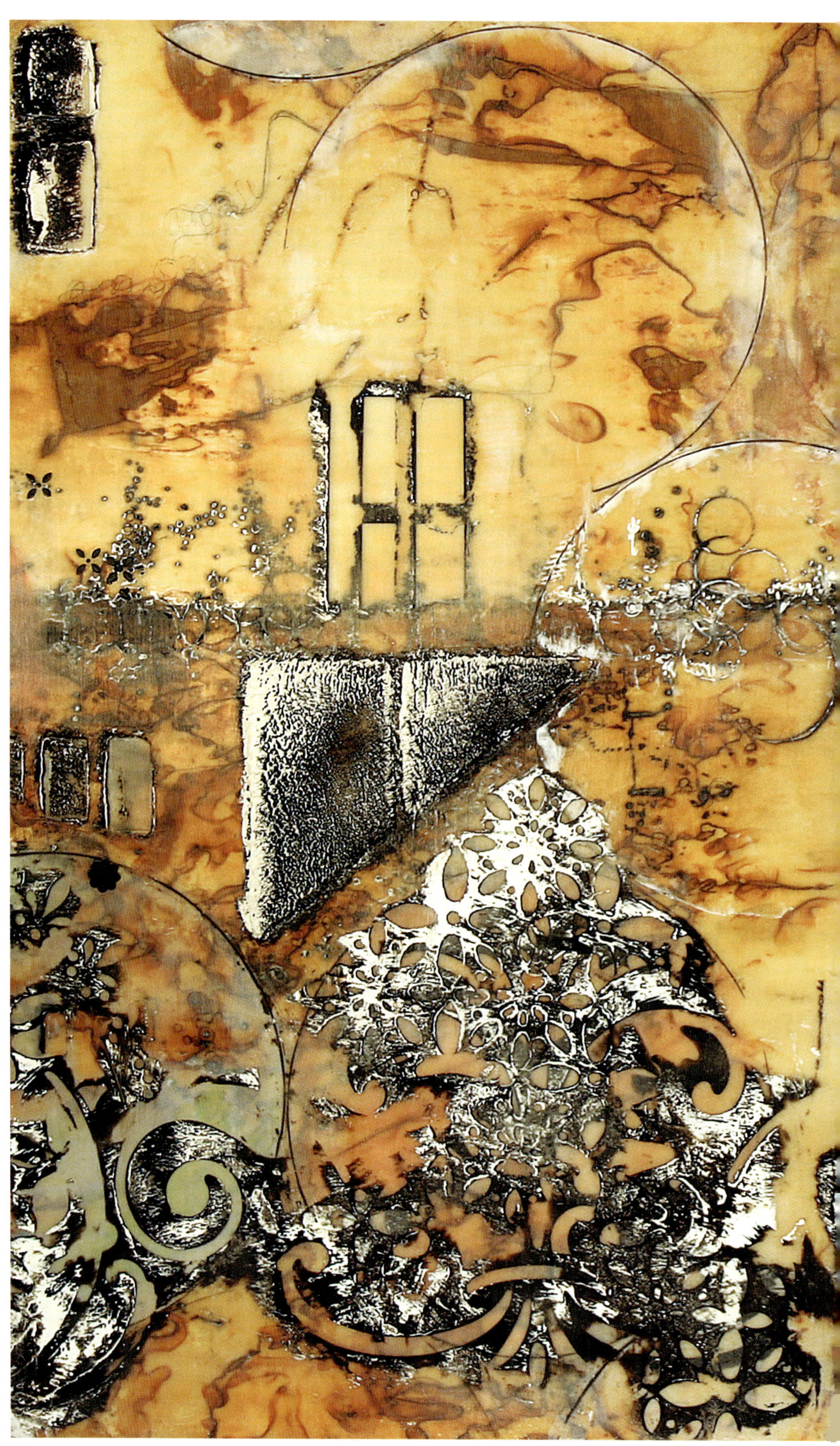

Lorraine Glessner, *Rows: Down Fifth Street Desert 2*, 2010.
Encaustic, horse and human hair, collage, mixed media on rusted and branded rayon on wood, 60.9 x 91.4 x 3.8 cm.

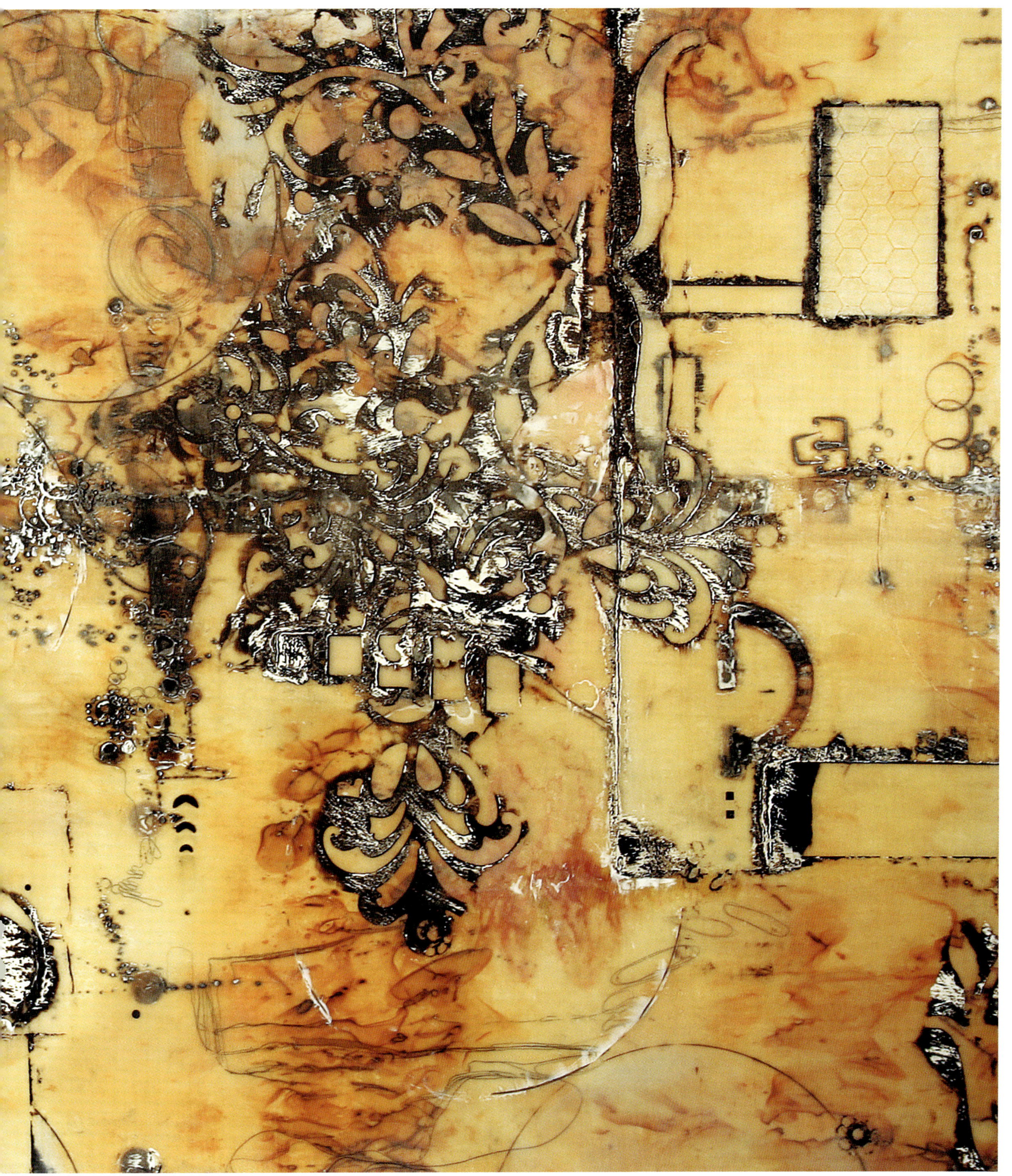

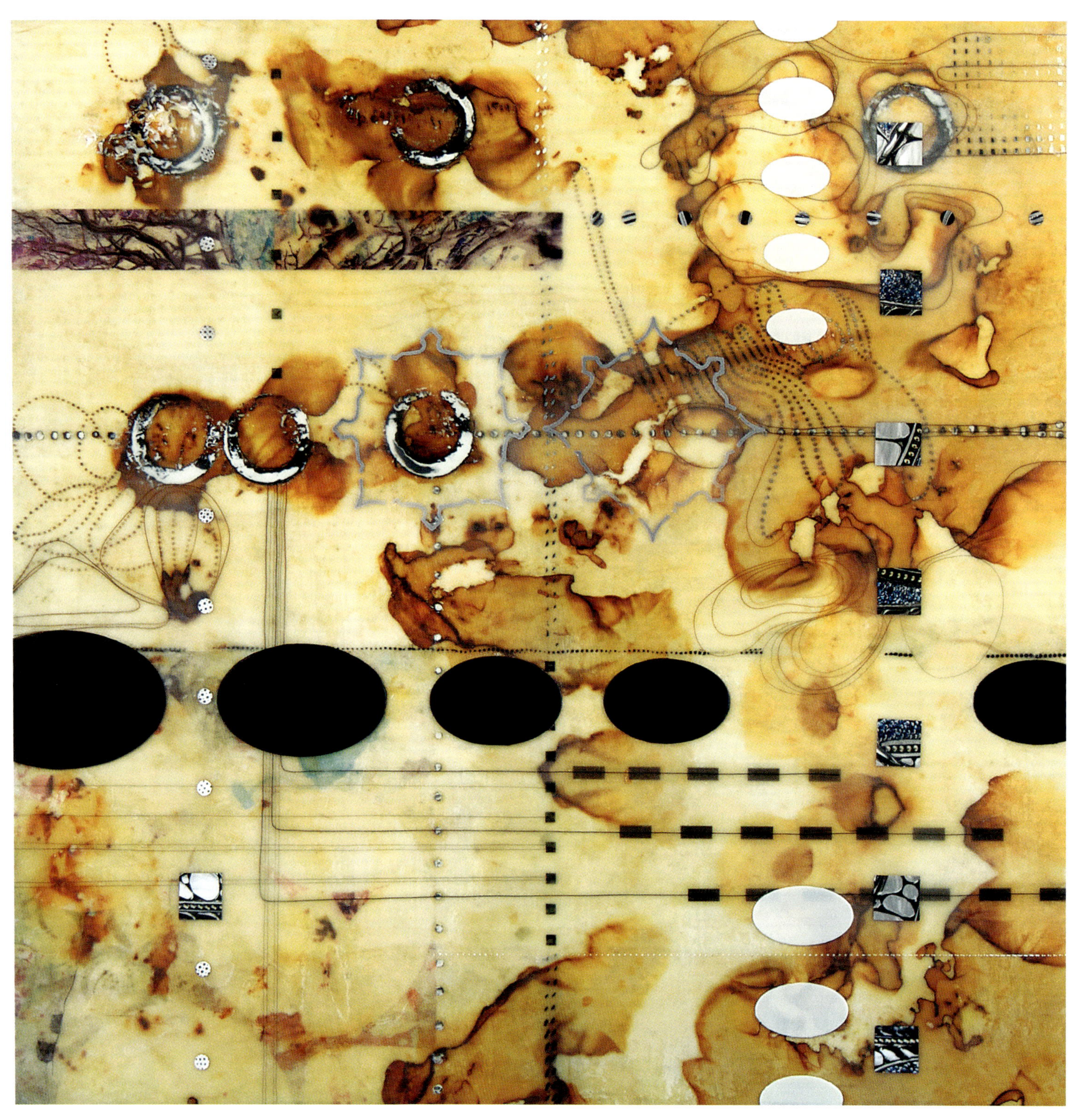

Lorraine Glessner, *Down Sixth Street: Window*, 2010.
Encaustic, horse and human hair, collage, mixed media on rusted and branded silk on wood, 45.7 x 45.7 x 2.5 cm.

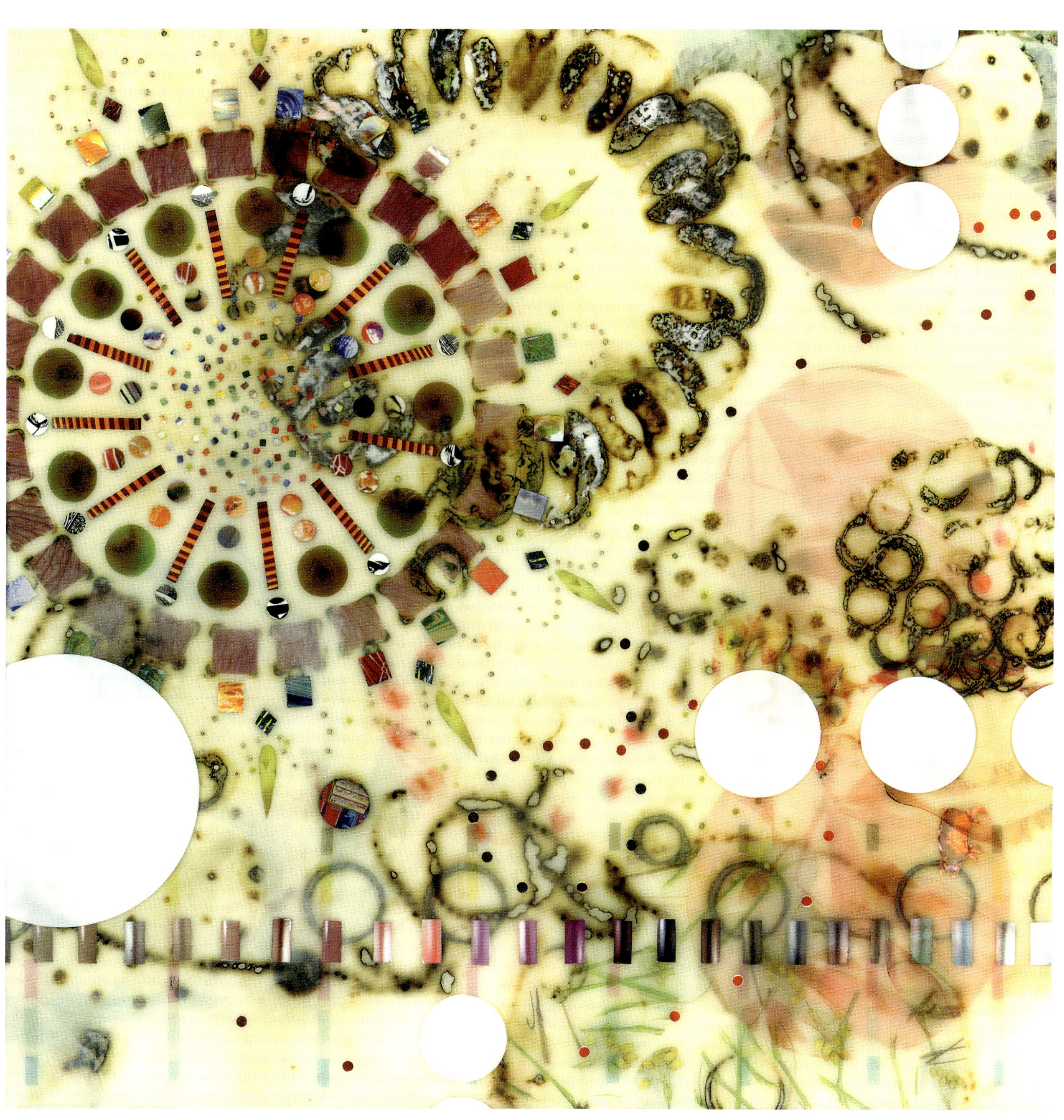

Lorraine Glessner, *Saccharine*, 2006.
Encaustic, digital prints, photographs, paper, oil paint on composted and branded silk on panel, 30.4 x 30.4 x 2.5 cm.

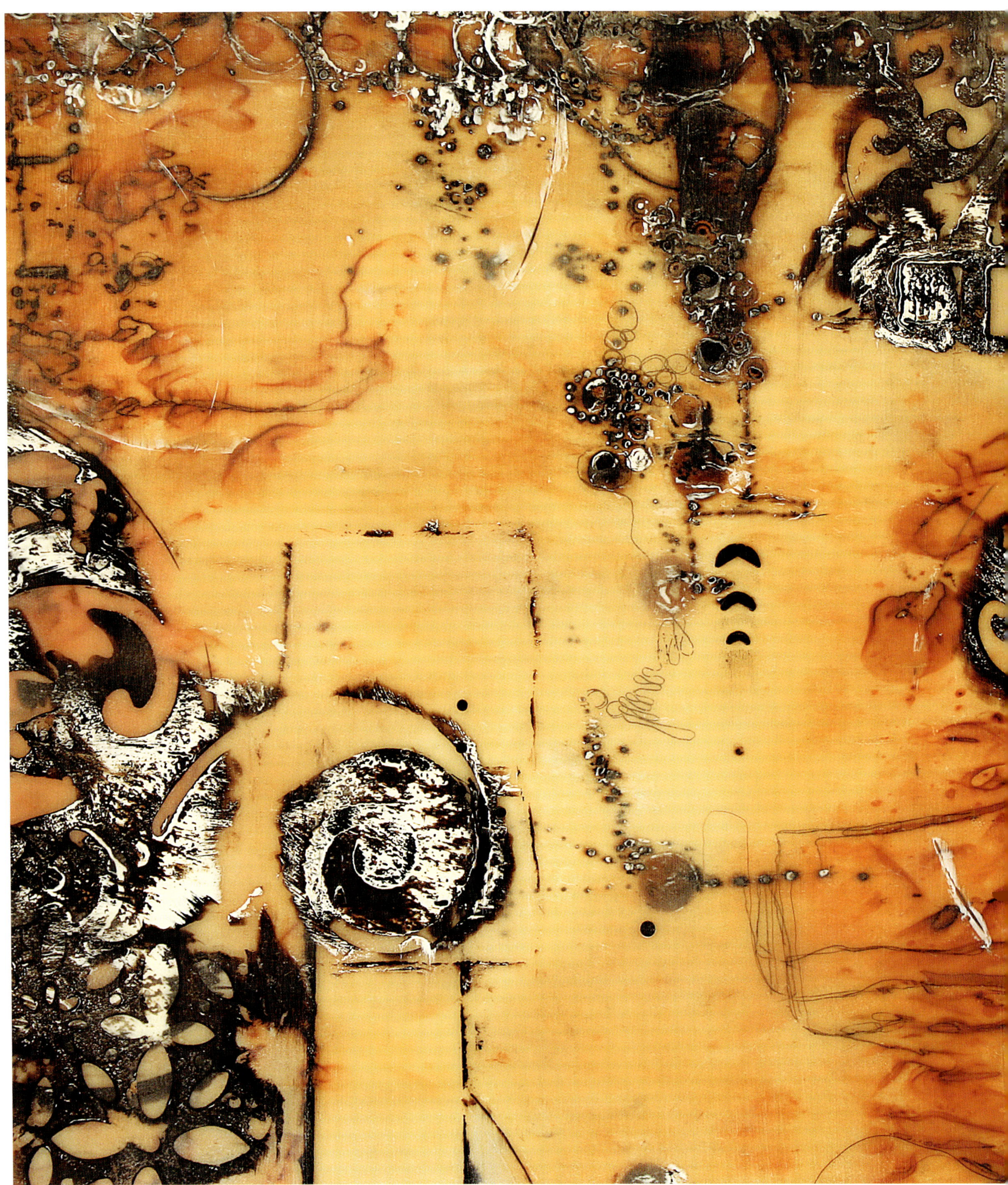

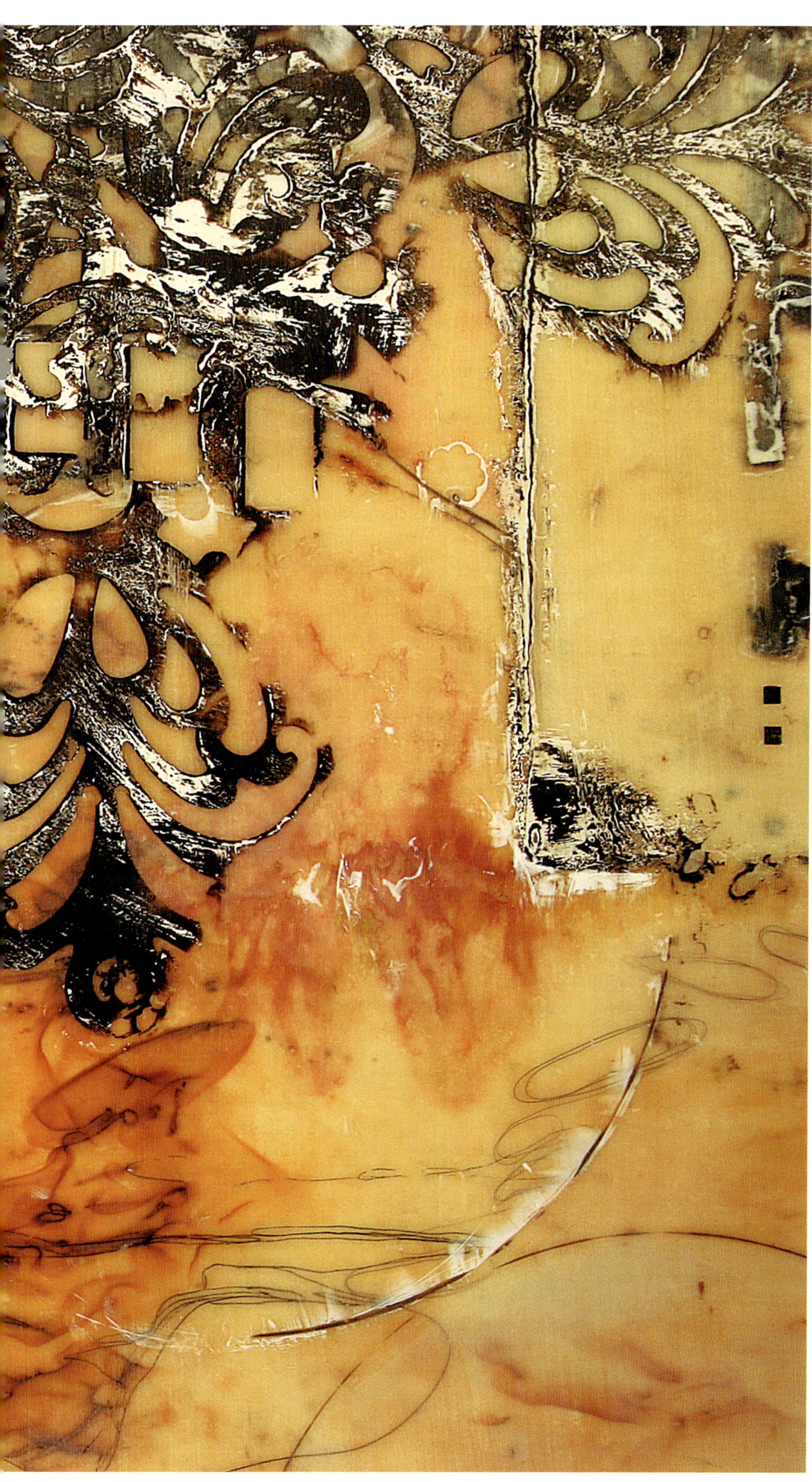

Lorraine Glessner, *Rows: Down Fifth Street Desert 2* (detail), 2010.
Encaustic, horse and human hair, collage, mixed media on rusted and branded rayon on wood, 60.9 x 91.4 x 3.8 cm.

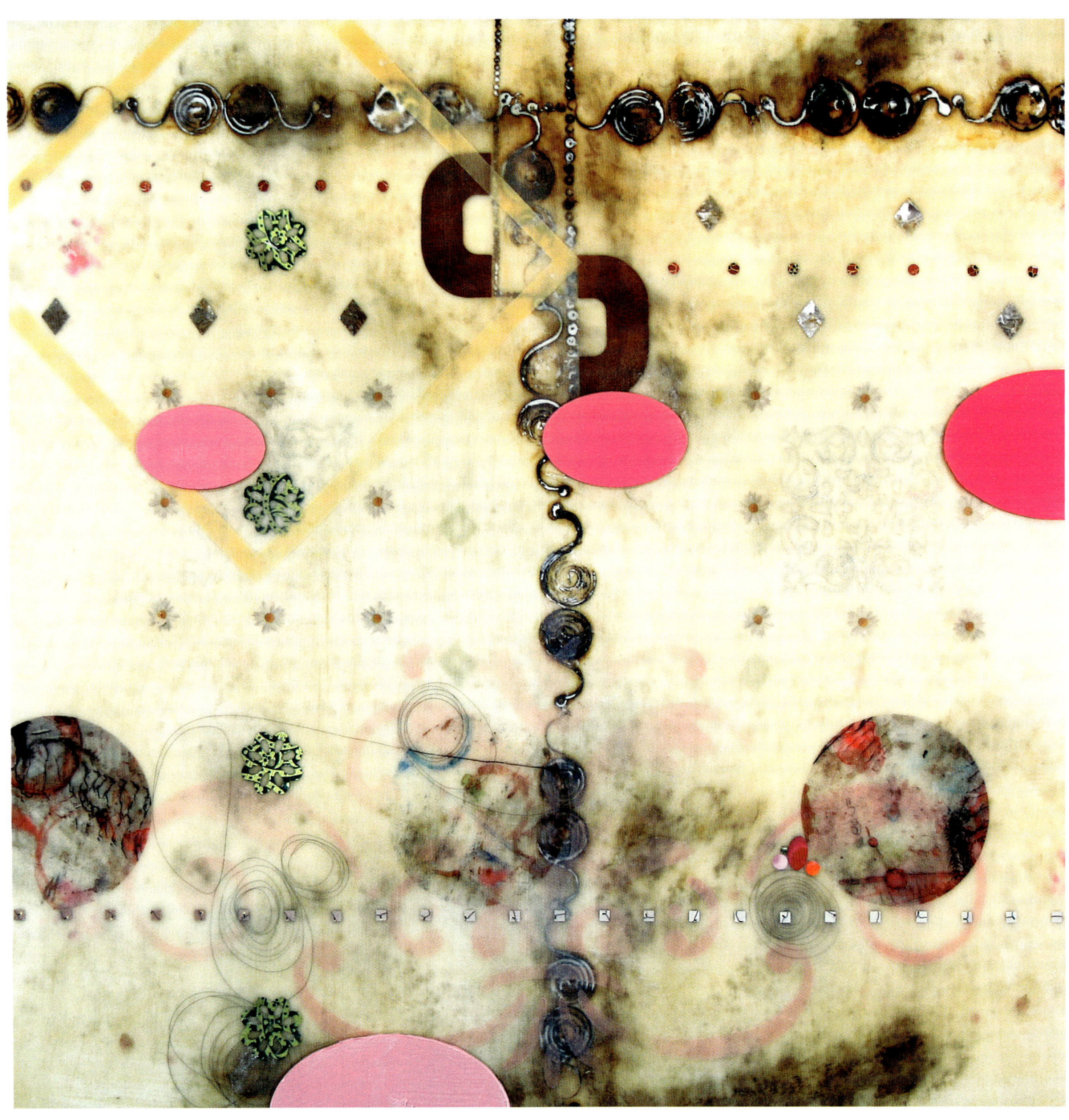

Lorraine Glessner, *Down Sixth Street: Fake Daisies*, 2010.
Encaustic, horse and human hair, collage, mixed media on rusted and branded silk on wood, 45.7 x 45.7 x 2.5 cm.

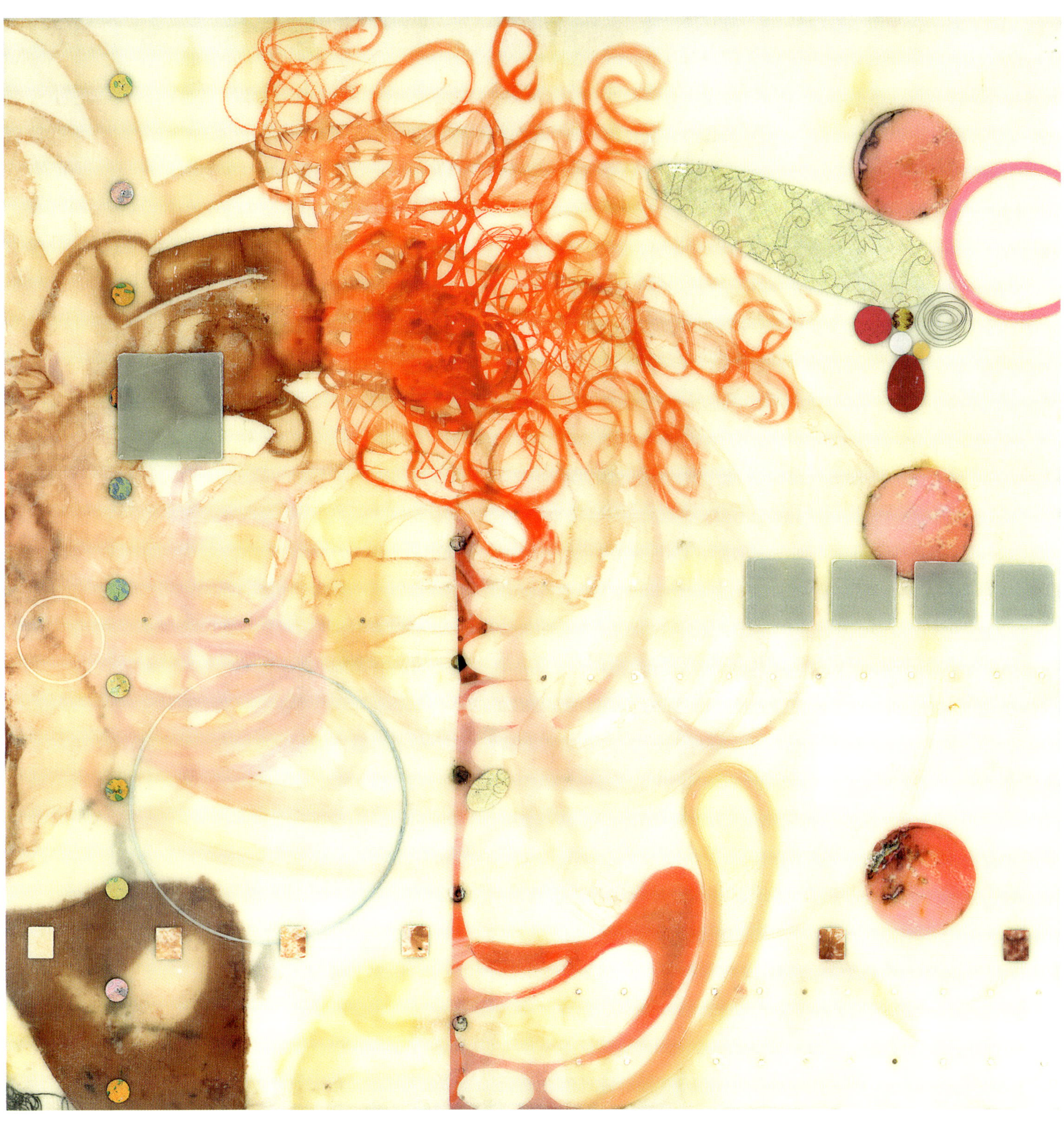

Lorraine Glessner, *Red Flower Box,* 2008.
Encaustic, horse and human hair, mixed media on composted and branded silk on wood, 30.4 x 30.4 x 2.5 cm.

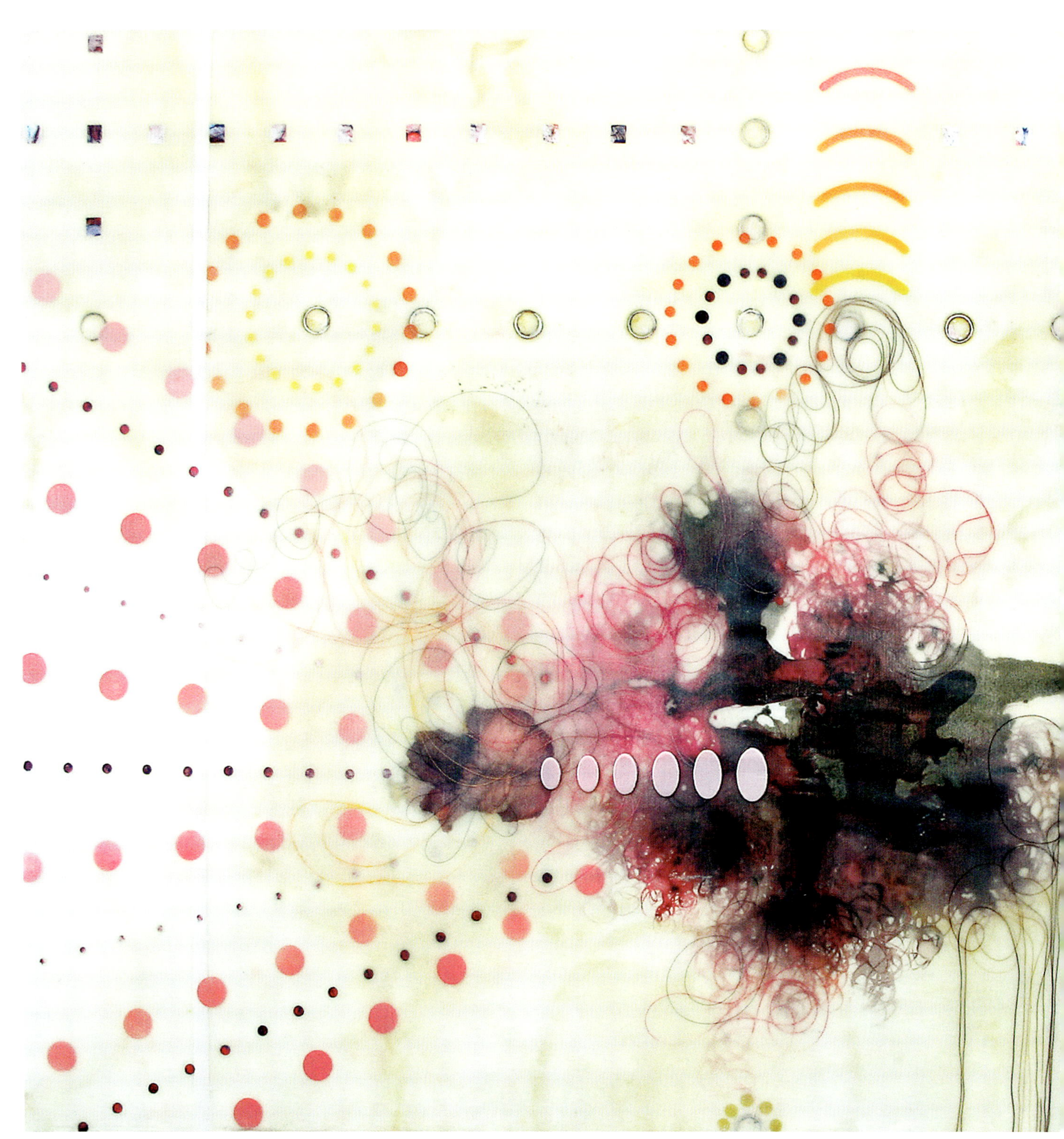

Lorraine Glessner, *How Much Time Do We Have?*, 2008.
Encaustic, horse and human hair, collage, mixed media on rusted and branded silk on wood, 50.8 x 101.6 x 2.5 cm.

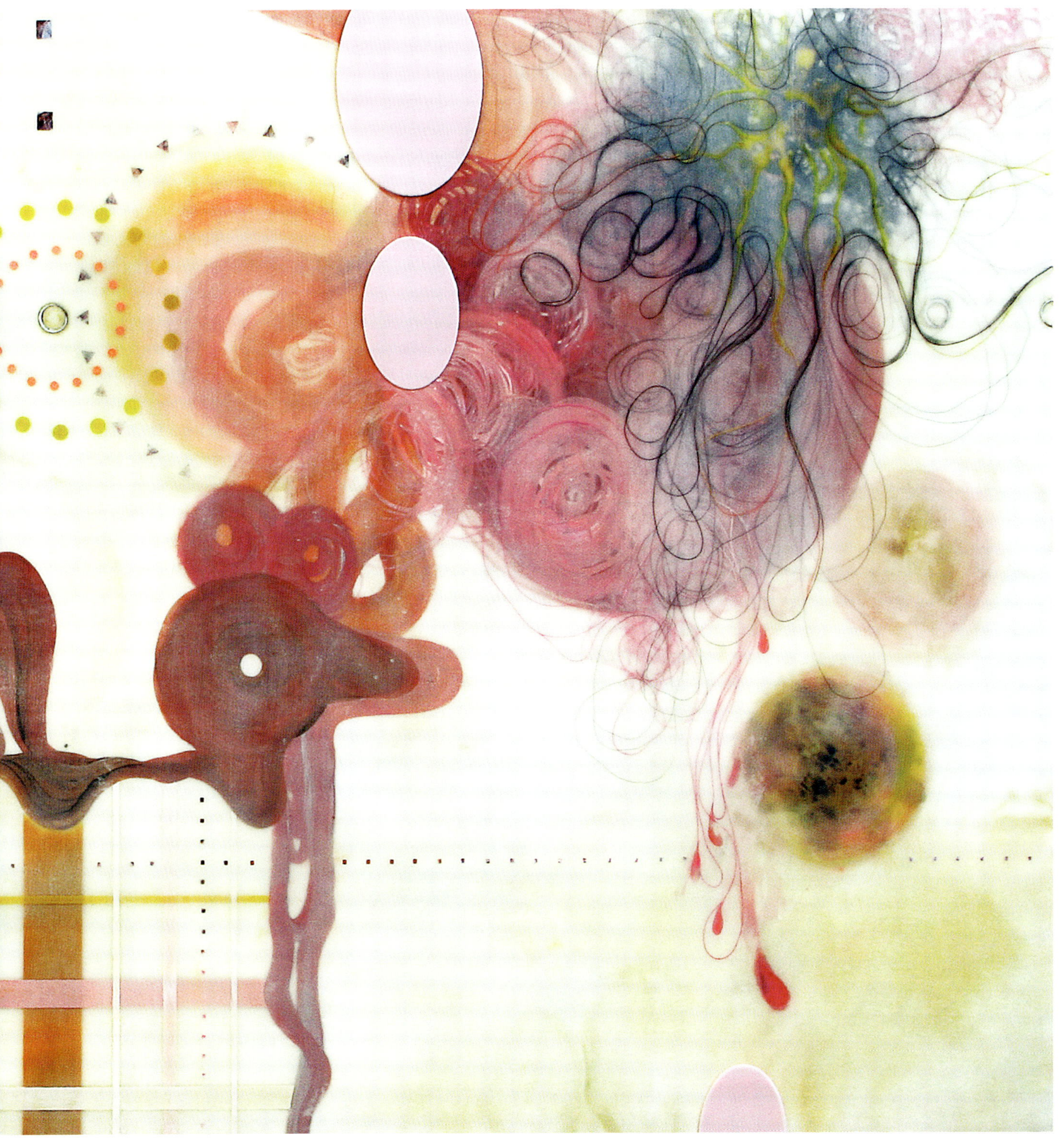

Adele Shaw

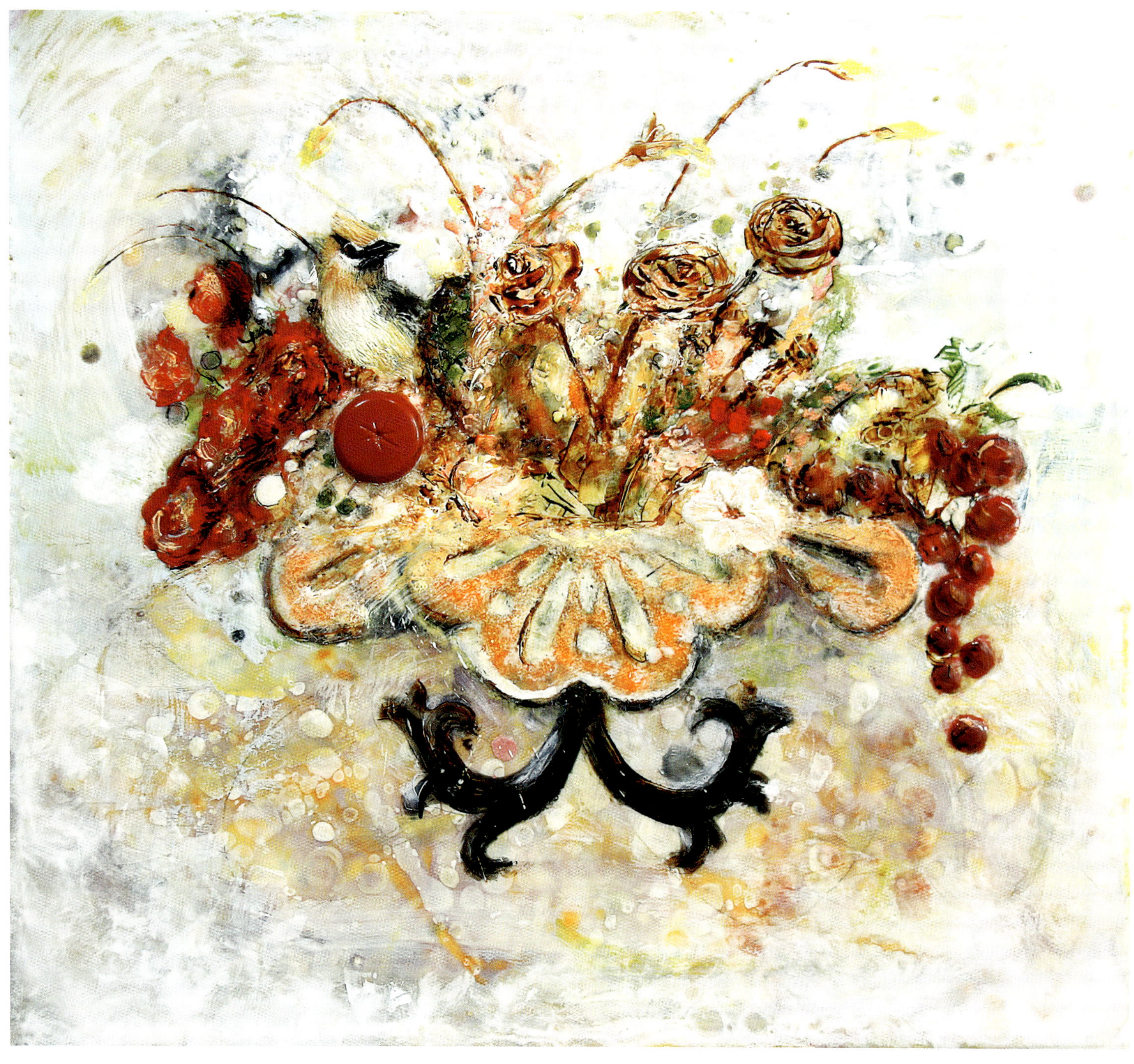

Adele Shaw, *Subtotal*, 2010.
Encaustic on wood, 40.6 x 50.8 cm.

Adele Shaw, *Sugar Bowl*, 2010.
Encaustic on wood, 45.7 x 81.2 cm.

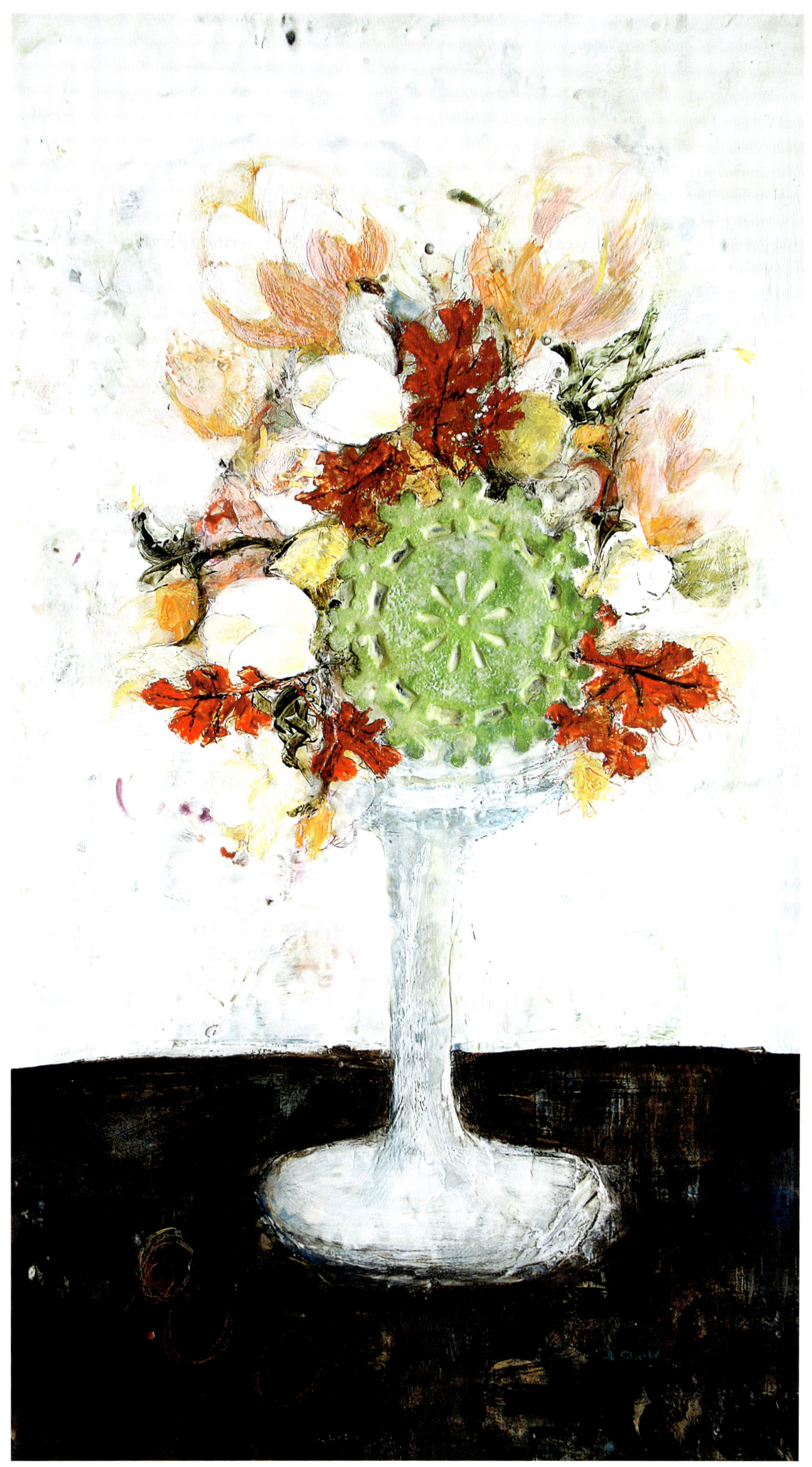

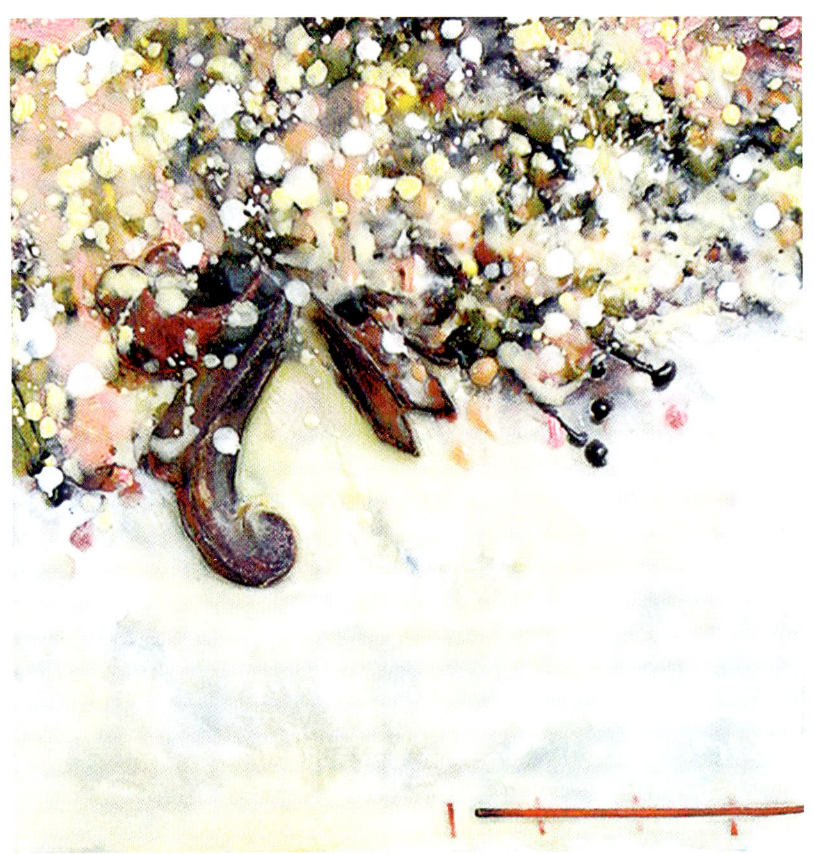

Adele Shaw, *Beaucoup Study #1*, 2009.
Encaustic on board, 20.3 x 20.3 cm.

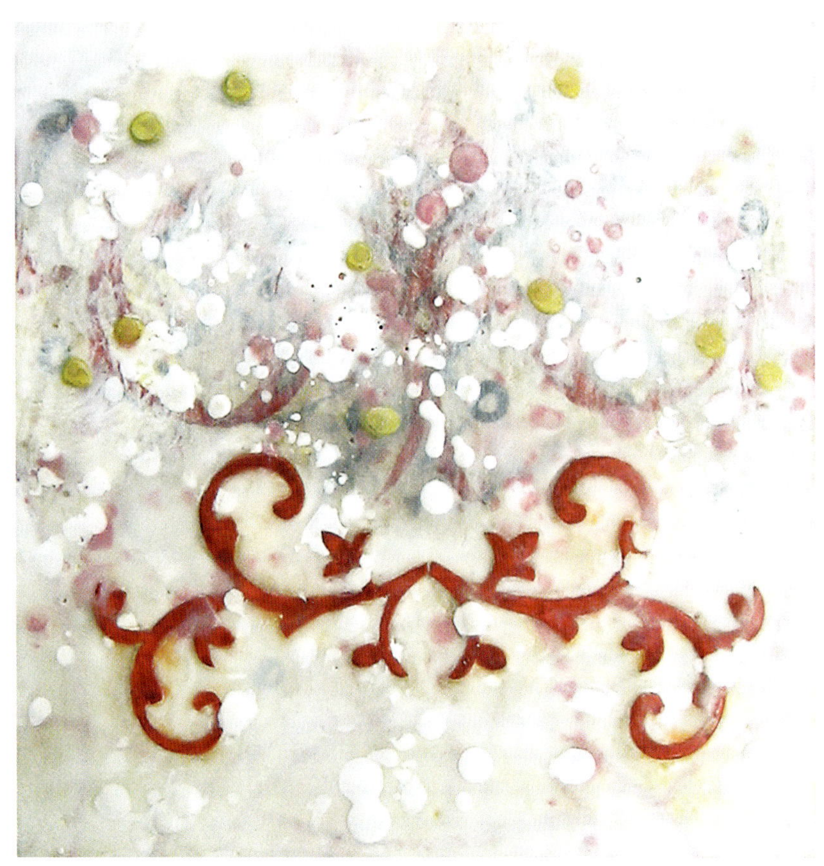

Adele Shaw, *Beaucoup Study #4*, 2010.
Encaustic on board, 20.3 x 20.3 cm.

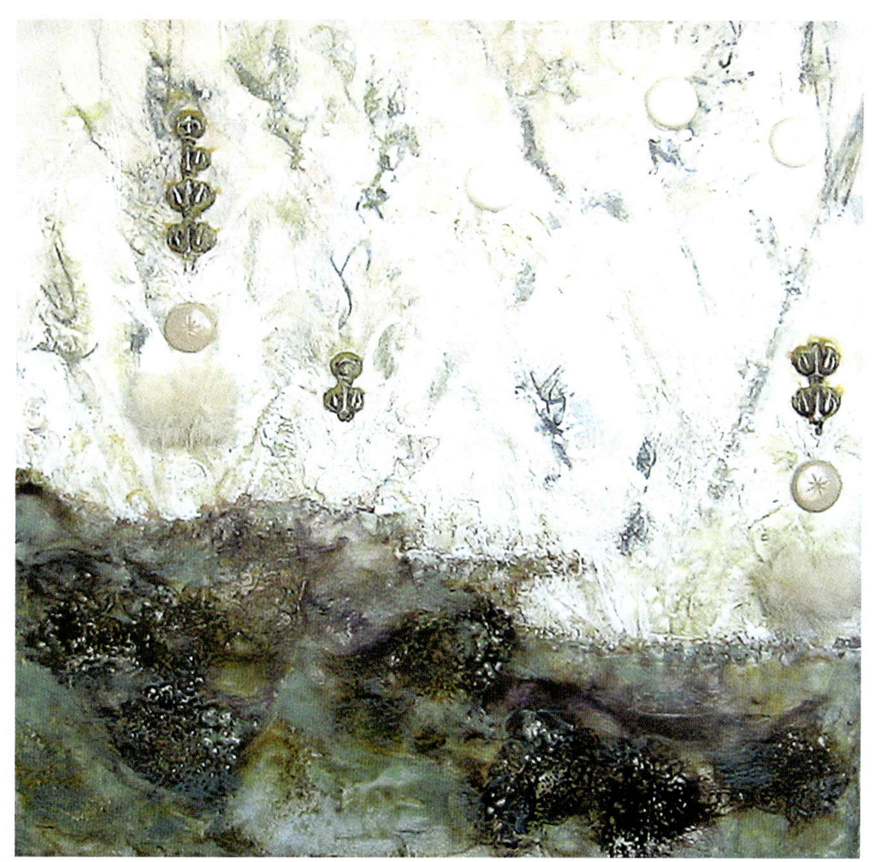

Adele Shaw, *This Occasion*, 2008.
Encaustic on board, 60.9 x 60.9 cm.

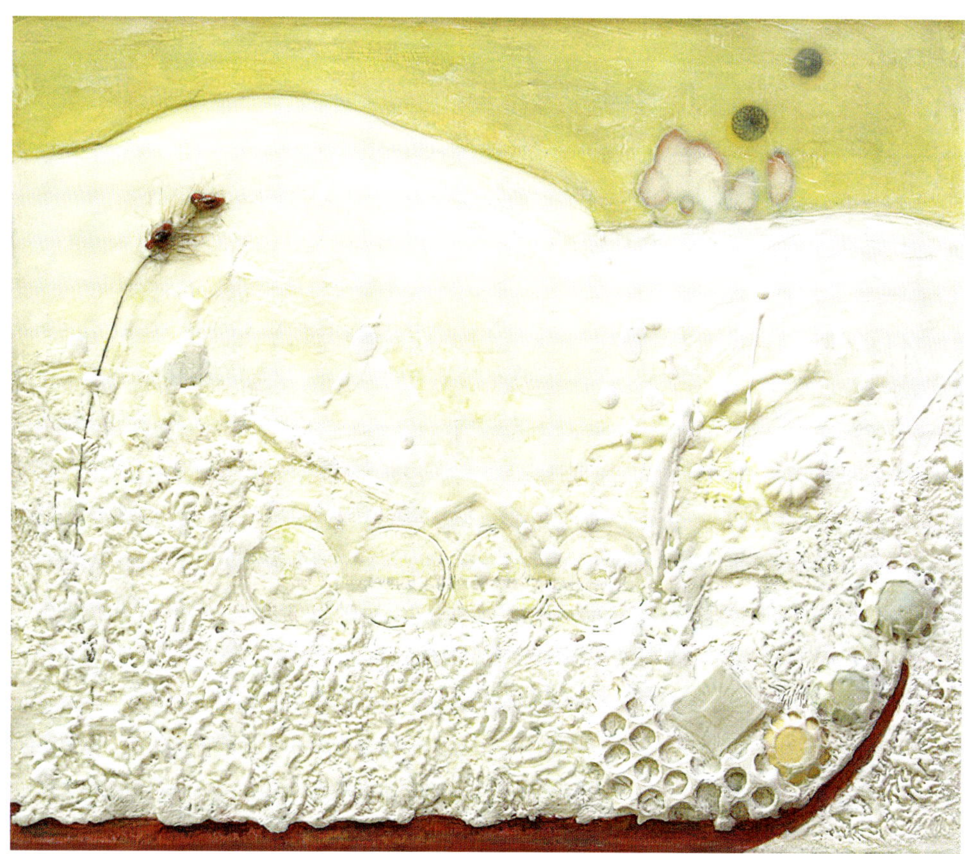

Adele Shaw, *A Matter of Small Things*, 2008.
Encaustic on board, 30.4 x 35.5 cm.

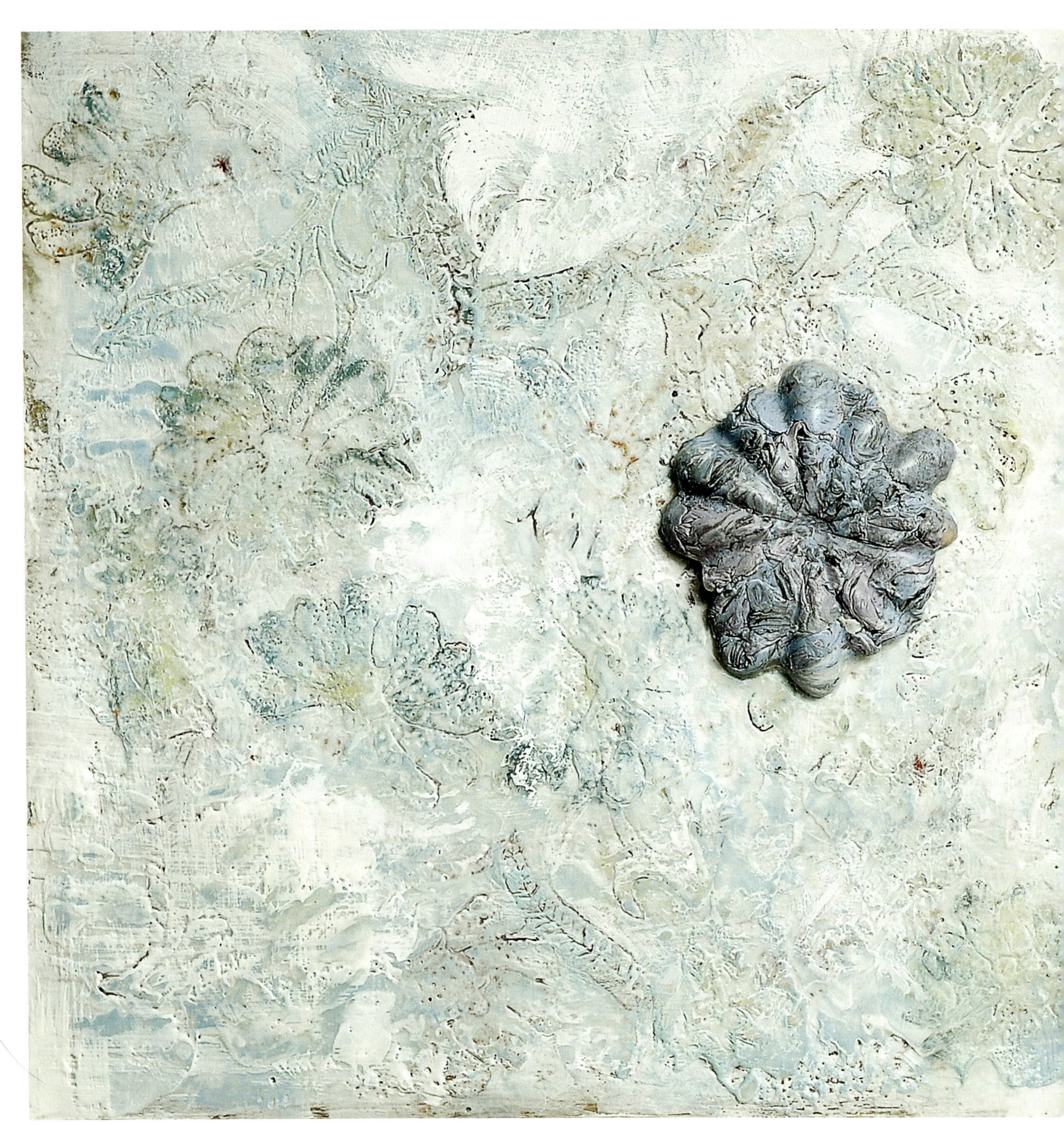

Adele Shaw, *Nature Could*, 2008. Encaustic on wood, 81.2 x 40.6 cm.

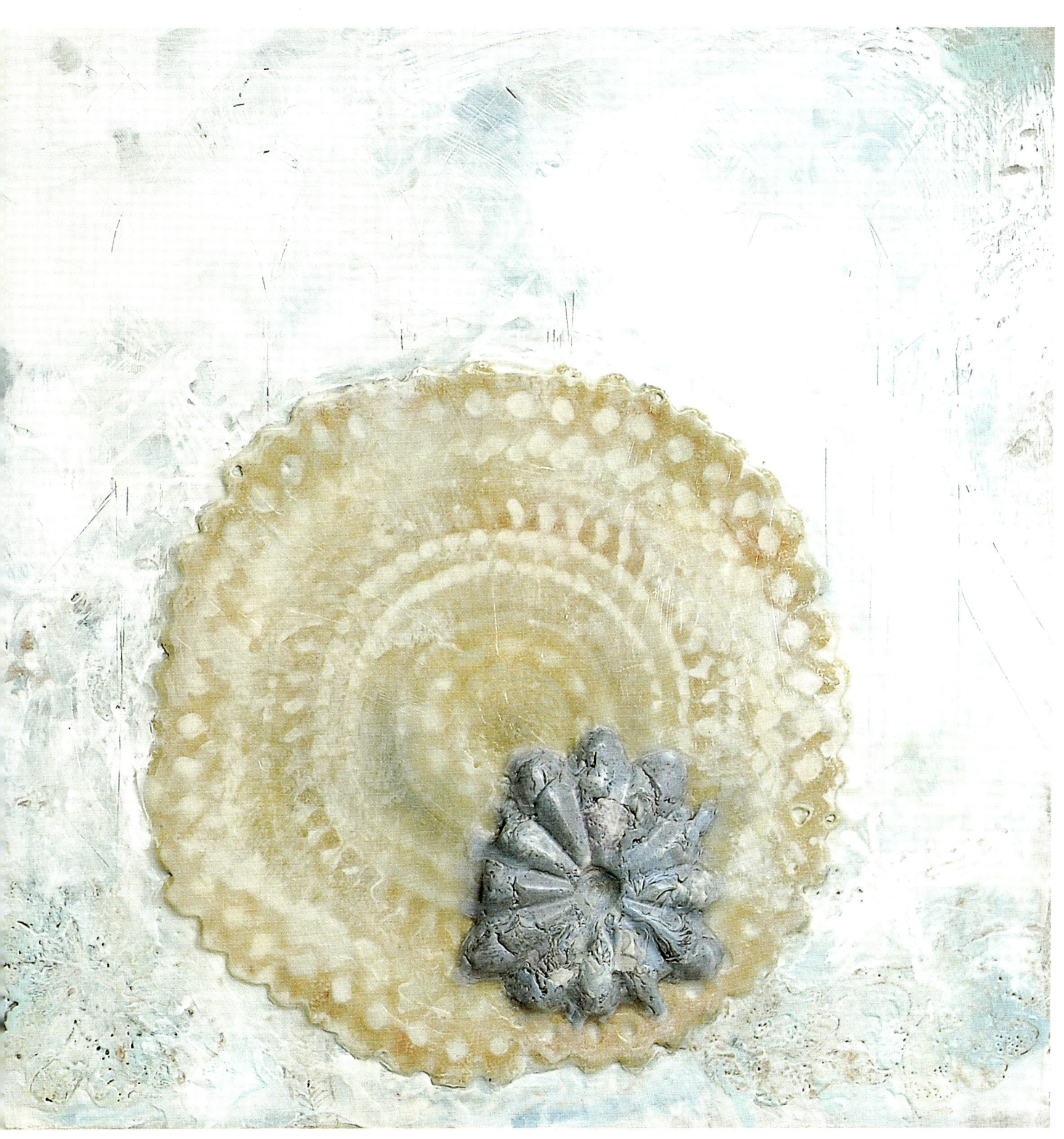

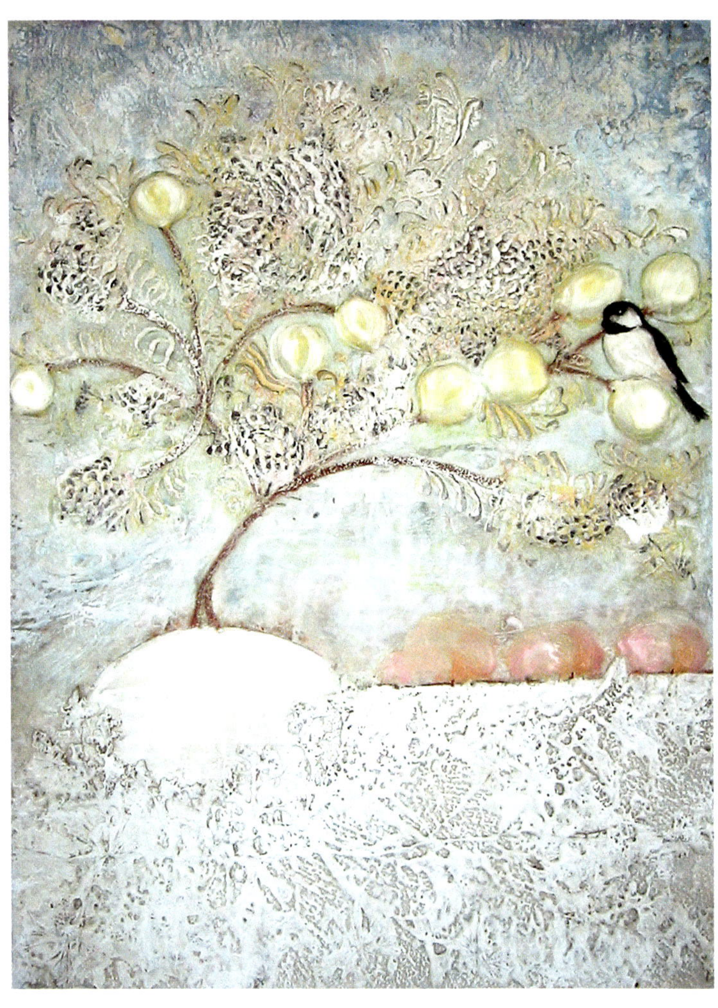

Adele Shaw, *This Hill*, 2008.
Encaustic on wood, 45.7 x 60.9 cm.

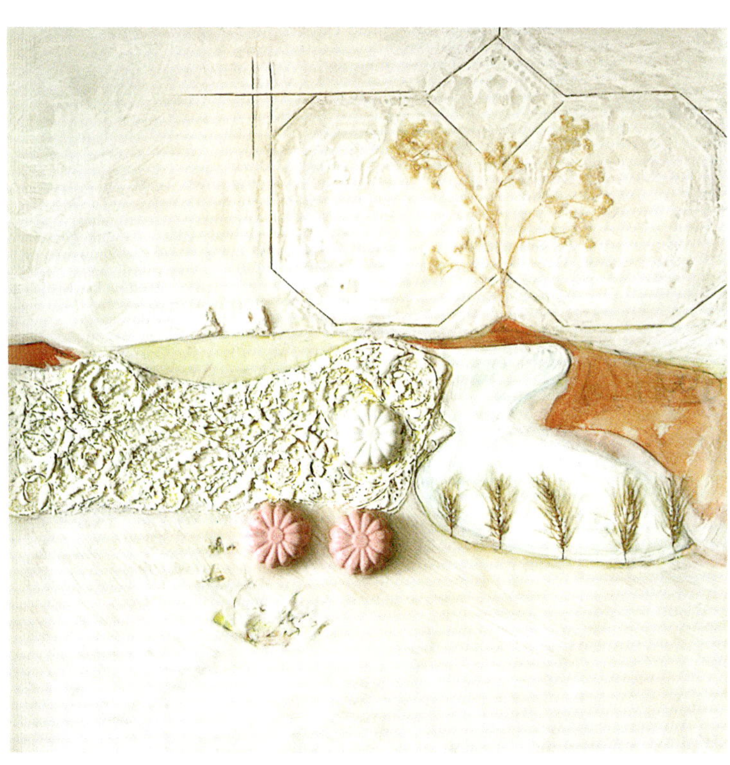

Adele Shaw, *This Praise*, 2008.
Encaustic on board, 30.4 x 30.4 cm.

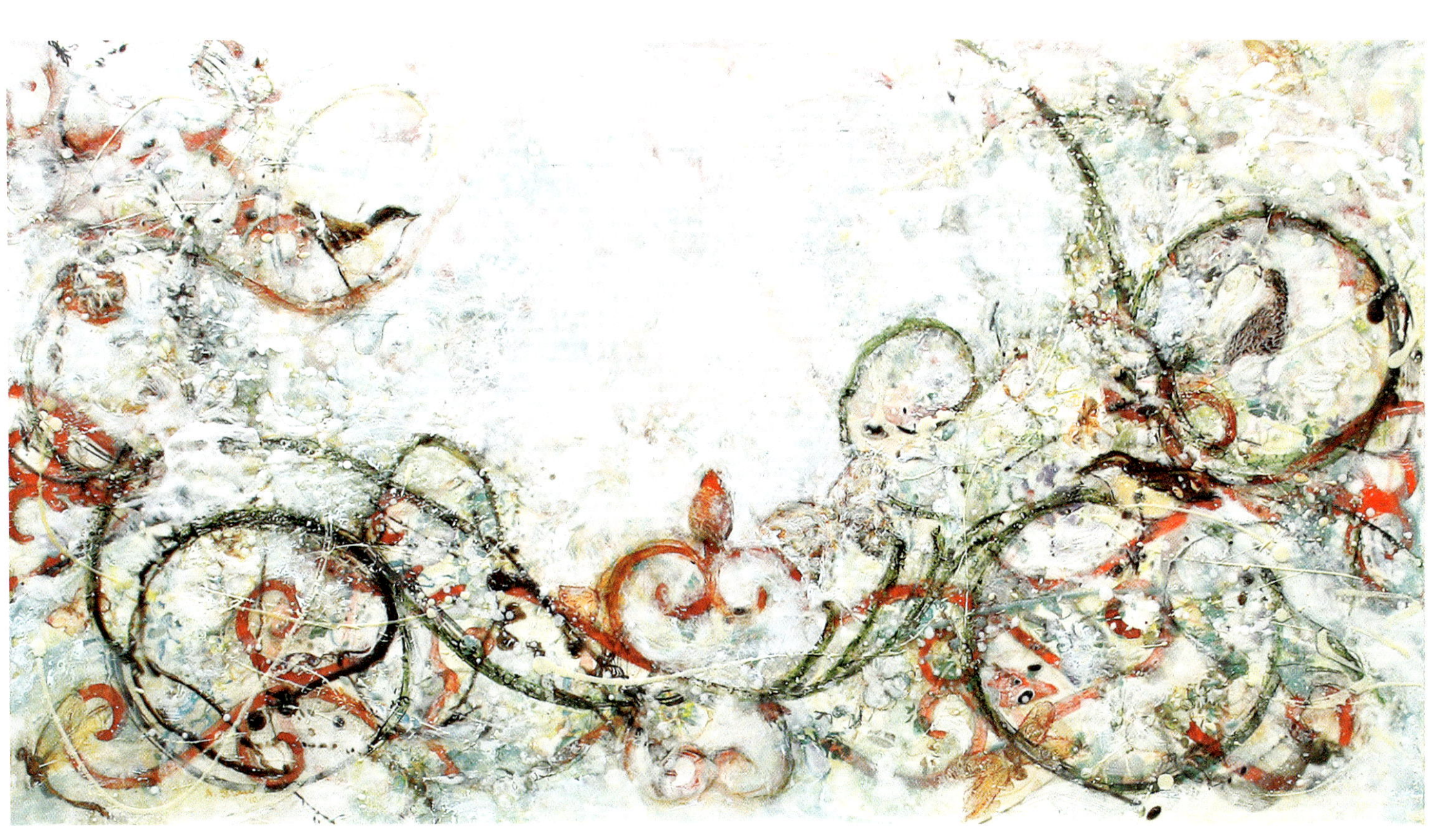

Adele Shaw, *Portal 1*, 2010. Encaustic on board, 50.8 x 81.2 cm.

Debra Neiman

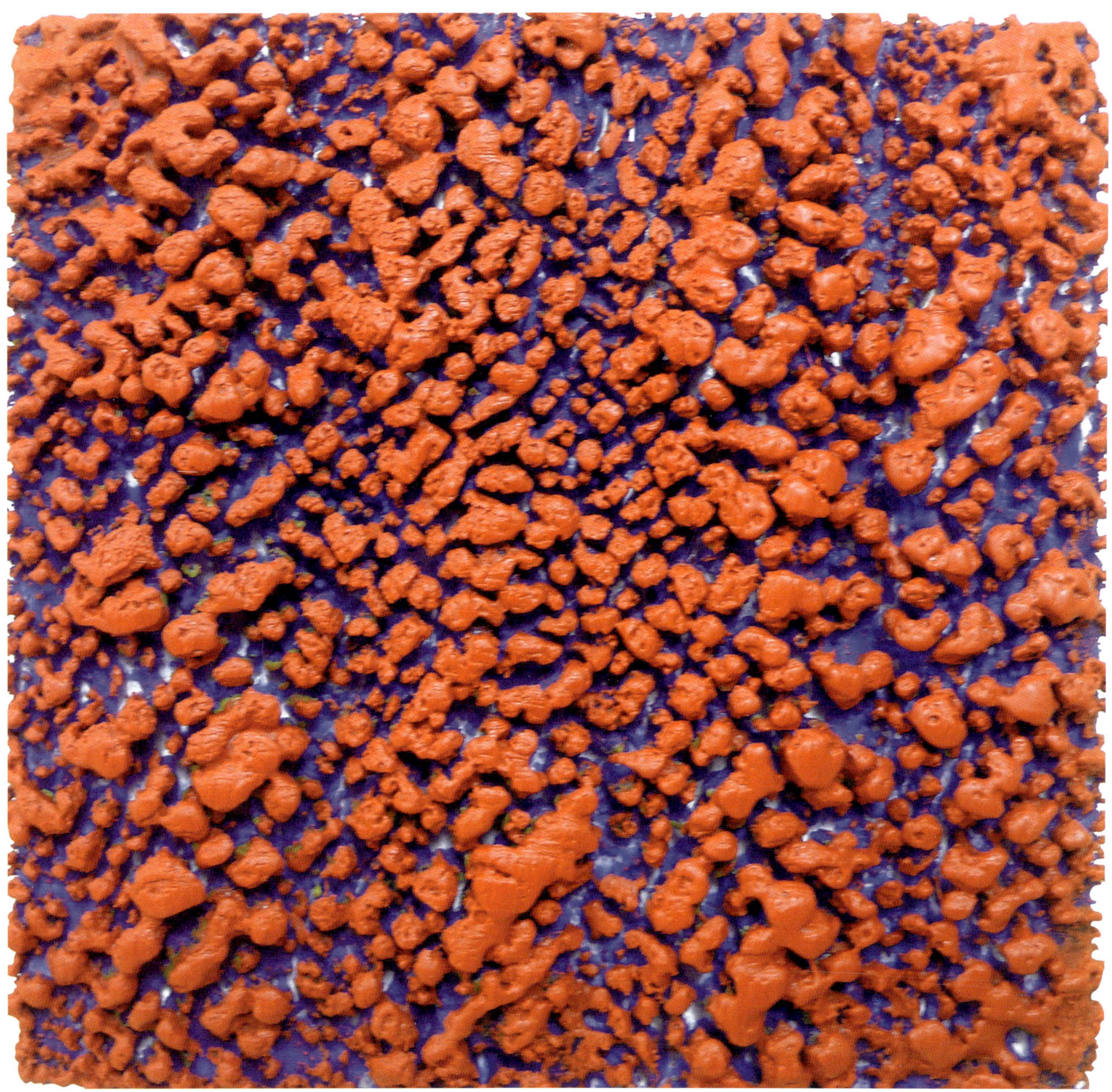

Debra Neiman, *Red Royal*, 2010. Encaustic on wood, 10.1 x 10.1 cm.

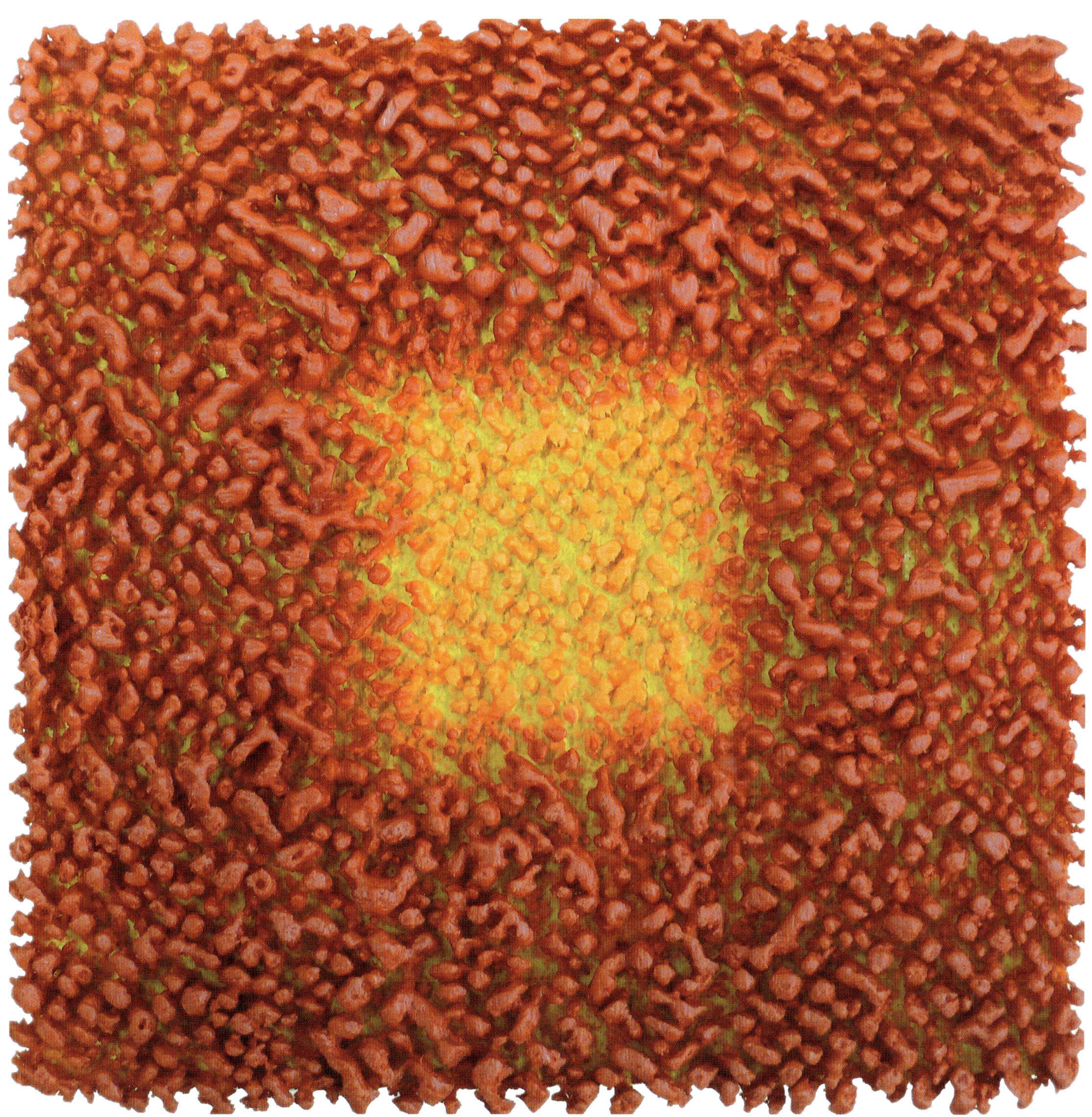

Debra Neiman, *Sunburst*, 2010. Encaustic on wood panel, 15.2 x 15.2 cm.

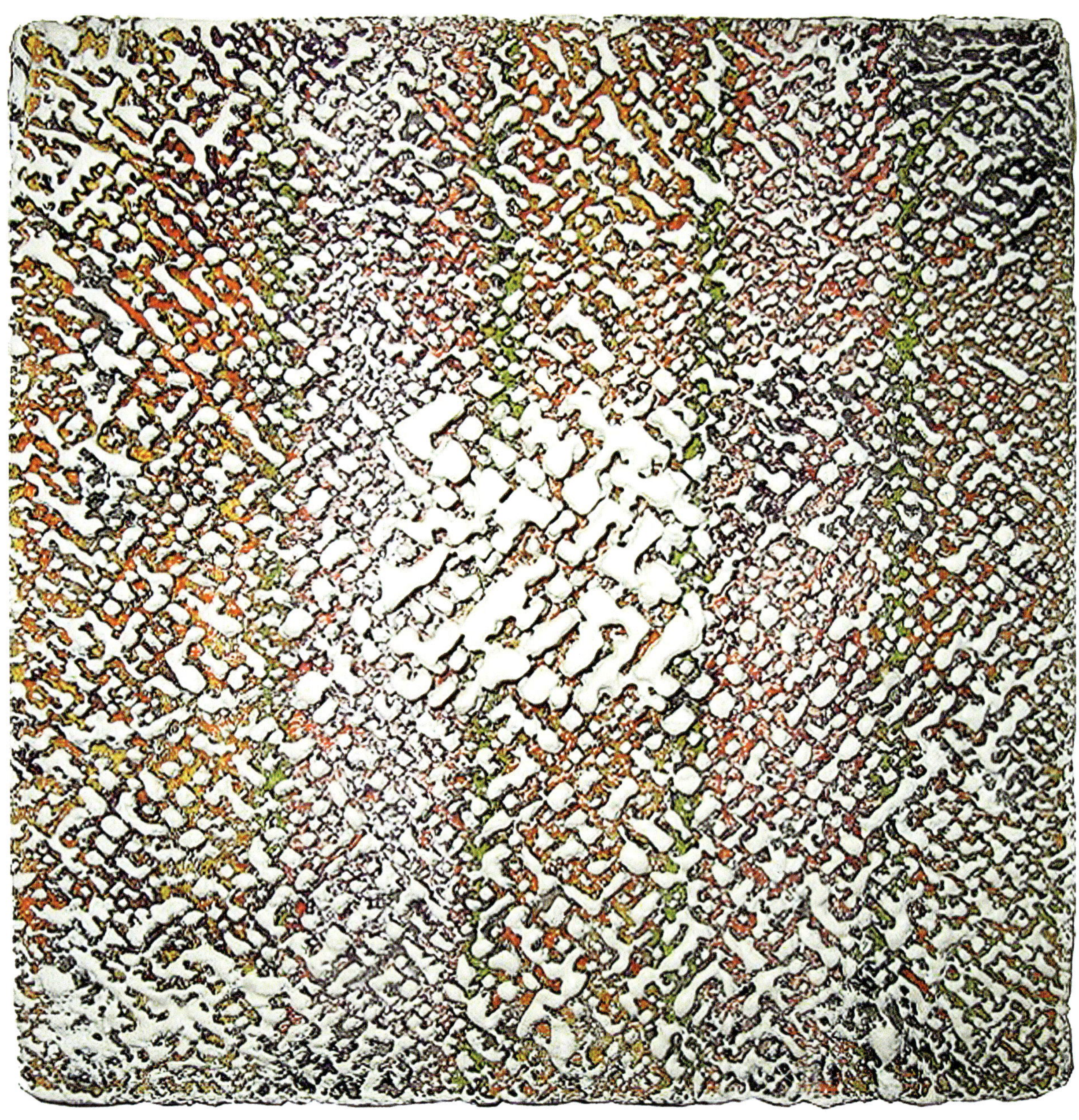

Debra Neiman, *Square*, 2010. Encaustic on wood panel, 20.3 x 20.3 cm.

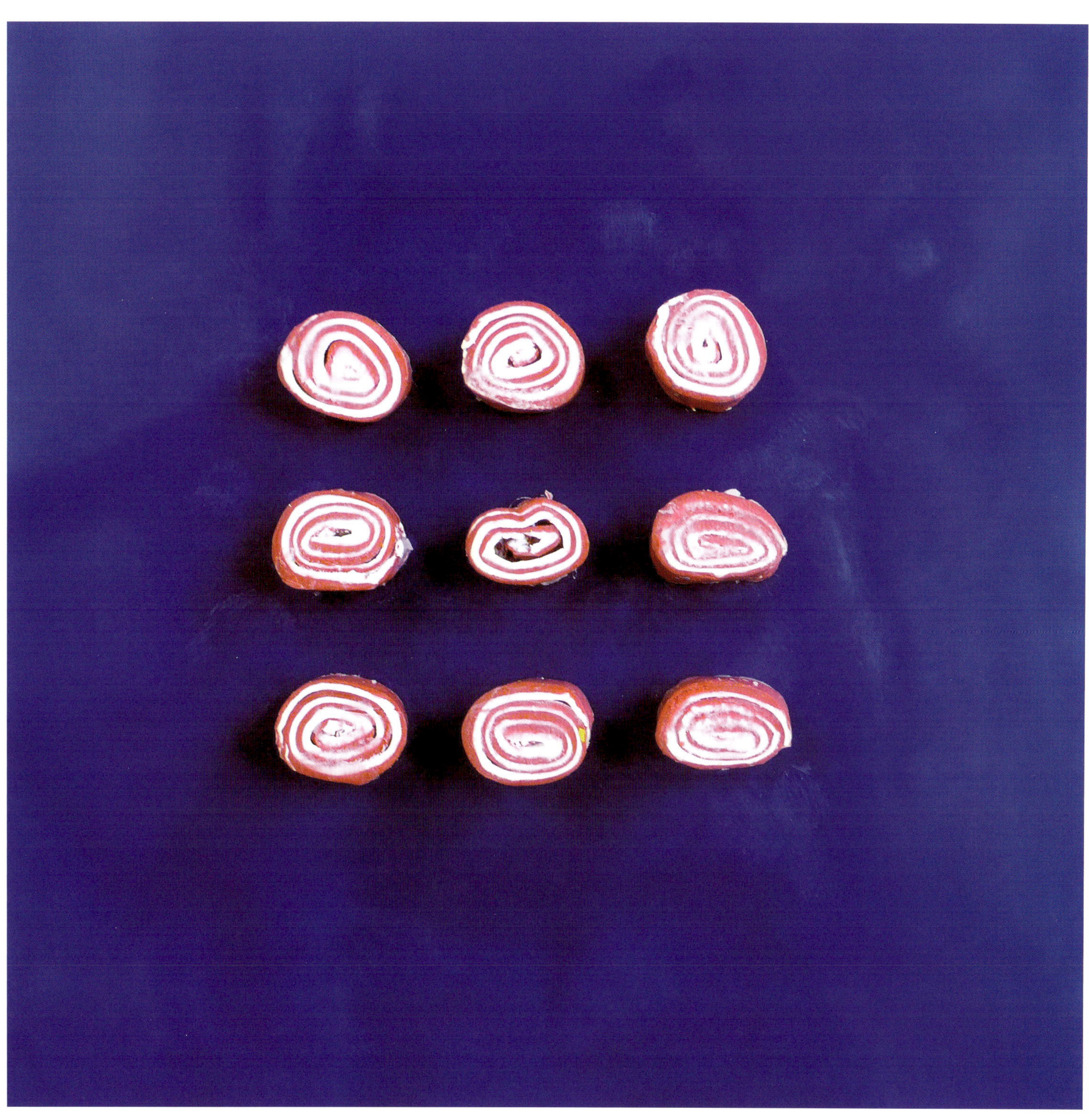

Debra Neiman, *Rollo*, 2010. Encaustic on wood panel, 12.7 x 12.7 cm.

MIRIAM KARP

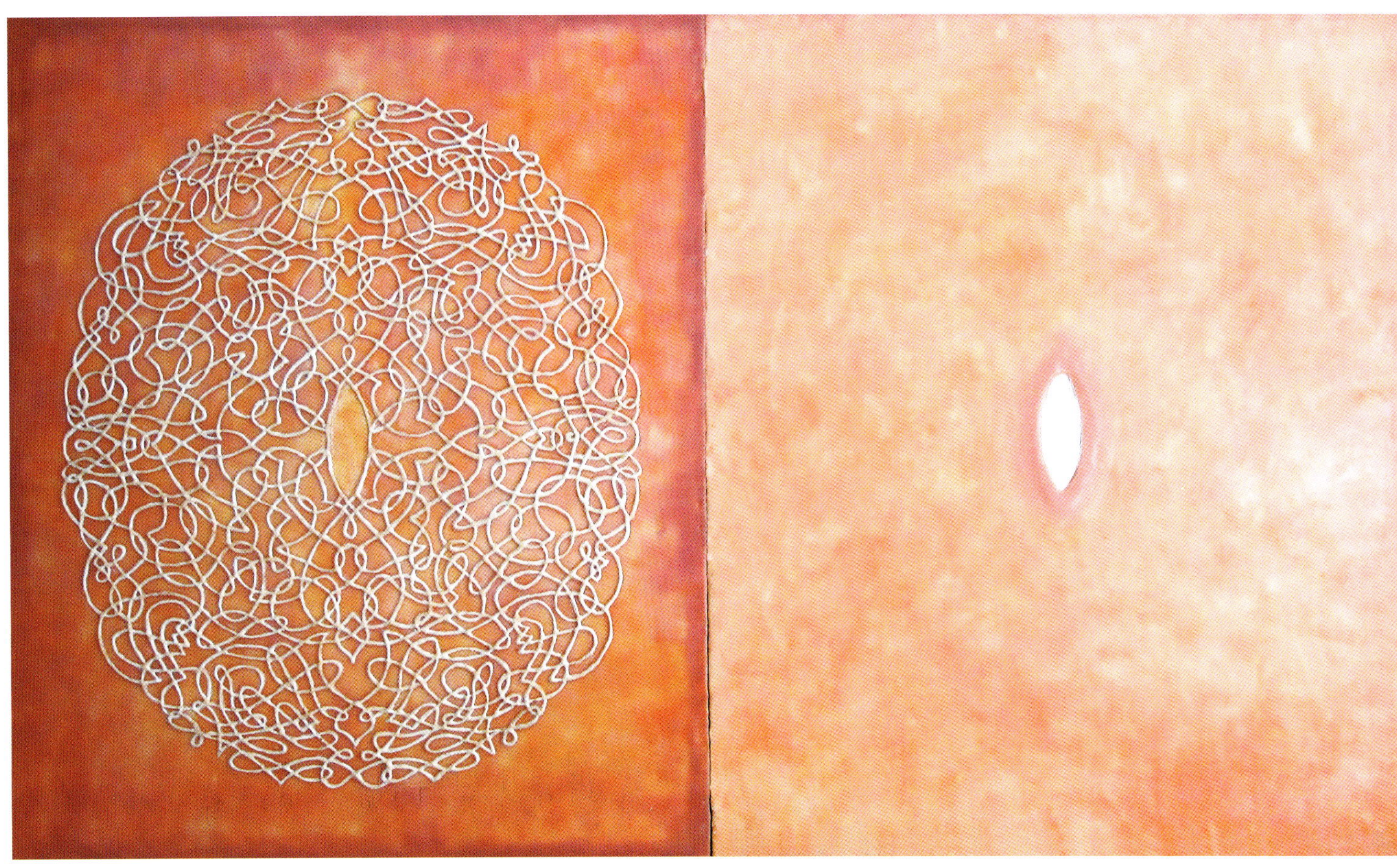

Miriam Karp, *Give and Take*, 1999.
Encaustic on wood panel, 71.1 x 121.9 cm.

Miriam Karp, *Elaborate Losses*, 2002.
Encaustic on wood panel, 91.4 x 60.9 cm.

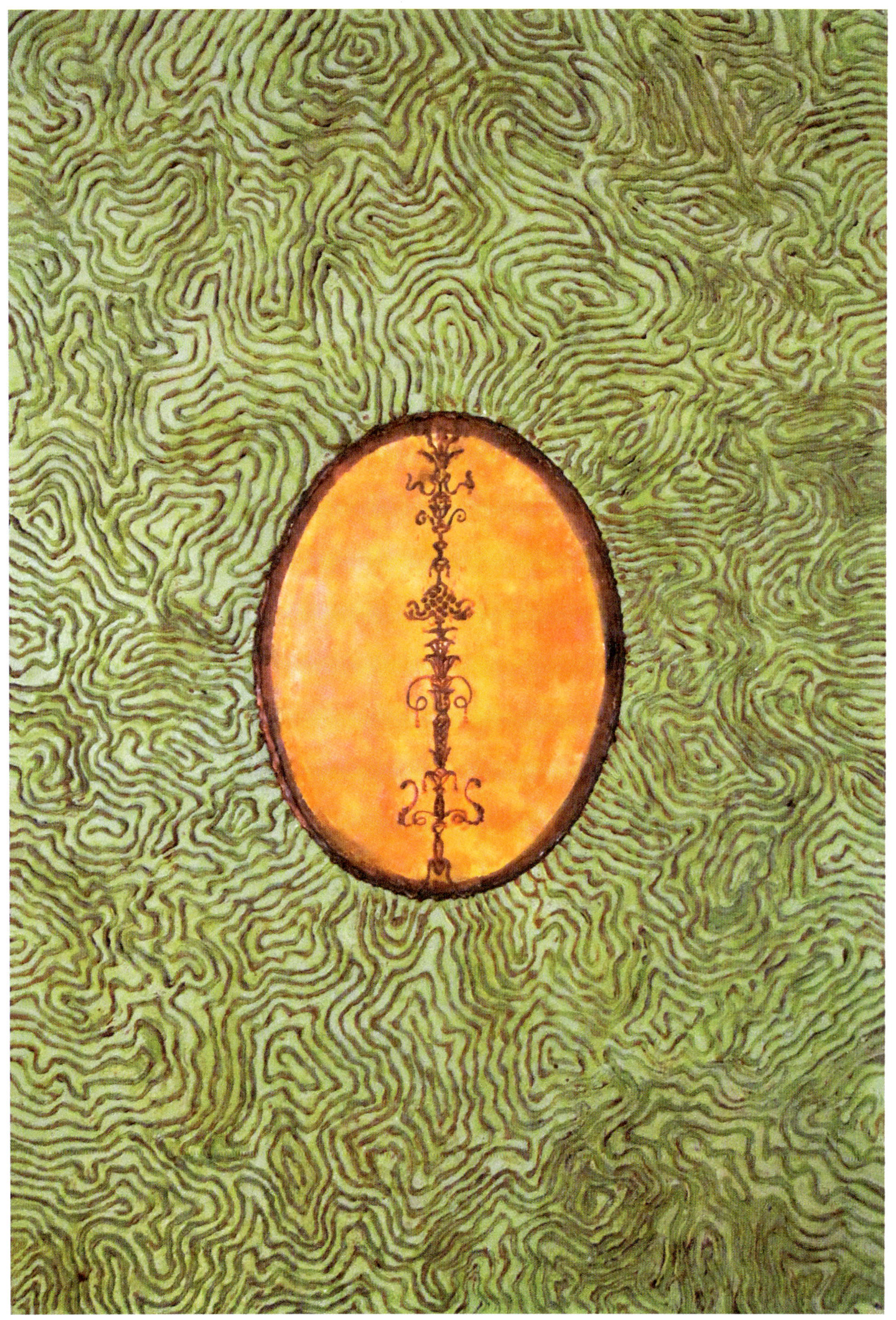

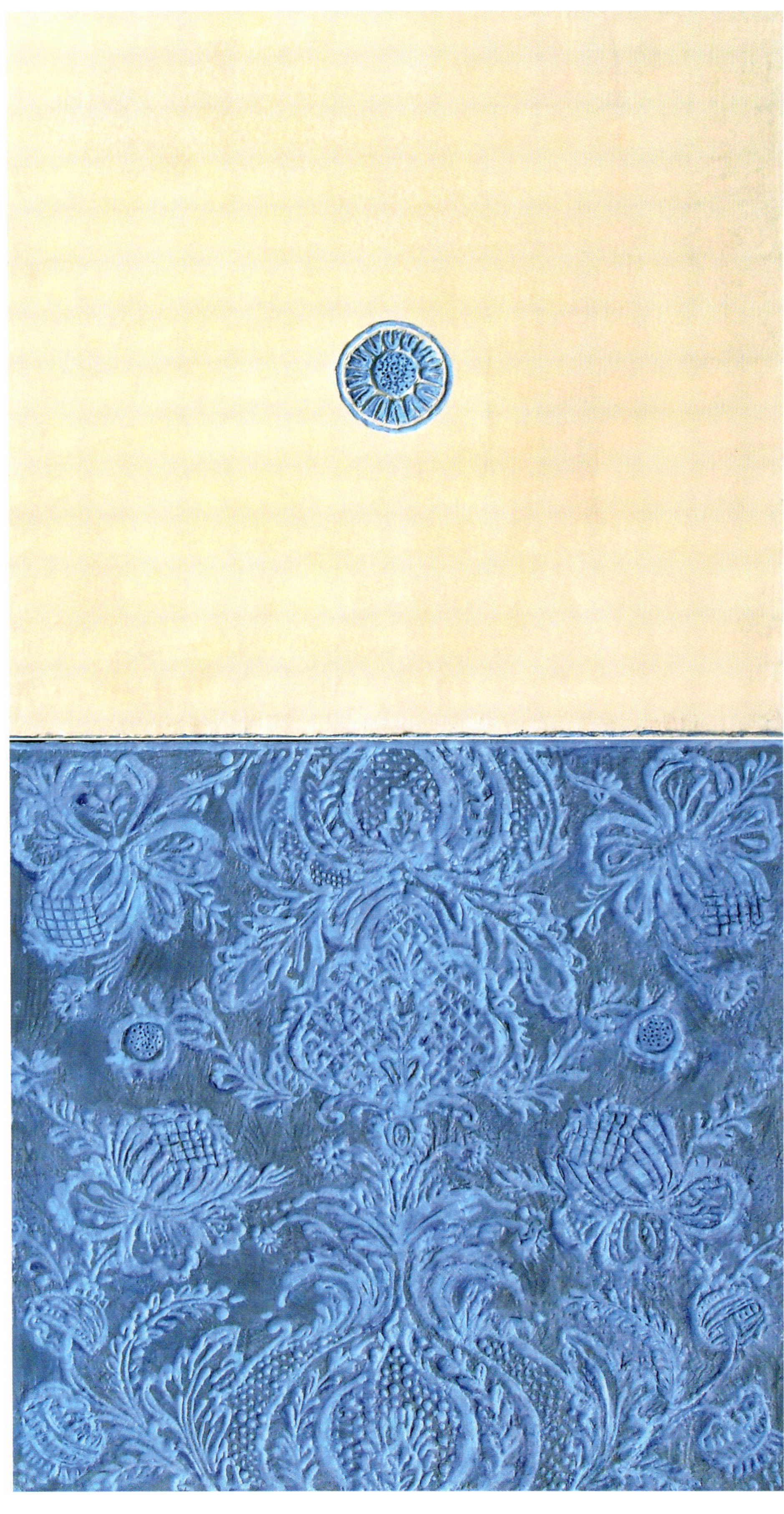

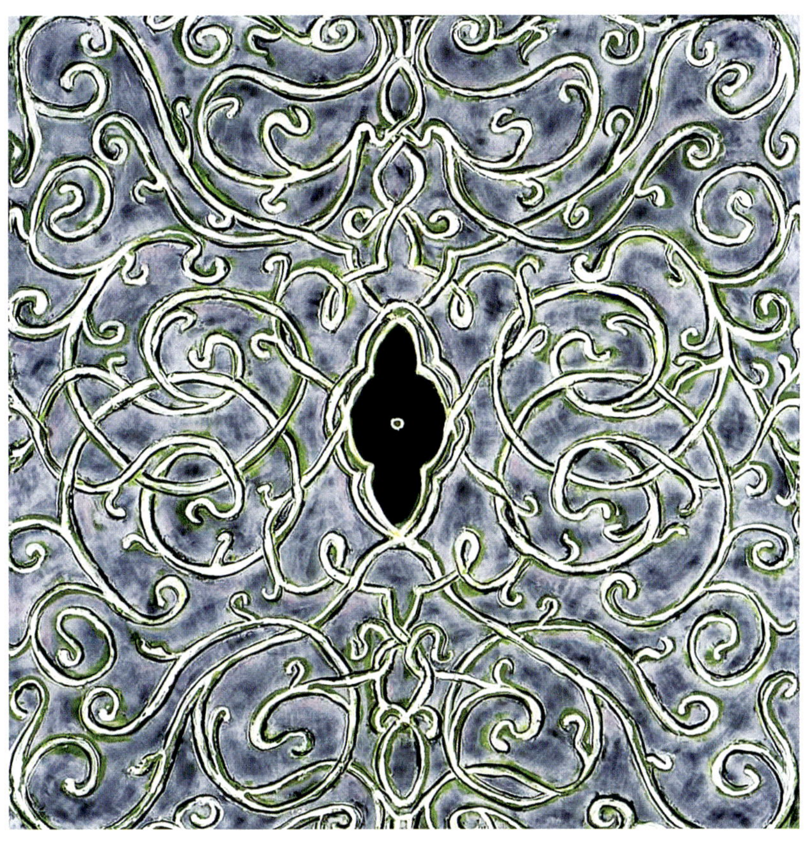

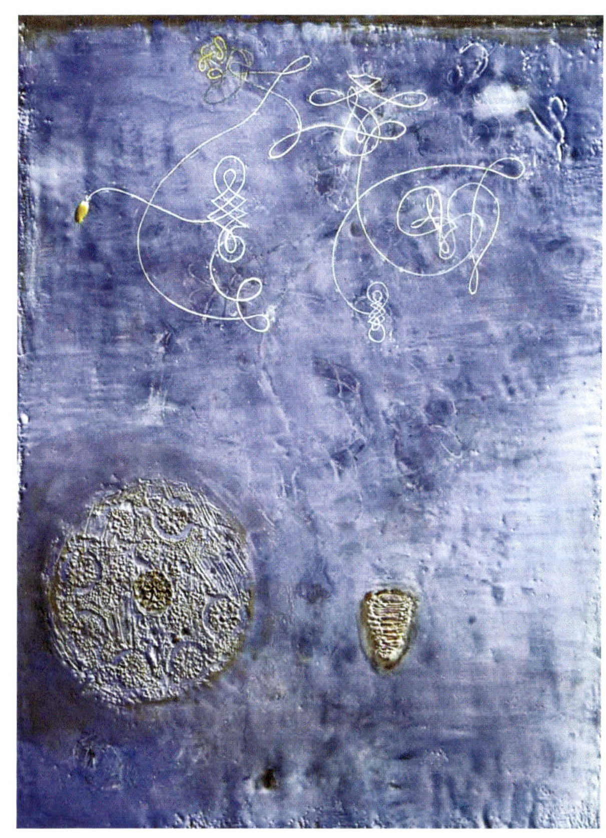

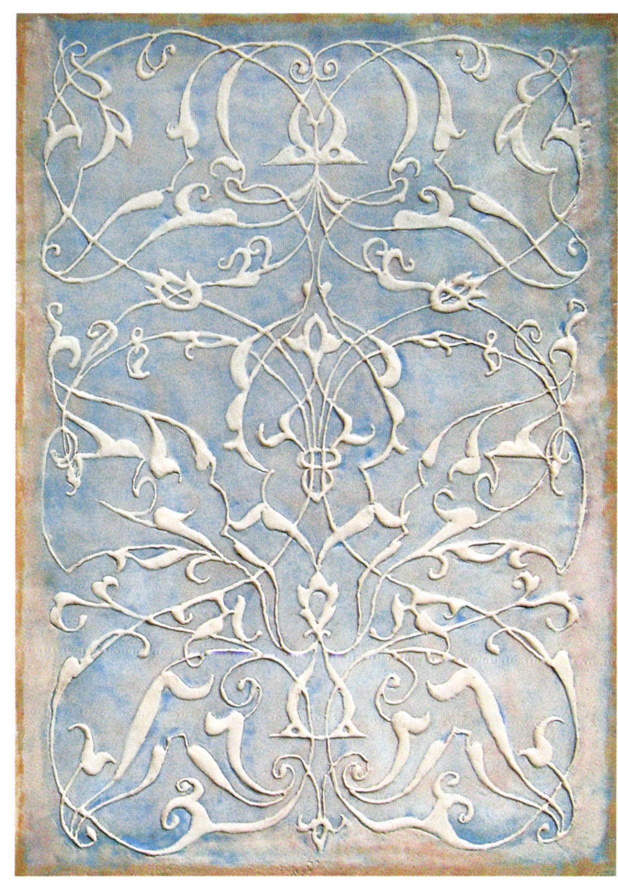

Miriam Karp, *Brocade*, 2000.
Encaustic on wood panel, 76.2 x 40.6 cm.

Miriam Karp, *Black Glass*, 2000.
Encaustic on wood panel, 40.6 x 39.3 cm.

Miriam Karp, *Thin Ice*, 2000.
Encaustic on wood panel, 60.9 x 71.1 cm.

Miriam Karp, *Veiled*, 2002.
Encaustic on wood panel, 60.9 x 45.7 cm.

Richard Purdy

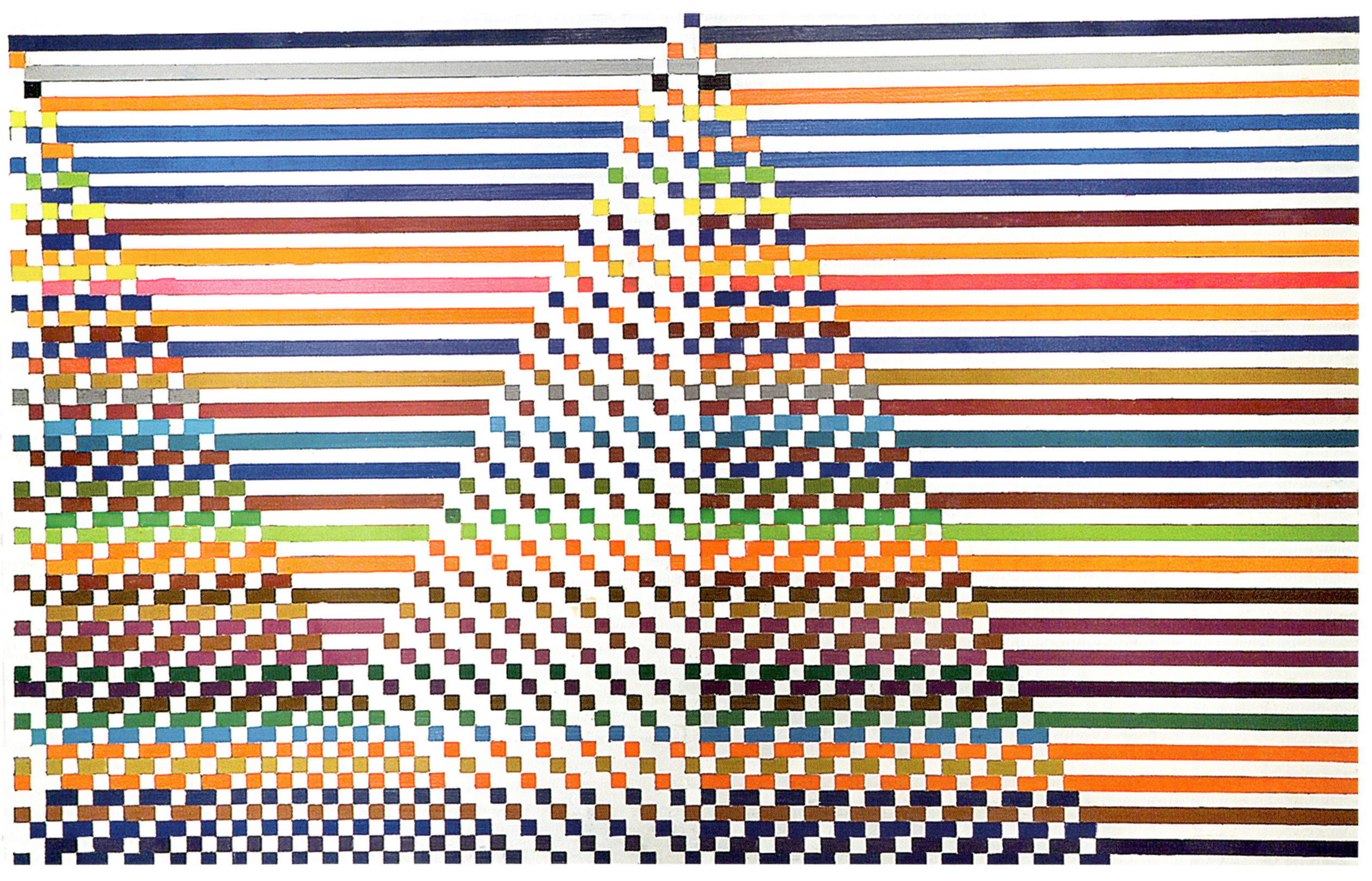

Richard Purdy, *198*, 2005.
Encaustic on wood panel, 50.8 x 76.2 x 5.1 cm.

Richard Purdy, *156*, 2004.
Encaustic on wood panel, 72.3 x 44 x 5.1 cm.

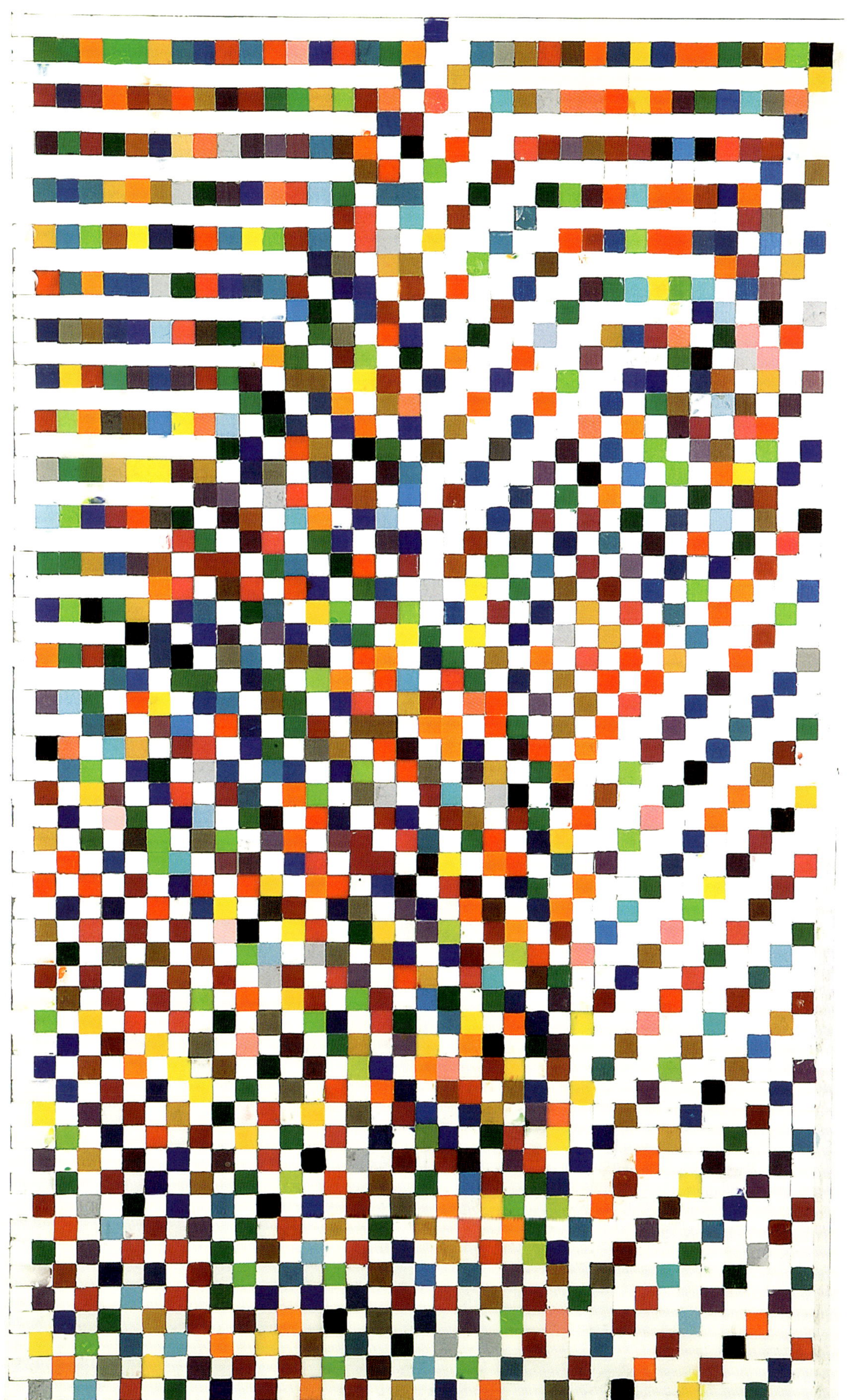

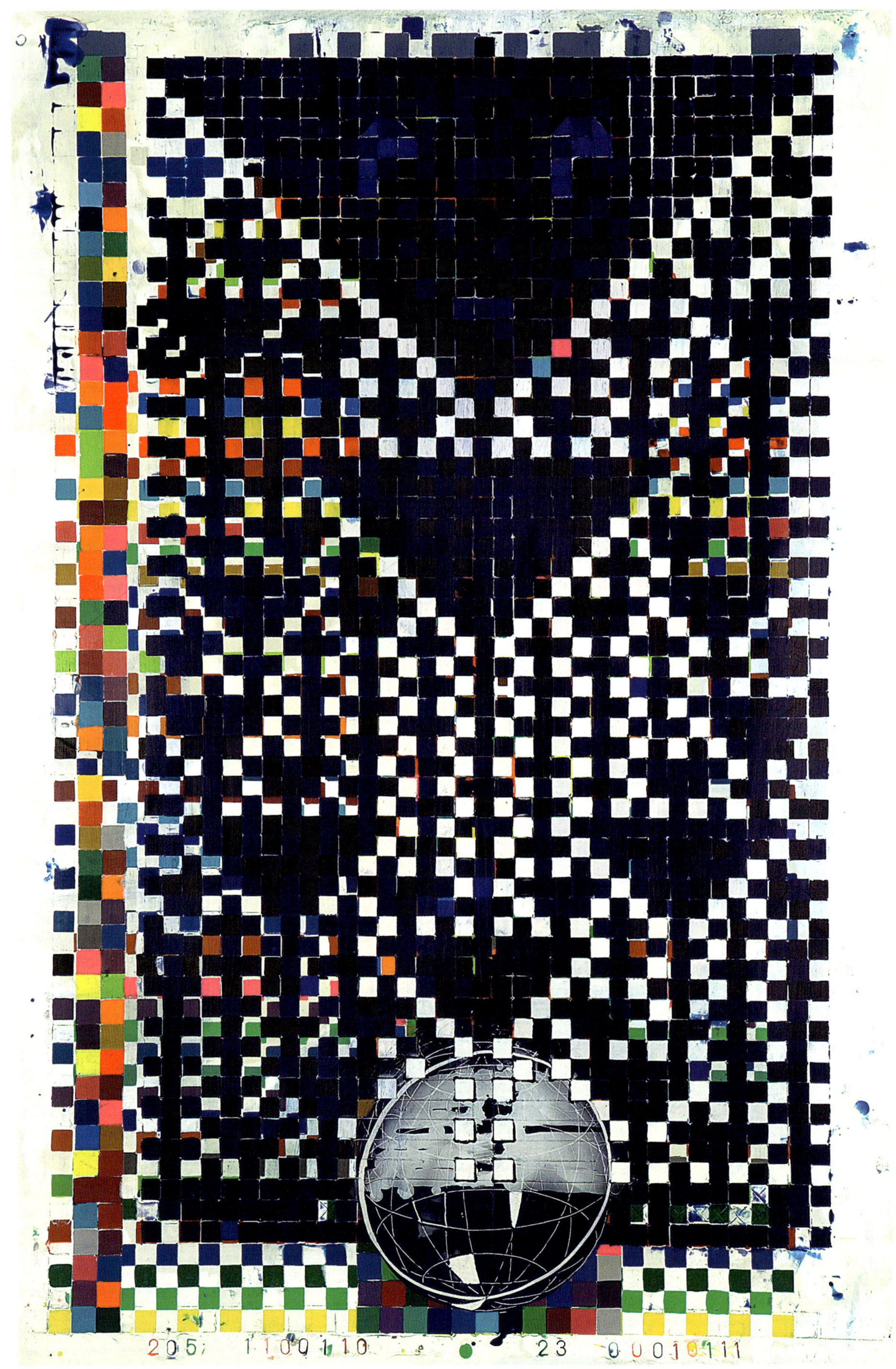
205 1100110
23 00010111

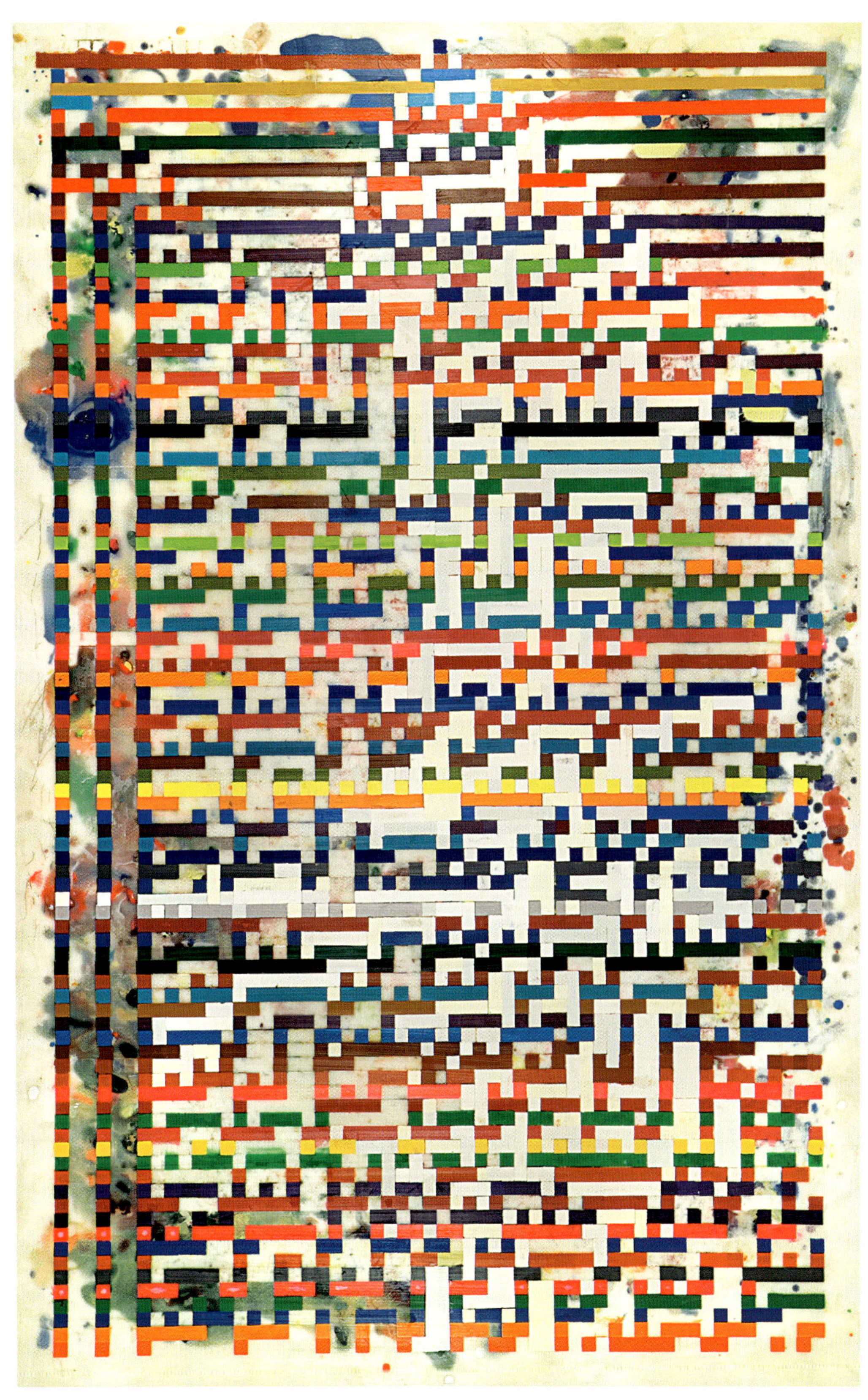

Richard Purdy, *Trio*, 2008.
Encaustic on wood panel, 65.5 x 61 x 5.1 cm.

Richard Purdy, *Gleason 7*, 2009.
Encaustic on wood panel, 150 x 94 cm.

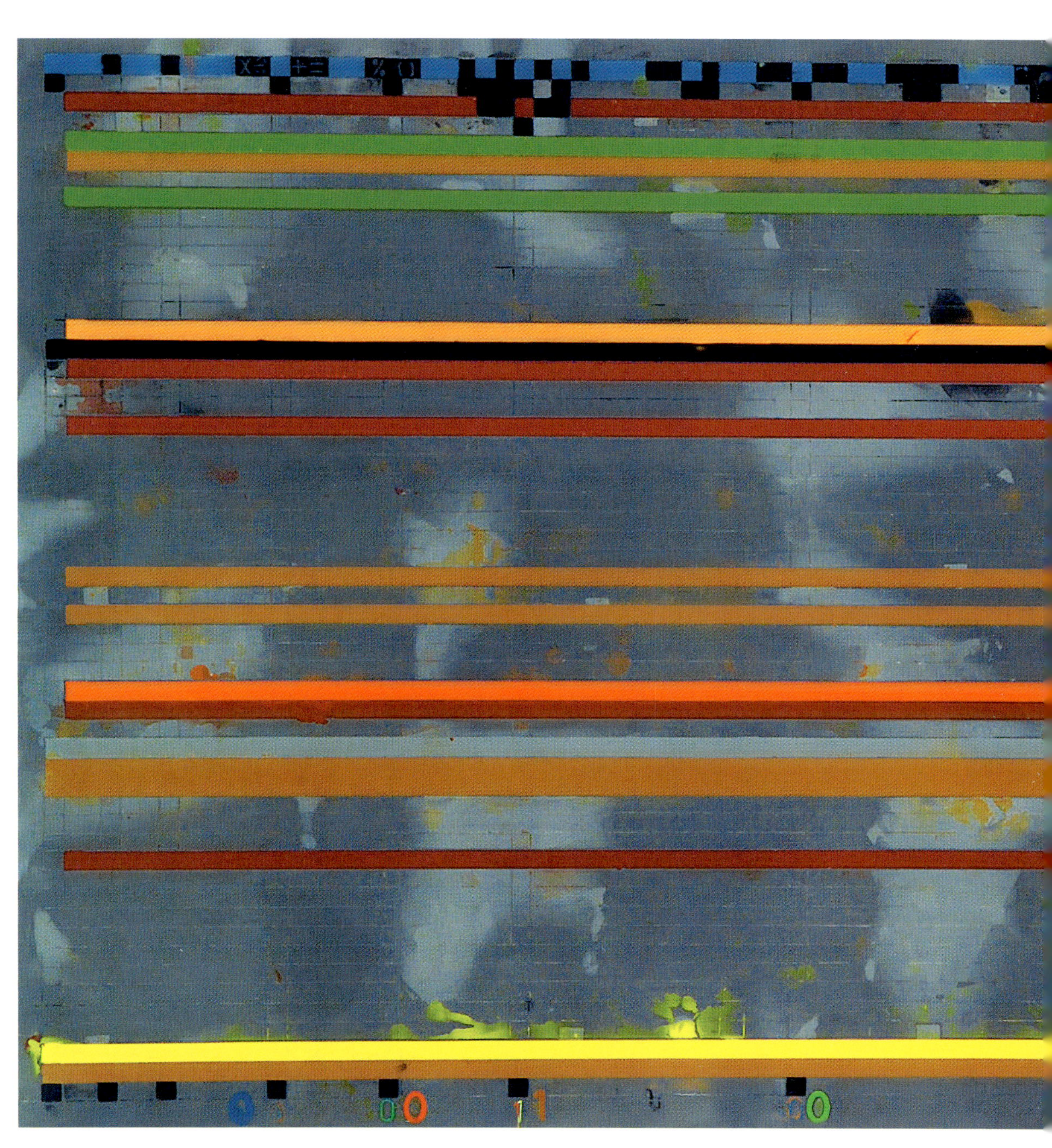

Richard Purdy, *Skeleton 37*, 2006. Encaustic on wood panel, 52.1 x 100.3 x 5.1 cm.

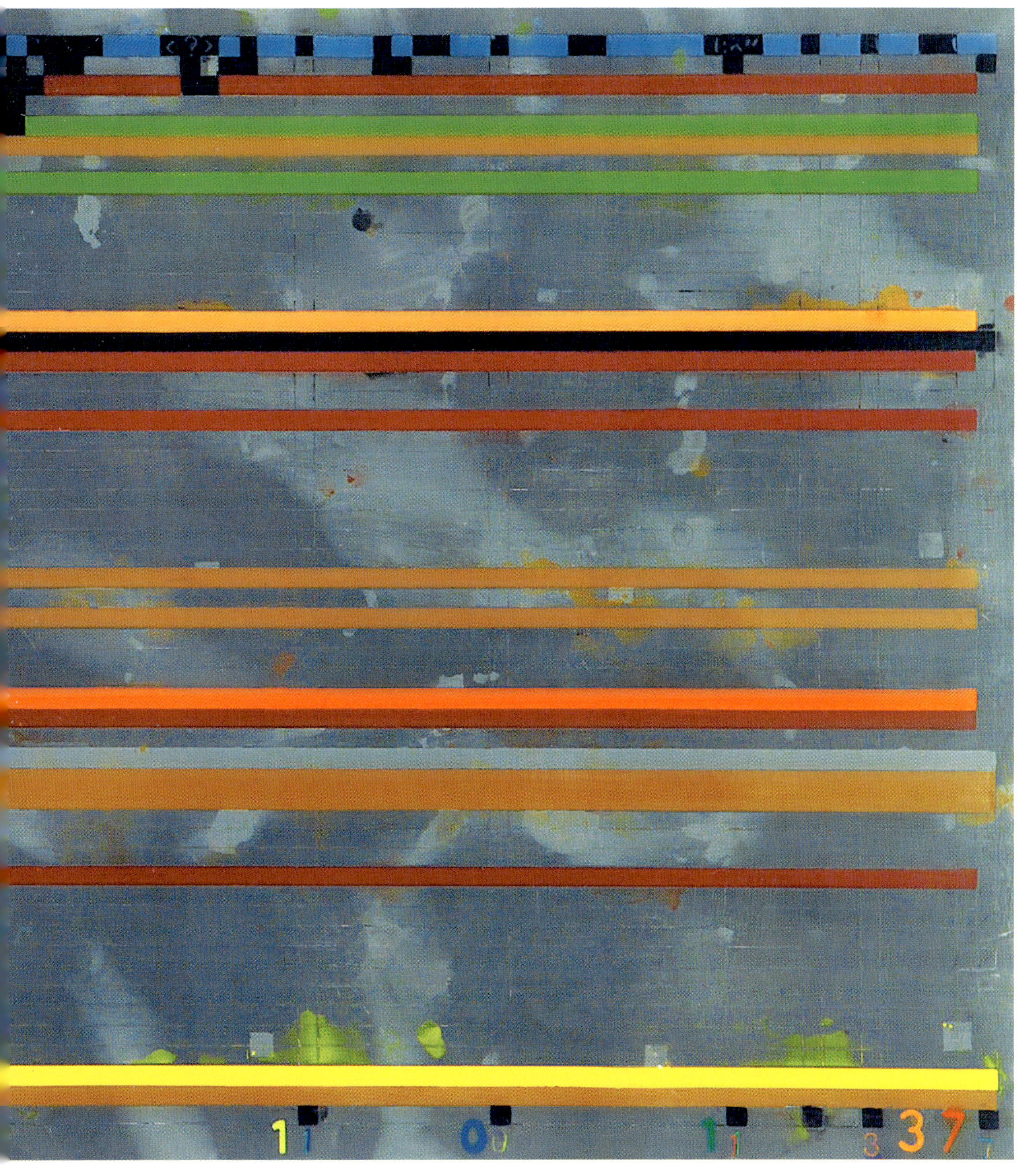

Resources

ENCAUSTIC SUPPLIES

Dadant & Sons
888.922.1293
www.dadant.com

Daniel Smith
800.426.6740
www.danielsmith.com

Rochester Art Supply
800.836.8940
www.fineartstore.com

Earth Pigments
520.682.8928
www.earthpigments.com

Evans Encaustics
707.996.5840
www.evansencaustics.com

R&F Handmade Paints
800.206.8088
www.rfpaints.com

Sinopia Pigments & Materials
415.824.3180
www.sinopia.com

Wagner Encaustics, Inc.
503.737.2400
www.wagnerencaustics.com

Art Boards
800.546.7985
www.art-boards.com

Custom Art Panels
www.rodneythompson.com

ARTIST ORGANIZATIONS

International Encaustic Artists
www.international-encaustic-artists.org

New England Wax
www.newenglandwax.org

Texas Wax
Dallas: texaswaxdallas.blogspot.com

BOOKS

The Art of Encaustic Painting
www.joannemattera.com
By Joanne Mattera

Encaustic & Beyond: A Guide to Creating Fine Art with Wax
www.LissaRankinArt.com
By Lissa Rankin

Enkaustikos! Wax Art
www.fineartstore.com
By Ann Huffman

Glossary

ENCAUSTIC PAINTING WORKBOOK

Beeswax (Filtered) – The product left after removing all of the impurities from natural beeswax. It often comes in pellet form. The color is bleached to a cloudy white. It is better to use filtered beeswax for encaustic painting than natural beeswax because there are fewer impurities.

Beeswax (Natural) – The product produced by young bees in the form of wax scales. The most natural raw state is available when it has simply been separated from the honey and main dross. The melting point is 144° Fahrenheit. It still contains some oils and dirt, is cloudy yellow in color, and exudes a strong beeswax scent.

Crystallization Point – The temperature required for a liquid to turn into a solid.

Dammar Resin – A refined crystal with a melting point around 175° Fahrenheit. It is a resin from the *Dipterocarpaceae* tree family found in India and East Asia. It is mixed with beeswax to create encaustic medium because it raises the melting temperature, toughens the wax surface, and improves adhesion and flexibility.

Encaustic Medium – A mix of beeswax and Dammar Resin. It is ready-to-use for encaustic painting. You can purchase encaustic medium or mix your own.

Encaustic Paint – A mix of encaustic medium with pigment. It is colored and can be purchased professionally mixed in various colors, or you can mix your own.

Fuse a Layer – When you melt the top layer of encaustic medium onto the base so that the layers of a painting become one. You can do this by heating the top layer gently using a heat gun or various other heat sources. This process increases strength and creates a more rigid painting.

Heat Gun – A hand-held device which projects very hot air. It is used in encaustic painting to melt layers of encaustic medium in order to fuse the painting together.

Melting Point – The temperature required for a solid to turn into a liquid.

Microcrystalline Wax – A petroleum-based wax with different physical properties than paraffin wax. It is denser, has better adhesion, creates a tougher surface, and has a higher melting point than paraffin wax.

Natural Bristle Paint Brushes – Brushes made from natural materials as opposed to synthetic plastics. Natural bristle brushes are used for encaustics because they do not melt when heated. Types of brushes include sable, squirrel, hog bristle, camel, and more.

Paraffin Wax – A white wax that comes from petroleum. It is not commonly used because of its environmental impact, increased prices, and the fact that better alternatives are available. It has a cloudy white color and melts around 133° Fahrenheit. It tends to shrink as it cools, creating cracking or buckling.

Photo Transfer – The process of transferring a photo or image onto a surface. There are various methods available for this process.

Support – A rigid surface on which to paint. Encaustic requires a hard surface such as birch wood, luan, bamboo, or Masonite.

Index